~ CHACO ECHOES ~
PERVASIVE KERESAN PRIESTHOODS

Language Identity,

Puebloan Prehistory,

and

Cosmic Ceremonials

©
© Jay Miller, PhD ©

© 2019

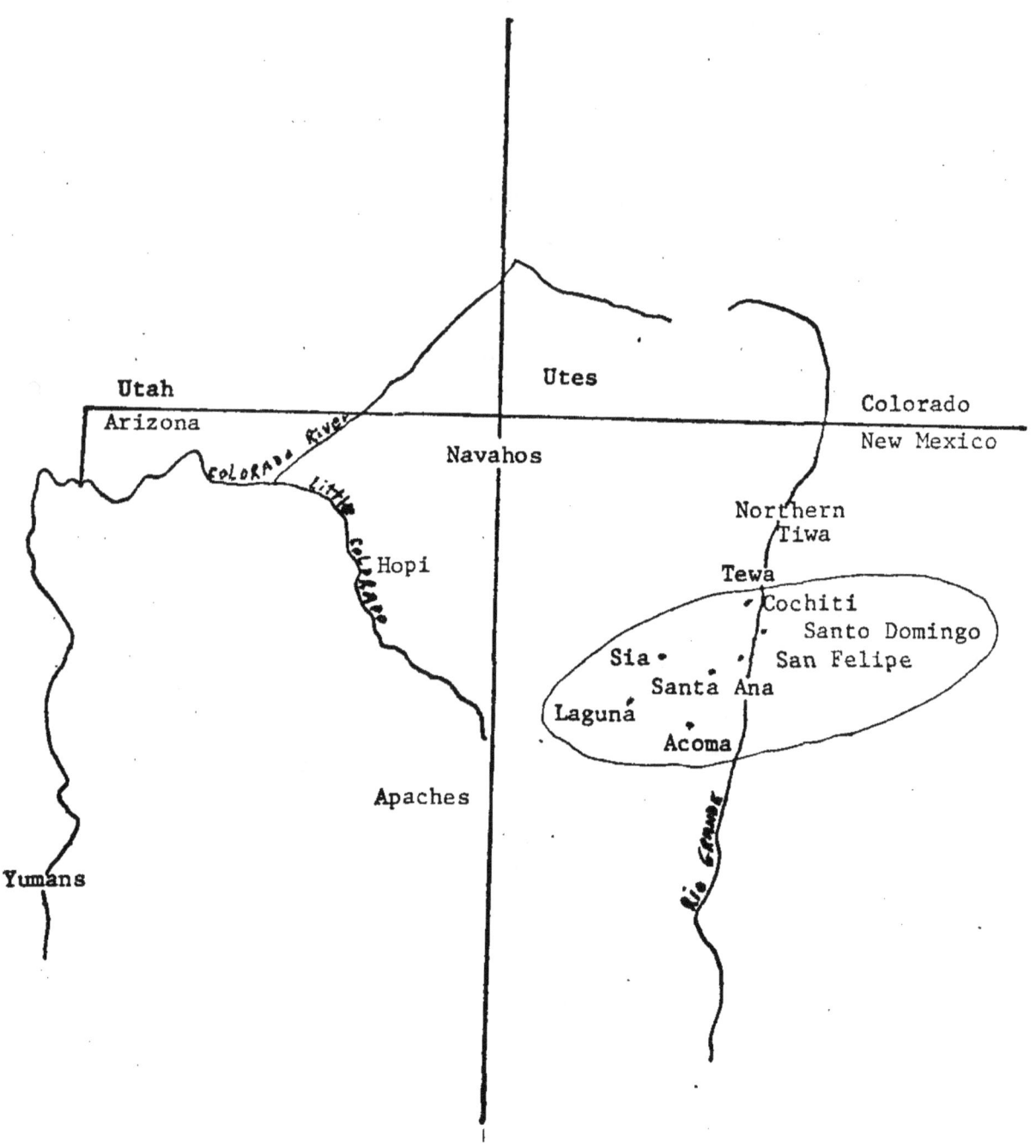

Keres Towns Today

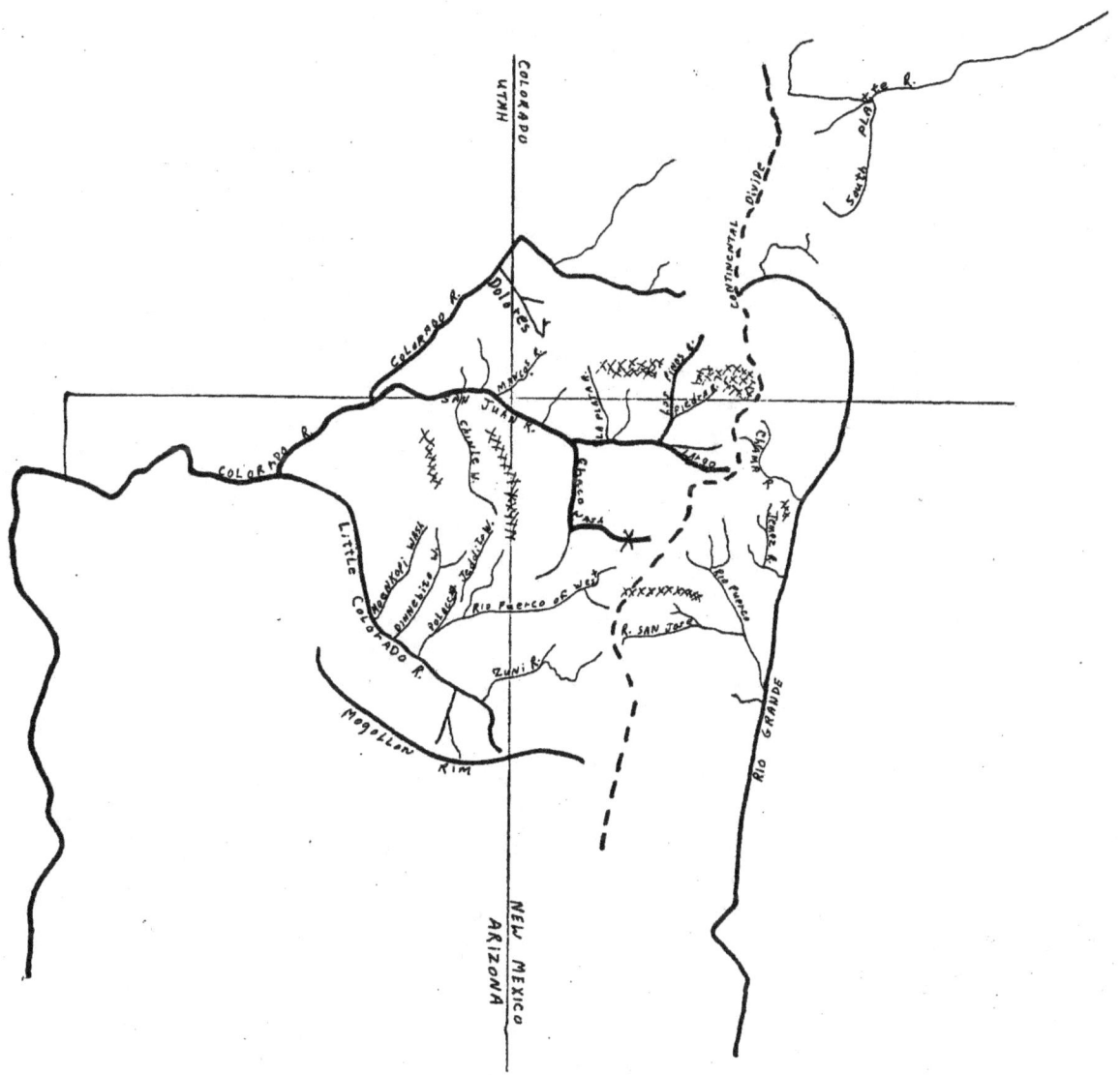

Chaco Centered Keres Homeland

"Four times they shouted, and each time an echo returned,
so they knew they had finally come to the center of their world."

Native Southwest Communities

KERES (Keresic)
  Cochiti
  Santo Domingo
  San Felipe
  Santa Ana
  Sia
  Acoma
  Laguna

TANOANS
TEWA
  San Juan
  Santa Clara
  San Ildefonso
  Pojoaque
  Nambe
  Tesuque
TANO
  Hano (at Hopi)
TIWA
  Taos
  Picuris
  Sandia
  Isleta
TOWA
  Jemez
  Pecos (at Jemez)
PIRO
  Tompiro
  Jumano

YUMANS
  Quechan
  Cocopa
  Mohave
  Maricopa
  Walapai
  Yavapai
  Havasupai

PIMANS
  Pima (O'odam)
  Papago (Tohono O'odam)

ATHAPASKANS
NAVAHO
  Eastern
  Western
APACHE
  Western
  Chiricahua
  Mescalero
  Jicarilla
  Lipan

ZUNI (Penutian)

HOPI (Numic)
FIRST MESA
  Walpi
  Sichomovi
  Hano (TANO)
SECOND MESA
  Shimopovi
  Shipaulovi
  Mishongnovi
THIRD MESA
  Old Oraibi
  Kykotsmovi (New Oraibi)
  Hotevilla
  Bacavi
  Moenkopi

Contents

Contents

Contents

Preface

Hallmarks of this work are detail, nuance, and complexity to highlight the role of Keresan Pueblos in the recent and prehistoric Southwest. Too much of this rich past has been slighted as scholars have hyper specialized. Instead, my efforts return to the wellsprings of Southwestern scholarship, and my lifelong concern with priesthoods of the Keresic language isolate nourished in Chaco Canyon to harness *iyaanyi* cosmic energy.

In his important study of Keresan kinship in its own terms, rather than the perplexing and problematic "matrilineage model" of Fred Eggan (1950), Robin Fox (1967: 138) noted that while scholars were confused by the match between their models and the behavior of the Keres, "among themselves the Cochiti had no difficulties and confusions." He wisely concluded, therefore, that the problem was not with the model or scholars, but turned instead to the Keres for understanding. I will do the same.

Starting over or, at least, reversing the process, seemed the best course for understanding the intertown diversity of the Keresan Pueblos of central New Mexico, their ancestral occupation of Chaco Canyon, and the pivotal role the Keres have played in the prehistory of the Anasazi and other archaeological complexes of the Southwest. Contra Eggan's homogenious model, Elsie Clews Parsons always emphasized four distinct Puebloan traditions, all agreeing that the language of Shipop[u], the primordial underworld, was Keresic.

Recent research along the Dolores River in western Colorado reveals paired man-woman burials on the floor of pitchambers vacated about 1200 years ago. Before and after this time, this population lived around Chaco, sustaining obvious engenderings as it spread what became Puebloicity. Both the ethnography and the archaeology have been reexamined because Southwestern academic research has slighted the unique contribution it has made to the appreciation of the Americas and the world.

This arid region, where the most fragile of human evidences can be found intact after thousands of years, once set the standard for tracing ancestral ruins to modern native towns. Now, however, archaeologists seek to use these superb remains to test "universal laws of human evolution and society," while arrogantly denying that modern descendants can provide important information about the nature of the archaeological record.

Other academics have not helped this provincialism since ethnographers have themselves been pursuing equally selective goals, and refraining from the type of sensitive synthesis attempted in this book. While the ancient Anasazi and the modern Pueblos comprise four different language families (Keresic, Tanoan, Zuni, and Hopi Numic) and disparate societies, shared patterns have obscured the importance of the dualities which pervade the Keresans.

Nor must we forget the long history of Spanish and American persecution of the native religion, which has effectively closed off much of the theocracy from contact with outsiders. Except at Hopi and Zuni, outsiders have not been welcome, especially those interested in native beliefs, rituals, and sacred objects (sacra). Fieldwork was done in private, away from the towns, and relied more on memory than on direct observation. These difficulties for research have meant that, despite volumes of publications, the Pueblos remain incompletely known, at their own insistence. Instead, we have a homogenized model of "The Pueblos" that is all but useless for understanding the dynamics of the very real differences it conceals. In the Southwest, therefore, archaeology is often a better indicator of religious behavior then ethical ethnography ever can be.

Still, as David Jessup (1985: 266) cogently argued "Though the changes which have occurred in Pueblo culture as the result of White dominance cannot be denied, I find this a poor excuse for failing to deal with problems of historical continuity."

Indeed, increasing dissatisfaction with what I saw as "ignorance of the obvious" has made the Keres a life-long concern. When I compared what I knew of these towns personally with the academic literature about them, I was baffled. How could the speakers of a language isolate, Keresic, be treated as a "bridge" between Eastern (Tanoan) and Western (Zuni, Hopi) Pueblos when their linguistic uniqueness clearly set them apart? How could societies like the Pueblos, defined as theocracies, be called egalitarian by scholars, particularly archaeologists? How could the Keres link to Chaco Canyon, the glory of Southwestern prehistory, be so widely-acknowledged but ignored? Why has the Keres's own recognition of Chaco Canyon as White House, albeit as a system of ruins rather than a single one, been slighted? How did all of these obvious oversights lead archaeologists away from the ethnographic analogies that had been the hallmark of Southwestern studies?[1]

My first response to these questions was my 1972 dissertation, The Anthropology of Keres Identity, but, over the decades, new data have changed my insights – and sometimes improved them.

---

[1] While ethnographic analogy can and has been abused by archaeologists, particularly when materialists ignorant of culture as a symbol system, the extend of human occupation of the Southwest, spanning over ten centuries, and the completeness of the artifactual record place a special burden on scholars to use it fully.

After the Spanish arrived, their word for town (*pueblo*) was applied to a variety of native societies in modern New Mexico and Arizona. At present, pueblo has three overlapping meanings as a type of person, an inhabited place, and a way of life, both now and in the past. Hence, Puebloan will refer to the lifeway that shared a tradition of farming corn, beans, and squash, of elaborate rain-making rituals, and of communal life in high-rise buildings made of stone and adobe, like a modern apartment ~ condominium. Yet, Puebloan cultures were as different as their languages.

Keresic stands out among the Puebloan languages, moreover, because no other modern language in the region seems to be related to it. Archaeological research, however, suggests that several thousand years ago, Keresan ancestors, represented by the Jay complex, moved eastward from the Colorado River region in southern California, which was the homeland of the Hokan stock of languages. At a more remote time, Hokan and the Siouian stock may have shared a common ancestral language.

Surrounding the modern Keresans are other linguistic groupings belonging to the Aztec-Tanoan stock. These languages were distributed from central Oregon to central Mexico, with a homeland along the southern border of Arizona and New Mexico in the Upper Gila River region. There, developing out of the Cochise complex of the Archaic period, over seven thousand years ago, the shift to farming and brownware pottery marked the Mogollon tradition.

Between about 1 and 1000 AD, some Mogollon began moving north along the Rio Grande Valley to scatter the Tanoan family of languages. Those who stayed in the lower Rio Grande became the Piro, Tompiro, and Jumano traders, now gone (Hickerson 1994), with the Tiwa in the central valley, divided between a northern dialect at Taos and Picuris or a southern one at Sandia and Isleta. Those who settled in present-day Colorado near Mesa Verde were Tewa ancestors. Speakers in the five modern Tewa towns of San Juan, Santa Clara, San Ildefonso, Nambe, Tesuque, and Pojoaque readily understand each other, suggesting long proximity. The exception is the southern Tewa ~ Tano, now living at Hano on Hopi First Mesa, who developed in the Galisteo Basin southeast of Santa Fe. They occupied that city during the 1680 Pueblo Revolt, then moved into the Espanola Valley after the 1692 Reconquest, and finally settled among the Hopi after 1700. With prolonged conversations, Tewa and Tano understand each other.

Most divergent of the Tanoans are the Towa, who lived in the Pecos and the Jemez valleys until they joined in 1838 at Walatowa (Jemez). This language developed in the Largo upland region of northwestern New Mexico, which long remained a culturally conservative region, using pithouses long after other regions were building stone pueblos.

More problematic is the relationship of Kiowa, famous Plains horsemen, to other Tanoans. Their ancestors came from the Pecos valley on the western plains (Jelinek 1967, 162-63), leaving farming for bison hunting six centuries before the Spanish brought back horses.

The Numic family, a member of the separate Uto-Aztecan branch within Aztec-Tanoan, consists of Great Basin peoples, including the ancestors of modern Hopi who moved south into northern Arizona after 1000 AD and occupied four mesa. Other neighbors of this branch were the Pimans, O'otam and Tohono O'otam (formerly Pima and Papago), who developed in southern Arizona from the Hohokam archaeological tradition.

Although the Zuni language has been remotely traced to the Penutian stock, these residents of west New Mexico indicate cultural links with ancient Mexico, particularly in terms of elaborated rituals and priesthoods. Indeed, their ancestors during the Archaic may have been related to the Frontera complex of Coahuilla, Mexico (Irwin-Williams 1979: 42).

By the 1400s, the Southwest was also settled by the ancestors of the modern Apache and Navaho, descendants of Athapaskans who fled south, after a central Alaska AD 800 volcanic eruption, along the Rocky Mountain corridor (Perry 1992). Their expansion further constrained life in the Southwest because their enforced claims limited the possibilities for Puebloan migrations into new areas, which had been the usual prehistoric strategy except on the northern frontier where Utes long raided. Instead, surrounded by Athapaskans, Pueblos built larger and more compact towns in defense. Still, trade and some intermarriage occurred, and, over time, Navahos separated from Apaches by adapting many features of Pueblo life, such as weaving and sandpainting rituals, to their own needs.[2]

After centuries of Spanish and American interference, however, Pueblos became understandably reluctant to discuss their religion, expanding upon more ancient practices of exclusion. Even among themselves, sacred topics were never common knowledge since native priests of these theocracies relied on the tight control of such information

---

[2] Though beyond the scope of this study, Strong (1927, 1972) noted that a leader-house-bundle complex, extending from the Pacific coast of California through the Pueblos, included priestly leaders, dry or sand paintings, cult objects, and integrative rituals. Among Pueblos, Parsons (1936) termed it the house-clan-fetish complex, involving elaborated sacred centers in terms of people, places, and sacra and it may well be the regional inspiration for the Chacoan elaboration. While less complex, Caddoans and other nations to the east also had a version of this complex, which linked people, places, and deities through sacra objects of *puwah*.

to provide the basis for leadership and authority. In the native idiom, such knowledge was guarded from harmful use by witches to better safeguard the community.

Scholars have concentrated on more public aspects of the Puebloans, such as kinship, ritual, and economy, but the result has been piecemeal, biased, and partial studies. Generalizing from these works to the society as a whole is fraught with difficulties. As Charles Lange (1959: 237) noted for Cochiti and the other Keresan towns, priestly authority is "extremely esoteric." Thus, while material is abundant on the importance of the Town Chief (also called the Tiamunyi, casik, and cacique), it is "confusing, contradictory, and incomplete" by native intent. Full, complete, and accurate information belongs only to the highest grade of the native priesthoods. It is forbidden to outsiders and uninitiates.

Even the Hopi (Whitely 1988: 65), regarded as classic examples of a loosely-structured society, separate the "powerful people" (*pavansinom*) from the "ordinary people" (*sukavungsinom*). As elsewhere, the basis for this distinction is access to and control of religious knowledge about how the world came to be, which spirits are responsible for what processes, and, especially, how these beings and places can be influenced by particular expressions of fasting, prayer, song, and ritual. When town populations became too large for the priests to monitor, schisms developed, such as the famous split at Hopi Oraibi in 1906, which resulted in the founding of several smaller towns.

Lastly, Edward Dozier (1970: 154, 189), himself a Santa Clara Tewa PhD, noted "despotic rule by the religious-political hierarchy did take place in virtually all the pueblos and across the years some Indians lost houses, property and land, and were evicted [for actions contrary to the sentiments of their community. However,] As priests, they do not act openly; the war captains and the secular officers are their go-betweens and mouthpieces with the people and the outside world."

This complex array of leaders was well known to earlier generations of scholars because the arid climate of the Southwest, preserving the most fragile of artifacts, along with continuous residence of native peoples, whose priests pilgrimaged to ancestral sites to leave offerings, reminded everyone that both the archaeology and the ethnography reflected the same people in different eras. Often, Pueblo workmen excavates and explained the significance of an artifact to scholars, and the analogy was accepted.

Parallels between ancient ruins and modern towns are self-evident, particularly in terms of the wide distribution of ordinary housing. In the case of the elaborate style and size of ruins in Chaco Canyon, however, such links have been denied. Arguing for a cultural complexity and technical sophistication unknown among modern Pueblos, several archaeologists have regarded the "Chaco phenomenon" as unique in the Southwest.

At the same time, over recent decades, most archaeologists have tolerated ~ accepted Chaco as a Keresan homeland. As presently understood, the Keresan population was scattered in the San Juan Basin, with the greathouse ruins of Chaco located at the center. The web of roadways and outlying ruins in the Chacoan style were aspects of a trade and exchange network that brought turquoise, pottery, and people into the canyon on a regulated basis. Indeed, for a survey of these San Juan ruins (Marshall, Stein, Loose, and Novotny 1979, 3, 359), Richard Loose

"predicted the location of Chacoan settlements based on their association with productive soils, and on a comparison with the spacing of historic Keresan pueblos [while in the final analysis of proximities] In the southwestern basin area where Chacoan sites are tightly patterned with drainage confluences, productive soils and modern communities, the mean value was 8.21 miles with a standard deviation(n = 6) of 1.9 miles. This value is not far off the Keresan spacing [8.1 miles] in the Rio Grande Valley – great food for rampant speculation."

Therefore, recent academic focus on aspects of ecology and economy has impoverished understanding of the cultural life of these Chacoans. To compensate for this, "archaeological analogy" (comparing the archaeology with the ethnography) will help to link small kivas with the priesthoods, small ruins with lineages, greathouses with the bases ~ "seats" of major clans, and the great kivas with town solidarities. Further understanding of Chaco's role in Keres culture must wait until the internal organization of the modern Keresan towns is reviewed in Chapter 3.

Recent scholars, however, have denied (and disparaged) the validity of any such present-to-past Puebloan analogies, citing the profound changes caused by epidemics and by the governments of Spain, Mexico, and the United States. While these objections are valid to some extent, they deny the continuity of the cultures, passed on from generation to generation in the same landscape. By maintaining their own places, spaces, and traces, the Pueblos keep their integrity and sense of on-going identity.

But, at the same time, professionals concentrating on Southwestern archaeology, ethnology, and history have themselves diversified, following the academic tendency to fragment and specialize in ways that discourage the kinds of all-encompassing integrative analysis promised by the earliest collaboration of natives and researchers. Instead of analogy, modern strategy involves "modeling the archaeological record, predicting change, and comparing it to the ethnographic record for fit" (Charles Adams 1991: 189). Thus, while Pueblos still emphasize the primacy of religion in their worldview, academics focus more and more on features of economy and ecological adaptation for narrowly defined purposes.

> "Pueblo ethnographies provide us with a wealth of information that is invaluable for formulating models and generating potential explanations. But the danger of ethnographic analogy is that we will short-circuit the process of model development, testing, and refinement and fall into the easy, unscientific trap of using ethnography as explanation" (Sebastian 1992: 4).

As a challenge to current academic interests, my work returns to "culture history" but benefits from a structuralist theory building on the beginnings of Southwestern research when the attraction for scholars was an bright and arid climate preserving thousands of years of Puebloan materials. Moreover, since these communities were studied, one at a time (ruin by ruin and town by town), the rich diversities within the Puebloan tradition became fully appreciated in terms of its archaeological and ethnographic complexities.

What has not been adequately treated (although Leslie White, Charles Lange, and Robin Fox have tried), however, has been the uniformities among these diversities, the larger patterns of intertown connections both for the prehistoric Anasazi and their Puebloan descendants. My analysis examines such uniformity for the Keres Pueblos of central New Mexico, a language isolate whose obvious distinctiveness has usually been obscured by broad comparisons with other Pueblos, each with equally varied origins and internal organizations.

Living in an environment whose vicissitudes were tempered by accumulated cultural knowledge, Pueblos had the advantage of priestly elites to guide them through fluctuations in natural conditions and, later, centuries of Spanish, Mexican, and American interference. While often regarded as changeless, these cultures have instead been highly resilient. During prehistoric times, they responded to impinging effects of climate, resources, neighbors, and enemies. Over centuries, Pueblo communities suffered and survived disease, dislocation, and repression to typify what is most conservative and traditional for Native North America.

Despite a wealth of detailed information, some Pueblos remain poorly understood, particularly the Keresans, mainstays of the Pueblo tradition for several millennia. To date, all the Keres towns have been treated as a single grouping only in the brief summaries of Leslie White (1947), Charles Lange (1958), and Robin Fox (1967a).

More unified accounts have been provided for other Pueblos, especially those removed from Spanish repression. These include the work of Fred Eggan and Mischa Titiev for Hopi; Matilde Coxe Stevenson, Frank Cushing, Ruth Bunzel, and Triloki Pandey for Zuni; Elsie Clews Parsons, Edward Dozier (of Santa Clara), and Alfonso Ortiz (of San Juan) for the Tewa; or Parsons and Florence Hawley Ellis for Jemez. Only the Tiwa lack a comprehensive survey, although work in this direction has been done by George Trager, Estelle Smith, and Elizabeth Brandt.

This book, therefore, intends, above all, to synthesize Keres tradition, informed by anthropological, particularly symbolic, theory. In lieu of extensive fieldwork, it uses almost a century of publications on the Keres to provide the burden of support for the argument. In this way, the logic of Keres culture emerges out of a variety of data whose value is enhanced by its disparate sources and dates. The primary advantage of this model is that it better accounts for more Keres data than any other.

My analysis has consistently benefited from the remarkably close fit between what Keres say and do, between what they believe and what they practice. Often, within their culture, instead of letting something fade away, Keres will sanctify it as a bit of the past, reverenced because it was ancient and "traditional." This means that the Keres themselves preserve a remarkably full range of their own prehistory, making it possible to see a wide range of contents for a particular form.

As useful conventions, several terms have been standardized in my text. In addition to Keres and Keresan for the people, Keresic refers specifically to the language. Prior publishing usage has anglicized words with cultural significance, such as Tiamunyi, Shiwana, and kiva. Proper names are capitalized, as are the names for classes of Keres supernaturals - Katsina, Kopishtaiya, Gomaiyawish, and for the mythic patrons of animal species – Locust, Bear, Cougar, and Beast doctors.

Throughout, our concern is the seven modern Keresan towns, now clustered near Albuquerque – most with distinctive regional developments elsewhere. To the north are Cochiti, San Felipe, and Santo Domingo; and, to the west, Santa Ana (Damaya), Sia, Acoma, and Laguna. While their names reflect the present blend of ancestral and Spanish Catholic influences, as a whole, Keres may well be the original source for the

Puebloan way of life, with a climax at sites in the ceremonial hub of Chaco Canyon about eight hundred years ago which echos today.

Indeed, rather than vanish, Chaco inspired Keresans to sustain intergraded towns for another thousand years and more.

Chapter One

INTRODUCTION

Orientation

Keresan culture is profoundly dualistic, engendered as manly and womanly. After analyzing features of Keres kinship and mythology, Claude Levi-Strauss (1967, 75), father of structuralism, decided it had "a system of polar oppositions." Robin Fox (1967: 69) concluded that the Keres in at least one town "seem to see the society as composed of a series of opposites." Such oppositions are, of course, the primary grist for the mill of structuralist research. Though found in every Culture, they are particularly well developed among the Keres, probably because they are in active use by an ancient theocracy to express the echoing reverberations of gender.

The research for this book started in an undergraduate course in Pueblo Ethnology taught at the University of New Mexico by Dr. Florence Hawley Ellis. There, I was surprised to learn that the Tiamunyi, the most important theocratic official in each Keres town is a man, a husband and father, who is installed wearing female ceremonial attire and, thereafter, is considered a Woman. The Keres call him the Tiamunyi, but publications also refer to him as the cacique ~ casik (from a native Jamaican word adopted into Spanish), and as the Town Priest ~ Inside Chief. Edward Curtis (1926: 84) reported that the cacique is addressed ceremoniously in Keresic words that translate as 'all-our mother' or, more simply, 'mother'. When Fox (1967: 143) asked the Keres of Cochiti if the cacique were "like a mother," they reminded him that this leader is a man and not "like" anything else, instead "He belongs to the same category as mothers proper." Fox (1967: 144) therefore proposed that the Keresan term for 'mother' means someone who is senior and nurturing, usually (but not always) a related female. Thus, the reasons for the Womanliness of this theocrat are partially answered in terms of a generic category.

Yet, everything is defined both in terms of itself and in terms of a contrast with something else. Among the Keres, the office of the Town Priest is balanced by the office of the Outside Chiefs ~ war captains. In the recent past, there was a single Outside Priest ~ Country Chief who complemented the Inside one. Now, however, this office survives only in the town of Acoma. In the others, it has lapsed and the two war captains, who probably were originally his assistants, now fill the defunct office in their own right. They represent the twin "war gods," Masewi and Oyoyewi, the heros of the second part of the Origin Saga. They hold office only for a year, probably because a longer tenure might lead to self-interest and haughtiness out of keeping with the inner peacefulness emphasized so strongly by the Pueblos. Above all, the Outside Chiefs are conceptualized as brave, strong, and, especially, manly. Thus, the womanliness of the Town Priest finds a complement in the manliness of the war captains.

Once I began to surmise that this Man/Woman tension might be relevant for an understanding of the whole culture, I turned to the corpus of Keres ethnography, because what little fieldwork I had already done convinced me of two things. First, it would take a lifetime of close contact with Keres priests, doctors, and townspeople to gather necessary data. Second, fieldwork among the Rio Grande Pueblos has always involved the ethical dilemma that revealing "secrets" to "outsiders" might have potentially fatal consequences for the native intellectuals. Indeed, the authority of a Keresan town theocracy was and is such that there are several unconfirmed reports that some informants were punished or killed on orders of their town officials. As Lange (1968: 21) astutely noted for the Keres, "An already well-developed faculty for keeping rituals secret even from their own people who did not belong to a particular [priesthood] was readily transferred to their concealment from Europeans, who attacked them as being both pagan and immoral." Most especially, "Power is concentrated within a small group of officers and societies, who rule the pueblo. Their power is both political and religious; disobedience is sacrilege and heresy as well as treason" (White 1932a: 11).

Hence, I turned to the published record and, in the process, discovered that a comprehensive analysis of the Keres was not only possible, but worthwhile since more and more of the data supported a consistent model of Keres culture that was far more complex than scholars had proposed.

I once tried to broaden the categories into male/female, but the data did not support these more generalized concepts. Instead, what was indicated was a metaphorical extension of the human genders throughout the Keres cosmos. For instance, as will be seen in details of the Origin Saga and social organization, manly is regarded as marked and exclusive, while womanly is unmarked and inclusive. They are bound together by the shared property of Mind – as thought ~ consciousness ~ intelligence. So pervasive are these categories that animals are described in myth and ritual as humanoids wearing skin cloaks. The mediation of Mind as the inclosive (all-embracing) category is deified as Consciousness Deity (also called Thought Woman), the head of the Keres pantheon, as discussed in a later section.

Within Keres society, the importance of consciousness is reflected in the distinctions among three social strata – priests, initiates, and others – related to their degree of religious training to enhance mental awareness. At the highest level are elite priests with complete knowledge because they have gone through the full series of initiations into the most esoteric lore. Other members of a priesthood also have claims to knowledge. Otherwise, the basic stage involves initiation into the cult of the Katsina, gods embodied in masked dances. Adults are initiated into the knowledge that visiting Katsina are being impersonated by members of that community. At puberty, in half of the Keres towns, both boys and girls are told this secret, while the other towns initiate only boys.

Knowledge of how the cosmos works and details of its creation, particularly the circuitry of powerful energy (*iyaanyi*),[3] constitute the valued lore belonging to the various priesthoods, each of which includes at least three grades of initiation. At the top is the leader ~ head priest (*nawai*), next are the doctors ~ established members, and lowest are the novice initiates. The priesthoods and internal grades have different functions associated with various uses of power to enable members to manage rituals, cure various sicknesses, oversee hunting, or, in the past, deploy warriors and strategy.

Different priesthoods had different degrees of power. At Sia, Flint, Giant, and Fire had full honawai-aiti [ho-nawai-aiti], which enabled them to "control communal diseases, cure illness caused by 'lost hearts,' participate in winter and summer rain-making and fertilization activities, and perform funeral rites. Fire Society members 'swallow' hot coals and Giant Society members push 18-inch digging sticks down their throats 'to prepare the soil for spring planting'" (Hoebel 1979: 413).

Based on access to such knowledge, Keresan social or class divisions span the extremes of nature and culture. Children are least aware of culture and behave in ways perceived as closer to nature. Uninitiated women have only their natural abilities. Initiated men, and sometimes women, learn the general outlines of Keres theology by virtue of the limited exposure given by Katsina initiation. They are commoners (Keresic: *hanU sischti*) who are 'raw' and 'know nothing'. Aside from novices, the full members of the priesthoods are the doctors (*tchaiyanyi*) who are 'cooked' and 'know something'. At the apex are the priests (*hotchaiyanyi*) who are

---

[3] This term, also translated as "life," is the basis of *chaiyanyi* (priest, doctor, shaman, "having-power") and *hocanitsa* (the cacique's office, probaby *ho-chaiyani-itsa*, "head priest place").

'well done' and 'know' as the real purveyors of Keres culture; the leaders of the town, country, and religious specialties. Their knowledge is supremely cultural, enabling them to understand, interpret, and predict meaning in the cosmos. Thus, overall, the range is between babies, dominated by natural functions, to priests, enmeshed in the complexities of the cultural system. Periods of fasting, prayer (pure thoughts), and celibacy – denying biological functions – added to the cultural aspects of the priesthood.

More generally, it is encouraging that my model of Keres culture is very similar to that proposed by Claude Levi-Strauss for global Culture, the distinctive adaptation of the human species. While some anthropologists remain skeptical of structuralism, its usefulness for the Keres data cannot be denied, particularly given the success which Alfonso Ortiz (1969) had in using it to understand his own Tewa culture, neighbors of the Keres to the north.[4]

The differences between the axiomatic echos of the Keres and the Tewa were particularly instructive for my analysis. Several of the important relationships are reversed or mirror opposites, as though by deliberate intent. For example, for Tewa, male is unmarked and has qualities of both sexes, while female is marked and has strictly feminine qualities.[5] Among the Tewa, "the standard phrase of encouragement to men about to undertake a demanding task is "Be a woman, be a man," while the phrase to a woman in similar circumstances is simply, "Be a woman" (Ortiz 1969: 36). In other words, among the Tewa, Woman is a special case within Man; while for the Keresans Man is a special instance of Woman.

---

[4] Structuralism, while now out of favor for most academics, continues to provide insights in the Americas, most recently for Classic Maya cosmology (Schele and Freidel 1990). Indeed, Levi-Straus universalized what is a very Indien philosophical outlook.

[5] Marked and unmarked are special linguistic terms applying to any semantic field. The unmarked is the more common in usage. Thus, you ask "How long is it?" because 'long' is the unmarked and 'short' is the marked category for 'length'.

Sources

Written records on the Keres, including ethnographic observations, began with the Spanish _entradas_ into the region, but I have made little use of these because they lack the reliability of later accounts by trained professionals. Though many of the features reported by the Spanish are substantiated in the later record, they were not understood by scholars until this century. For example, it would be interesting to know more about the observation of the 1540 Coronado Expedition that women owned the houses and men owned the kivas (_estufas_ = ovens), in which the unmarried men supposedly slept apart (Winship 1896: 520). Thus, while not attributed to any particular town or region, the importance of gender considerations among Pueblos was long standing.

Similarly, Onate referred "to a captain of several Pueblos", suggesting political groupings larger than a single town existed even before the coordination necessary to undertake the 1680 Pueblo Revolt (Schroeder 1979: 246). At the time of the Revolt, records name "Alonso Catiti, governor and head of the Queres nation" (Hackett quoted in Strong 1979: 392). Such references to intertown leaders help to deny the charge by archaeologists that modern Pueblos lacked the kind of inter-community leaders assumed for the archaeological phenomenon associated with Chaco Canyon. Keresic names for such positions will be treated in chapter 4.

The Benavides Memorial of 1630 (Forrestal 1954: 34, 36) confirmed the importance of the sexual division of labor: "women build the houses ... While the men spin, weave blankets, go to war and do the hunting." While these observations strengthen our appreciation of the persistence of Pueblo tradition, many Spanish writers lacked cross-cultural sensitivity. The forceful, sometimes fatal, impact of the Spanish colony and the Catholic church had important consequences for the Keres: the ecclesiastical capital of New Mexico, by 1604, was located in the Keres town of Santo Domingo (Hodge and others 1945: 260, 261).

Yet, the Keres cultural order has an integrity and vitality that has thrived in both old and new situations. This is witnessed by the example of the directional shrines used to fix community boundaries and reclaim Pueblo space when the Spanish capitol of Santa Fe was captured and occupied during the successful Pueblo Revolt of 1680-92. In this account, Queres is an older, Hispanic form of Keres.
Governor Otermin interrogated captive Piro and Queres men who told him that following the departure of the Spanish from Santa Fe the Indians built stone shrines in the center of the plaza and on its four sides, where prayer

plumes were deposited and offerings made of corn meal (quoted in Hayes 1974: 8).

While such details are helpful, they are not intelligible by themselves. That understanding comes from the work of professional anthropologists, such as Matilde Coxe Stevenson, Elsie Clews Parsons, Florence Hawley Ellis, Matthew Stirling, Franz Boas, Charles Lange, Robin Fox, Leslie White, Fred Eggan, and many others. To familiarize the reader with the Keres towns and ethnography, I have charted the major sources, by author and first date of publication, as cited in the bibliography.

TOWN	DATE	AUTHOR
Sia	1894	Stevenson
	1962	White
Cochiti	1890	Bandelier
	1919	Dumarest
	1926	Curtis
	1927	Goldfrank
	1931	Benedict
	1959	Lange
	1967	Fox
Laguna	1920	Parsons
	1923	Parsons
	1926	Curtis
	1928	Boas
	1959	Ellis
Acoma	1926	Curtis
	1932a	White
	1943	White
Felipe	1932b	White
Domingo	1935	White
Santa Ana	1942	White

This list, largely chronological, gives priority to the study of Sia by Matilde Coxe Stevenson, who began her work in the Southwest in the company of her husband, Colonel James Stevenson, during a collecting trip for the Bureau of American Ethnology. By all accounts, she was a strong (sometimes bullying) and dedicated woman, who helped found the 1885

Women's Anthropological Society. Her political clout with American officials was such that she got away with barging into esoteric Pueblo rituals for much of her life. Earlier, she studied women and children at another pueblo for "Religious Life of the Zuni Child." After the death of her husband, she continued alone, researching a full range of ethnographic topics. Nevertheless, I agree with Nancy Lurie (in Helm 1966: 62) that these "researches were fragmented and scattered."

In the introduction to his own monograph on Sia, Leslie White assessed the work of the Stevensons at this pueblo. Prior to the Colonel's death in 1888, the couple gathered artifacts and data in 1879 and 1887. Before she published the volume on Sia in 1894, Matilde came back for a visit in 1890. She also returned in 1904, but these notes were never published. Because she had a keen, if impolite, interest in the native religion, her volume has been particularly important for my analysis. Otherwise, as White noted, the data on social organization and daily life are weak and that on political organization is meager. White also discovered that she had altered a photograph of the altar of the Flint priesthood because it included two porcelain Chinese lions. Instead, she published a sketch of the altar in which the lions are conspicuously missing. She was so devoted to the "science" of ethnography that she routinely forced her way into sacred chambers, dislodged and photographed secret paraphernalia, and, very likely, browbeat natives. Additionally, both White and I heard rumors that the few Sia who had worked closely with her were killed on the orders of the theocracy, a grim reminder of the moral dangers of fieldwork among the Pueblos.

By the time that Elsie Clews Parsons began her comprehensive work in the Southwest, academic anthropology, founded at Columbia University, was in the process of supplanting self-taught, museum-based ethnographers like the Stevensons. Parsons became an anthropologist after a vacation in the Southwest, returning again and again to devote her time and personal fortune to the study of all the Pueblos, concentrating on folklore, social organization, and ceremonialism. All of this research culminated in her classic two volumes of Pueblo Religion (1939), where Keres data are compared by topic with that from other Pueblos. She also gave short summaries for every Keres town but Santa Ana. Earlier, she had published a series of short notes on each of the towns but Sia.

By far, her best work among the Keres was done at Laguna, famous for intense factionalism between Protestants and Catholics, which split it apart around 1880.[6] The Protestants stayed in Old Laguna, while some of the others founded the town of New Laguna ~ Mesita. The rest went to the Tiwa town of Isleta, near Albuquerque, where they established an internal colony. Although she never published a full monograph on Laguna, Parsons sketched the pre-schism ceremonial pattern (1920) and kinship system, augmented by census data on buildings and genealogies (1923).

Since Parsons, the scope of data on Laguna has been broadened by the work of Byron Harvey (1963) on the Laguna colony at Isleta, and, particularly, by information gathered for the Laguna Land Claims by Florence Hawley Ellis (1959, 1974) with the consent of town officials. Ellis effectively refuted the mistaken idea that Laguna was founded in 1699 by refugees from the eastern ~ Rio Grande Keres towns. The internal consistency of Laguna, along with a local archaeological chronology covering several thousand years, suggest instead that the Spanish sources were only noting the 1699 founding of a Catholic church there.

Laguna and Acoma, sometimes called western Keresans (Eggan 1950), have also been the source for invaluable information on Keres mythology. Particularly important for my own analysis is the Acoma Origin Saga collected in 1928 from a family visiting Washington, D.C. by Matthew Stirling (1942) and Daryll Ford, together with about 70 songs, details on the initiation of officers, membership in the Katsina cult, and the Koshari priesthood. This Acoma version of the saga is the fullest one yet collected from the Keres.

In his curious book, John Gunn (1917) includes other sections of the Acoma and Laguna Origin Saga, along with some folktales and dubious history.[7] Gunn lived with Lagunas and Acomas, collecting Keresic terms

---

[6] According to Florence Hawley Ellis (1979: 447) "The Rev. Samuel Gorman had taken residence in Laguna as a missionary in 1851 and stayed approximately 10 years. In 1868 Walter G. Marmon came to work on a boundary survey for Laguna Pueblo and in 1871 was appointed government school teacher to supplant the Spanish-American teacher whose school was private, requiring parents to pay. Robert G. Marmon, Walter's brother, arrived in 1872 as surveyor and trader, and George Pratt (Pradt), also a surveyor, at about the same time. The Marmon's cousins – John, Elgin, and Kenneth Gunn – then settled at Laguna. John establishing a flour mill. Pratt, the Gunns, and the Marmons all married Laguna women, their families forming a small colony on the northeastern edge of the village. Walter's wife later attended Carlisle while Ohio relatives by marriage cared for their children." Each Marmon served a term as governor, and Pratt was initiated into the Chakwena religious society.

[7] Paula Gunn Allen (1986: 282-3, note 1) identified Gunn as her great uncle, who later married his brother's widow and became her step-grandfather. Since he spoke Laguna Keresic and lived in the community, his information deserves serious consideration.

and song texts which he presented in anglicized, hyphenated transcriptions. Among these is a most interesting list of deities that includes not only the all-important Thought Woman (deified Consciousness), but also deities called Memory, Force, Evil, Charity, Sleep, The Yellow Earth, and The Hills and Mountains, none of which are reported elsewhere (Gunn 1917: 89). Parsons (1920) thought enough of Gunn's work to cite him and to reproduce from his book six sketches of supernaturals done by native artists.

Laguna mythology and cosmology is also presented in carefully written Keresic and English texts collected by Franz Boas (1928). His final summary of "Beliefs and Customs" extracted all the myths and interviews, presenting a plan of the Keres world, characterizations of the classes or personalities of various supernaturals, and some descriptions of officials and priesthoods (which he called shamanistic societies).

For the eastern Keres, Parsons added to our knowledge by editing a manuscript by Father Noel Dumarest on Cochiti, where he was Catholic priest, describing details of the life cycle, priesthoods, and ceremonials.

Considering the difficulties inherent in doing ethnography among the Pueblos, there has been an astounding number of scholars who have published data from Cochiti. Among them were Adolph Bandelier, Edward Curtis, Ruth Benedict, and Esther Goldfrank. Lange did a great service, in the full monograph (1959, reissued 1968), by combining their findings with his own fieldwork. He has had the rare privilege of occasionally residing in Cochiti (1947, 1948, 1951), an advantage denied by all the other towns. Nevertheless, by living inside Cochiti, he was denied certain religious information gained by others working in private with people away from the town. In other words, constant surveillance by the community and his duties as a guest left little opportunity for esoteric information to be transmitted.

Lange's book uniquely presented both a synchronic and diachronic analysis of this community. Growing out of his dissertation on economic factors effecting social change at Cochiti, his treatment expanded to include

---

After all, he was the only writer to assert, concerning White House (Chaco) (1917: 75):

> From the earliest times the Queres were governed from one central seat called "Kush Kut-ret," or the "White Village." The ruler or "Ho-chin" was elected for life, selected for his knowledge and executive ability. At his death another was selected in a similar way. His duties, besides governing the people, were to keep the ancient traditions and history of the people of the nation. He was also the head of the medicine orders. He had one officer, the war captain (Sah-te Ho-Chin).

geography, ecology, archaeology, history, ownership, farming, diet, subsistence, political offices, religious organization, ceremonies, social and kinship organization, life cycle, and numerous appendices listing property frequencies, supplementary descriptions, and socio-religious memberships. In sum, Lange produced the best general and accessible work on the Keres. Complementing it is the plausible novel – The Delight Makers, a synonym for the Koshari priests ~ sacred clowns – about ancestors of Cochiti by Adolph Bandelier, based on his personal experiences and observations in this town.

Among the appendices to Lange are a treatment of song and dance by Gertrude Kurath and of sociolinguistics by J.R. Fox, who later went on to study Cochiti and Keresan social organization and to argue against the position taken by Fred Eggan that the Keres form a gradient ~ bridge between the matrilineal, clan-based Western Pueblos like Hopi and Zuni, and the more bilateral, family-based Eastern Pueblos like the Tewa, who are supposed to be acculturating to the descent system of Spanish and American settlers in New Mexico. Rather, Fox (1967: 187) decided that the Keres have "an intelligible system in its own right, based on a form of double descent and dual affiliation, and an organization of extended families." More specifically, "it turns on the twin axis of mother-child and father-son, linked by the indissoluble bond of husband-wife" (1967: 129) at one level, and of matriclan-kiva complementarity at another (1967: 121-24).

The analysis by Fox represented a major breakthrough for understanding Keres culture, although he did not fully explore its ramifications. While Dozier (1970: 124) accused Fox of some wild speculations and others have criticized the briefness of his fieldwork, they overlook the value of his insight into the importance of a dual axis for understanding Keres culture.

Indeed, throughout this book, the equations established by Fox will be expressed by the basic Keresan institutions of the priesthoods (father - son, real and ceremonial), clans (mother -child lineages), and kiva wings (husband - wife) aligning these components of a town into moieties.

While Cochiti by Lange was the best general work, the life-long Keresan research of Leslie White detailed most of the Keresans. In all, he produced monographs on five of the seven Keresan towns, albeit uneven in size and content, after he began his work in 1928 under the scholastic and financial guidance of Elsie Clews Parsons. To assess his overall contribution to Keres research, each monograph will be treated separately before his career is summarized as the preeminent Keresanist.

Acoma was the first town described by White, establishing a model for his other ethnographic treatments. After a historical summary of Spanish and American sources, he described the layout and contemporary situation of the town, then turned to the matriclans, native leaders and priesthoods, pantheon, ceremonies, Katsina organization, medicine priesthoods and their cures, distinctive paraphernalia, life cycle, and, finally, myths and tales. Almost a decade later, he published new material to augment our knowledge of Acoma in terms of leadership, priesthoods, life cycle, tales, and a short biography of a 73 year old man.

Acoma has a fascinating position among the Keres since it still maintains the office of Outside Priest and has a problematical number and shape to its kivas. One of the advantages of my model is that it places these anomalous features of Acoma within the overall Keres pattern. For example, White (1932a: 100) noted that Acomans sometimes divide up between Eastern Town Kiva and Western Fire Chamber, which agrees with the general division into East and West kivas among the other Keres. At the other towns, kivas are round, but at Acoma they are square. Explanation of this is deferred until later, however, because it requires an understanding of the cosmology and local terrain. Acoma, and possibly Laguna, are the only towns known to celebrate elaborate rites enacting the mythic fight between humans and Katsina, the visitation of supernaturals called Kopishtaiya, and a Corn clan sponsored ceremony called Shuratsha Lights The Fire. Both the Corn and Antelope clans sponsor rituals and have separate clan houses, perhaps vestiges of Chacoan greathouses. While the house and ritual is under the nominal authority of a clan, participants are recruited through a variety of fictive and ceremonial kinship ties. Such a parallel will be treated fully in the final chapter, where relations between clans, clan-sponsored rites, and greathouses are explored.

Published in the same year as his first Acoma monograph, White's San Felipe report is the shortest (70pp) and least detailed of his five studies. It includes a brief sketch of history, political organization, priesthoods (which he calls fraternities), and ceremonies concerned with the solstices, scalp dance, rabbit hunt, buffalo hunt, birth, and death. Appendices treat names for places, birds, and colors, together with what could be learned about the styles of prayersticks. San Felipe seems unique among the Keres in having three Katsina groups, while the other towns have two. Felipe has the same two, Turquoise and Squash, associated with each of the kivas, plus a third called _yaashstcha_ 'all kinds of beads.' This is the smallest group and has only a house where its masks are stored. As discussed later, these data from Felipe make most sense in terms of the comparative evidence from Cochiti and Santo Domingo.

In his work on Domingo, White discusses historical and contemporary periods, social organization, life cycle, ceremonialism, and mythology. Appendices are devoted to the question of possible relations between the Katsina and the dead, along with lists of terms for numerals, colors, reptiles, animals, corn, birds, places, and some body parts. While thicker than the work on Felipe, the Santo Domingo monograph lacks the sweep of the later books. Among the most interesting features of this pueblo has been its willingness to accept migrants from other Pueblos, even though it is reputed to be very conservative and notoriously inhospitable to Anglos. Evidence for outside influences include an internal colony of Tano (Southern Tewa) from the Galisteo Basin to the east,[8] the Boyakya priesthood with curing songs in Tano, its role as the past Catholic ecclesiastic capital, a crucial role in the Cerrillos turquoise mine and the modern jewelry trade, especially on its feast day, and its modern position as headquarters for the All Pueblo Council. A cultural reason for this kind of receptivity will be explored later.

White apparently regarded his volume on Santa Ana as his best, and he had good reason to do so because it is the fullest treatment of the esoteric lore so crucial to understanding the Keres. He was able to improve on it later, however, after he had worked with a priestly initiate at Sia, adding a few important concepts. Along with his usual chapters, he included others on Corn and the Cosmos, Hunting, Warfare, Sickness and Witchcraft, and Paraphernalia. His Introduction includes a fine discussion of the difficulties of doing ethnography among the Keres, both in terms of the problems for the researcher and of the potentially fatal consequences for informants who speak about "secrets" to which they do not have a legitimated right. The volume presents our fullest discussion of cosmology, the pantheon, selection and instillation of the Tiamunyi (cacique) and "her" successor (the Gowiye), kinship terminology, songs sung by specific Katsina, the Christmas and Easter ceremonies, and esoteric paraphernalia.

White thought Santa Ana unique among the Keres by virtue of its two Shikame priesthoods, kiva membership determined by clanship, and allowing initiated women to wear the masks representing female Katsina. All of these bear on my argument for a Keresan unity, and become understandable when compared to those of Sia, Acoma, and Laguna, all of

---

[8] The Boyakya priesthood originated among the Tano or Southern Tewa of the Galisteo Basin. In 1706, 18 Tano families living at Tesuque resettled Galisteo Pueblo, but epidemics and Comanche attacks forced them to abandon the basin between 1782 and 1794, when 52 Tanos joined Santo Domingo (Schroeder 1979: 248). The Tano majority had joined the First Mesa Hopi in 1700.

which also link matriclans with kivas. Sia also seems to permit women to impersonate female Katsina. Furthermore, Santa Ana continues a version of the otherwise lapsed Warrior Priesthood (the *Opi*) by initiating hunters who kill a cougar, bear, or eagle into the Animal *Opi*. The only other town to do this is Cochiti, a manly hub for the overall Keresan pattern.

Moreover, while this theoretical consideration of Keresan interactions generally lacks mention of inter-town hostilities, and since each pueblo stood alone for economic and some political purposes, conflicts obviously developed with neighbors.

Tamaya ~ *Damaya* (Santa Ana 1994) has chronicled some in a history of their land use and title, specifically mentioning abuses by some Sia, Cochiti, and San Felipe. In the 1400s, a Sia town (*Kiticina Tsiiyame*) asked Navajo help for a planned attack on *Kwiiste Puu Tamaya*, across from them on the Rio Salado near Borrego Springs. On 8 October 1687, Pedro Reneros de Posada led a force north from El Paso that kidnapped Tamaya young children while a Cochiti man had lured the men of Sia, Tamaya, and Jemez off on an antelope hunt (1994: 71, 233). Native officers later insisted that they received land rights to the Espiritu Santo (Holy Ghost Spring) grazing area near Mesa Prieta (*siiku*) in compensation.

During the last century, San Felipe repeatedly tried to sell off farmland owned and purchased by Santa Ana (1994: 99). In 1900, the Masewi war captain had to threaten off Anglo developers and others trying to steal water rights. Indeed, at the 1936 All-Pueblo Council meeting with John Collier, Tamaya leaders pleaded that "we find ourselves in the bewildering wilderness of modern civilization."

The Sia study was, in many ways, the culmination of White's career, a final refinement of his total understanding. While his Santa Ana report remained definitive for religion and society, the Sia volume presented philosophy and semantics, thanks to the assistance of a member of a native priesthood. The Introduction, in addition to assessing the work of the Stevensons, has a useful discussion of the linguistic use (and "abuse") of English and Keresic by Sias. He noted that Keresic does not develop neologisms (new coinages), so foreign words must be adopted for introduced items. This practice is curious because other Pueblos strictly keep foreign words and objects away from their communities, and absolutely forbid them in religious contexts, particularly inside the kivas.

The Sia were discussed in terms of subsistence and cash economy, degree of Christianity, health care, life cycle, sickness, and ceremonialism. White refined our understanding of the two so-called solstice ceremonies, proposing that they be called solar rites because their timing is intended to anticipate the turning points of the sunrise along the horizon, as prelude to the actual solstice standstills (see the last chapter).

In addition to these monographs, White also published many articles. Among the more important of these was one describing an esoteric ceremonial language ~ vocabulary among the Pueblos, illustrated by Santa Ana examples, one discussing Keresan color terms, including the merging of blue and green under one word,[9] and others treating ethnobotany, ethnozoology, age and sex terms, numerals, and minerals. While White did the most to round out our knowledge of the Keres, he never provided an overall synthesis.

As White himself recognized, his work suffered in two areas. First, the bulk of his data came from native statements about what should or ought to happen, but he could rarely if ever observe and verify it. His ethnography, therefore, represented the ideal rather than the real, the cultural rather than the practical, the normative rather than the statistical.

A second detriment to the work of White was his lack of women sources, which had as much to do with Keres reluctance to deal with outsiders and the modesty of Keres women as it did with White's methodology. Compensating for this absence, however, was the research of Stevenson, Parsons, and Ellis, women involved in long term fieldwork with Keresan women. In general, though, the Keres data were silent with respect to the everyday life of women and their overall position in the society.

Of related concern is the ethical dilemma of collecting data from the Keres. Fox, somewhat unfairly, wrote that "White has carried the art of pumping informants to a fine degree." White himself admitted that he often patiently coaxed information from people, but he always clearly identified himself as an anthropologist. His sources were helping him for intellectual as well as financial reasons; they were as curious about their own traditions as White was. Shortly before he died, White (1973) discussed the financial deprivations by his wife and himself to conduct the fieldwork, marking further that

I have produced a few comprehensive studies of some of the Pueblos; they stand (with all their faults and shortcomings) as enduring memorials of what was once their world. Devoted Indians helped me to make these studies and others treasure them as reminiscences of the lives of their mothers and fathers.

---

[9] Using the same word for both blue and green is common in Native American languages, but the Southwest also valued turquoise with the same color range. The color is often called "grue" (green + blue).

White always compensated informants, either formally with money or informally with gifts of food. Keres particularly liked cans of sweet corn. While I admire White's data and his ability to acquire them, there is no easy solution to the ethical problems involved. Surely, the wishes of native intellectuals must be considered along with those of commoners and priests. Of all the researchers, only Lange, Fox, and Ellis have had anything approaching community approval. Such approval, of course, actually rests in the hands of the theocracy since they have authority and sanctions over ordinary people. As Adamson Hoebel made clear in his study of Keres law, these are highly centralized communities.

Allied research among the Keres includes the work of Francis Densmore on the music of Acoma, Cochiti, and, particularly, Santo Domingo. Linguistic studies have been done on Keresic as spoken at Acoma by Wick Miller and Joel Shiner and at Santa Ana by Irvine Davis. Miller and Davis collaborated on a reconstruction of the proto-phonology. General outlines of Keresan glottochronology have been done by Davis (1959), who suggested that Keresic diverged at least 500 years ago into four slight dialects: Cochiti, San Felipe - Santo Domingo, Santa Ana - Sia, and Acoma - Laguna. Earlier work on Keresan language includes the comparative study by Robert Spencer (1940) and brief comments by Ales Hrdlicka, Nixon Toomey, and Robin Fox (see bibliography).

Theories

My model argues for the cultural unity of the Keres, emphasizing the similarities and continuities of the pattern while also accounting for important local differences and diversity. As such, this argument runs counter to all previous statements, which were devoted to the comparative study of all the Pueblos or to a few diagnostic traits. Only after I had a model for Keres integrity did I turn to these comparative and tribal studies to trace ramifications of a Keres nexus for all the Pueblos, as discussed at the end of Part One.

Previous theories were based on the occurrence of particular features and all, to some degree, argued for acculturation. Except for the implicit unity provided by their unclassified, unaffiliated status as a language isolate, Keres have been regarded as internally more diverse than similar. My own view, however, grew out of an appreciation of the engendering of the various social and ceremonial organizations among the towns.

At various times, Leslie White tried to trace the inter-relationships among the towns. Initially, he (1928: 619) wrote "I feel that Santo

Domingo and San Felipe are most typical ... Cochiti and Sia, however, are not far behind ... Sant'Ana, Laguna, and Acoma diverge most widely." Later, he (1935: 21, notes 49, 51) explained "For some time I have felt that Santo Domingo is the most important of the Keres pueblos ... the population of Laguna and her colonies is larger than that of Domingo. But the old pueblo of Laguna is almost deserted, and her culture quite disintegrated and Americanized ... Sia is quite small and considerably disintegrated. Cochiti and Santa Ana are variants of what might be termed a Keresan norm. San Felipe is quite close to Santo Domingo." In the same pages, White referred to Acoma as marginal. Later adding, "Sia and Acoma have been especially closely related, historically and culturally" (1962: 83).

White emphasized Domingo for its large population and ongoing ritualism, conservative haughtiness, and central location. In short, his classification seems to be based on resistance to outside influences. This has to be a relative argument because no Keres town has fully given up its language, religion, or theocracy. Acculturation is carefully limited to work in the cash economy, purchase of factory-made goods, and use of conveniences such as cars, electricity, and indoor plumbing. The cultural heart continues to beat strongly.

Other theories compared the Keres with all other Pueblos or with the entire Southwest as a culture area.

Karl Wittfogel and Esther Goldfrank discussed evidence for the Pueblos as an incipient hydraulic ~ waterwork society based on irrigation. Goldfrank had already published the first major work on Cochiti to detail its tripartite organization, then considered unique and problematical. The importance of this anomaly will be discussed under the Towns. Considering Pueblo mythology and society, these authors remarked
The importance of maternal clans in Hopi, their lesser significance in Zuni, and their gradual replacement in the east by social organizations of a different type, certainly do not mechanically reflect the basic diversities in the structure of the miniature Pueblo waterwork societies. But variations in the irrigation pattern and the kinship systems of the different pueblos show too striking a correspondence to be dismissed easily" (Wittfogel and Goldfrank 1943: 27).

Edward Dozier (1970: 131), an anthropologist born into the Tewa Pueblo of Santa Clara, restated the irrigation hypothesis more forcefully "I believe that intensive irrigation practices utilizing water from permanently flowing streams have brought about the centralized orientation of the Eastern ~ Rio Grande Pueblos." While this ecological argument has considerable merit, I will argue below that it represents a development along lines already basic to Keres culture, reinforcing clans, priesthoods, or kivas where they were long entrenched.

The most famous theory applied to the Pueblos is that of Fred Eggan (1950), building on past publications and his own fieldwork among the Hopi. His model argued for the degeneration or progressive acculturation from a universal Pueblo type, which remains strongest among the Western Pueblos, particularly the Hopi. It was based on the matrilineage but has been changing to accord with Anglo-Hispanic bilaterality, especially among the Tewa, who had the longest contact with the foreigners. As the Keres occur in the middle of its range, he called them a "bridge" gradually shifting among themselves from matrilineal Western Keres at Acoma to more bilateral Eastern Keres at Cochiti. Corollary to this main argument is another Fox (1967: 25) dubbed "time of arrival: length of survival," meaning that as successive waves of Pueblo peoples moved into the Rio Grande Valley, each of them shifted from clan- to moiety-based organizations because this greater flexibility was better adapted to successful irrigation.

In keeping with such recognized importance of the prehistoric record for understanding the Southwest, and in lieu of ethnographic analogies, the second half of this book will attempt an "archaeological analogy" to fit modern Keres into their past. Once their modern society has been detailed in terms of its threeway structuring of priesthoods, clans, and moiety kiva wings, the archaeological development will be traced primarily through architecture. Specifically, discussion will focus on the shift from pithouses to chamber kivas for the priesthoods, from matrilineage smallhouses to clan sponsored greathouses as shrines and fetish repositories, and of great kivas as integrating mechanisms for all these components.

Overall, greater comprehension of Keresans requires careful review of the Puebloan Southwest. While Fox began by considering several empirical flaws in Eggan's model, there are other difficulties, including comparative ones. While all the Pueblos are characterized by an farming economy, multi-storied architecture, theocratic polity, kivas, and masked cults, they are by not uniform, representing four language stocks with considerable dialect diversity. Chartering mythologies and cosmologies differ, including deliberate reversals evident by "playing off" Keres against Tewa or Hopi, one often a mirror opposite, the later often parallel, since Hopi were "puebloized" by neighboring Keresans (below).

Chapter Two

THE ORIGIN EPIC

To understand the Keres, their universe, as explained in their chartering saga, must be described. While full accounts are not available from each of the towns, versions have been published for Sia (Stevenson 1894, White 1962), Laguna (Boas 1928, Ellis 1974), and Cochiti (Benedict 1931), together with an especially rich account from Acoma (Stirling 1942). White (1960) published an overview of the saga, which he called a consensus account because it was based only on common features found in all the available variants. Such a comparison indicates that all Keres have the same saga, varied according to the local conditions of each town.

Among these distinctions, the most important characters have names and attributes that vary according to the spoken dialects. Thus, to proceed with the analysis, but forestall overly biasing the account, I have decided to use capitalized letters for each of these deities since the initial sound of the names seems to be consistent throughout the towns. Therefore, T represents the deity various called Tsityostinako, Tsichtinako, Sussistinnako, and Ts'its'ts'ciinaak'o. A lengthy exegesis will be devoted to this high god, later in this section, because this is the crucial mediator of Keres culture (Miller 1989). Usual translations of this name as "Thought, Prophesying Woman," however, are inadequate because they ignore its full semantic range. For now, "it" will be androgynous, since it has been variously described as a man, a woman, and a spider (White 1962, 113).

Other actors were U for Uretsiti ~ Utctsityi ~ Utset ~ I'tc'ts'ity'i, and N for Naotsiti ~ Nutsityi ~ Nowutset ~ Nowshsiti. In most accounts, U and N were sisters. The Acoma version translated their names: U as "Crammed Full (In A Basket)" (Stirling 1942: 1, note 4) and N as "More Of Everything (In A Basket)" (1942: 3). Some versions add I, another deity called Iatiku "Bringing To Life" (1942: 3), although Gunn (1917: 89) said E-yet-e-co means "Earth." The same name was also applied to the sacred fetish, made of a perfect ear of corn, given to members of the priesthoods to serve as a badge of initiation.

The attributes of these last three personages also varied among the accounts. White's (1960) summary referred to U as elder and N as younger sister, as do most sources. Stevenson (1894) had N as elder and U as younger in her Sia version, but White (1962: 115) reversed this order and had U as the elder. At Laguna, U was the father of Anglos (whites, Euro-Americans) and N was the Mother of Indians (Ellis 1974: 24). At Cochiti, N was the elder sister and mother of whites and Navahos, while U was the younger one and mother of Indians (Benedict 1931: 203). At Acoma, U was the masculine creator of the universe, and T seems vague and androgynous, finishing the work of creation through the medium of two sisters: N, the younger one associated with whites, and Iatiku, the older sibling associated with the Keres (Stirling 1942). These characters and attributes will be sorted out by sex, age, and function at the end of this section.

Unfortunately, the consensus account by White missed much of the well-ordered diversity in the variants. Therefore, I assembled a composite of all of them by relying on internal evidence to establish a relative chronology for events.

Composite Epic

Only the Acoma version mentioned the actual creation of the world from a void ~ nothing when U threw a clot of his own blood into space and used his supernatural power to make it grow.[10] This earth was metaphorically a Woman, whom he hung from the Milky Way with her head to the east, feet to the west, and arms to the north and south (Stirling 1942: 29). One Laguna version began with only water, from which land emerges spontaneously and the sisters appear (Boas 1928: 8).

While a Woman, the earth is also a cube, divided into four layers. From bottom to top these are identified by color as the White, Red, Grue (Green-Blue), and Yellow Worlds. At Sia, however, these colored worlds are listed in an order that is exactly the reverse. At Acoma, four layers of sky are also mentioned above the earth, with U living in the highest of these sky levels.

All versions agree that at the center of the White World is a place called ShipopU, the spiritual heart of the Keres world, their first and dearest home. T created the sisters at ShipopU and charged them with finishing creation according to unspoken instructions ~ thoughts from T. At Sia, T created the sisters by drawing a line of cornmeal from north to south and bisecting it with another from east to west. Then, a bundle of unspecified contents was placed in the northeast quadrant, another in the northwest one. Sitting in the southwest one, T began to sing and, soon, the parcels began to shake like rattles and grow into the sisters. When the song ended, all animate life had been created by the sisters (Stevenson 1894: 27). Therefore, it seems that creation became measured and modulated by

---

[10] A fascinating parallel suggestive of a remote common ancestry is the Lakota creation of the earth from blood drained from Rock. The Keres belief is strikingly similar.

the song, thought by T, which instructed the sisters in their task. Even now, a priesthood conducts its cure in time with a series of esoteric (secret and sacred) songs. Presumably, songs have the ability to create and cure because they catch the flow and rhythm of power (*iyaanyi*) coursing through the cosmos.

According to the Acoma myth, U placed the sisters at ShipopU in complete darkness. As they grew, they were nourished and taught language by T. Once, the sisters asked T "whether it was male or female" (Stirling 1942: 1), but received no response. When they were full grown, T somehow gave each sister a basket of seeds and animal images in gender pairs, from which they were to create animate life. They planted seeds for four species of evergreens, which grew rapidly until one of them pierced through to the next higher world, flooding the lowest one with light. The image of badger was enlivened to widen the hole, and the locust image was sent to plaster the inside of it. Locust, however, prematurely ventured into the higher world of light ahead of the others, and, for his presumption, locusts have spent much time in the dark ground.

Everything done by the sisters was according to the thoughts put into their minds by T. Creation moved from the lower worlds to the upper ones, passing through a hollow reed or a hole made by a fast-growing tree and new-made creatures. By convention, it is said that the sisters lived four years in each of the lower worlds, until they emerged into the present one. They came out in the north, at a spot called Gauwatsaishoma, directly above ShipopU (White 1943: 323). Sometimes, people emerge with the sisters, led by the priests of special cults. Otherwise, it is implied that separate people were created in each of the lower worlds by the sisters, then created one final time at the top level. Among the people, there was a distinct class of witches (*kanadaiya*), called 'left-handed' and 'two-hearts' because they had both a good heart like humans and the bad one of witches. Sometimes, witches slipped into this world unnoticed, or, when they were discovered by the people, they made a convincing case that witches perform a useful service, preventing overpopulation, and so they were allowed to stay. People tolerate witches as long as they keep things in balance; only punishing or killing them during spells of dire misfortune.

When the sisters first came out, this last world was raw, spongy, and incomplete so it had to be cooked ~ hardened. At Acoma, the Cougar image was animated to do this. At Sia, U asked, in turn, Cougar, Bear, Badger, Shrew, and Wolf to try, but each failed. Next, a female member of the Spider priesthood had some success building a cobweb bridge. Then, a male Spider fully hardened the world and four directions, progressing south, east, west, and north (Stevenson 1894: 36).

The sisters created the sun of white shell, turquoise, red stone, and abalone shell – directing it to travel from north to south, then west to east, before they decided it should move from east to west (Stevenson 1894: 35; Boas 1928: 2, 5). The moon was made of turquoise and black, yellow, and red stone. Stevenson (1894: 30) said the sun and moon were brothers. Stirling (1942: 27) said that the moon was female and weak, while the sun was male and strong. Some versions have Star People created to help the moon. Others have a bug, usually a beetle, leaving the underworld, entrusted with a bag containing the stars. Curiosity overcomes the bug, who opens the bag to look inside. Most of the stars rush out to take up disorganized positions in the sky (Stevenson 1894: 37). Those remaining become constellations.

After the sisters emerged, T named them at the first sunrise, together with the directions around them: east in front, west behind, north to the left, south to the right, and, lastly, above and below. The woman on the right was named U, who then chose to belong to the Corn clan. The woman on the left became N, associated with the Sun clan because she received its full rays and became white (Stirling 1942: 5). The sisters created the four sacred mountains at the north, west, south, and east to mark the boundaries of the Keres world. They went to these mountains with their baskets to populate them with plants and animals. Over time, they became careless, putting wild fruits in the mountains rather than near future habitation sites as had been intended, thus making life that much harder.

The Cloud People, Lightning People, Thunder People, and Rainbow People were created by I through the sisters to bring water and rain to the earth. A pair of each of these was sent to live in a spring at the heart of each of the sacred mountains of the six directions. Each mountain was also topped by a giant tree: spruce in the north, pine in the west, one kind of oak in the south, aspen in the east, cedar in the above, and another kind of oak in the below. In addition, all supernaturals were given the use of the Middle Sky, where they ride around on hoops proportional to their size (Stevenson 1894: 38).

The sisters continued to be involved with creating and instructing people in the proper use of things. Corn was a special gift from U to the people, said to be equivalent to milk from her breasts. Later, when U created priesthoods, she made a fetish from a hollowed perfect ear of corn for each initiate as a vital badge of membership. People were taught to roll mature tobacco leaves in corn husks to make cigarettes, and to smoke them to compel acceptance of their requests, the rising smoke and prayers ultimately merging with the minds of the deities (Stirling 1942: 7).

When the sisters began to create animal life, they enlivened the image of Kangaroo Mouse and told it to increase. People learned to kill, cook, salt, and eat these mice, which thenceforth "represented all animal food" (Stirling 1942: 38). After grass was planted to feed them, Rat, Mole, and Prairie Dog were animated. Images of larger animals were set in the mountains, among pinyon, cedar, oak, and walnut trees. Rabbits, Antelope, and Bison were placed on the plains, Elk and Deer in the lower mountains, and Mountain Sheep in higher, rougher terrain. If Cougar, Wolf, Wildcat, and Bear had not already been created to harden the earth, their carniverous images were enlivened at this point to keep the other animal populations in check. Next in succession, the sisters made Eagle and Hawk, smaller birds, cacti, and water creatures like Fish, Turtle, and Water Snake.

It was during this time that an image slipped unnoticed from the basket and activated itself to become the evil being called Pishuni at Acoma and Laguna. Other towns call him Poshaiyanyi, but regard him as a mythic hero who left the Keres and went to live in Mexico.

This was also the time that U felt she had been working harder than N, who was hoarding the images in her basket. Thus began selfish thoughts, and the sisters began to quarrel. Pishuni talked N into visiting the Rainbow, where she was impregnated by rain drops and gave birth to twin boys. By acting on her own, N caused T to become angry and desert them. N raised the son she liked, and gave the other to U. At Acoma, the sisters and these boys sired humanity. Elsewhere, the people came up from the lower worlds with the sisters, or were created anew at each level. In all cases, the priests were created before the ordinary people (White 1962: 116).

The sisters continued to quarrel about the relative strengths of their own powers. They decided on a series of tests. Commonly, the first one to be struck by the rays of the sunrise would be judged the stronger. U instructed Magpie to fly east and block the Sun with wide-spread wings, keeping N in darkness. In a Sia version, a feather was plucked from the left wing so rays would shine through onto U, but otherwise block them from N (Stevenson 1894: 34). Another time, they held a guessing game. N tried to baffle U by creating something under a blanket that had crossed legs and was neither male nor female, but U was not fooled (1894: 32).

Finally, U won all the contests. At Sia, U then killed N, removed her heart, cut it up, and turned the pieces into Woodrats (1894: 34). At Cochiti, U cut out the heart of N, split it open, and watched as "a squirrel came from the north side and a white dove from the south" of it (Benedict 1931: 204). At Acoma, after N was defeated, she went off to the east with domesticated plants and animals, writing, and metal, explaining how Europeans got them (Stirling 1942: 13).

At Acoma, U then settled down with her foster son and husband, who was named Tiamunyi. When she had her firstborn, she assigned it to the Sun clan in memory of N. Thereafter, this child and all others have been ritually presented to the sun on the fourth sunrise after birth. Her daughters founded the various matriclans, their names and rankings depending on the town member telling the saga. Each town also insists that its ancestors migrated by the most direct route from the place of emergence to the very center of the present world, while the other towns meandered along, unsure even now of their proper location.

Still not content with the world, U made personifications of the seasons, all of them ugly, and put them atop the sacred mountains: Winter in the north to send snow, Spring in the west to send warmth, Summer in the south to send heat to ripen crops, and Fall in the east to send frost to erase the smells of fruits and plants. Later, Summer and Winter fought to establish which was stronger. Summer won and controls the seasons for seven months, winter for only five (Boas 1928: 245).

Next, U made the Katsina, who were handsome. The first one created became their leader: a left-handed male, named Heruta (Curtis 1926: 110). Other Katsina were made in pairs, man and woman (Stirling 1942: 15) sent to live in the south and west at a place called Wenimatsa, under a lake filled with weeds, where they were given animals to hunt. People seeking them had to make an offering consisting of a basket of corn meal, pollen, tobacco, and prayersticks. With such offerings, people could summon them, asking for rain, summer clouds, and food. During visits, they were given human produce in return for those gifts.

U created Kopishtaiya and his wife, who are ferocious, to control winter clouds. They too receive a stipulated basket of offerings when people pray to them for a long, healthy life and for bravery. Later, when several Kopishtaiya gambled with witches to recover the body of dead girl, they had to renounce sexual relations forever in return for winning the body from the two-hearts (White 1932a: 65).

After emergence, the Keres began to move south until they collected again at a town called White House, where U began her preparations to leave humans and return alone to ShipopU. As her representative, she appointed a good man to be mother and father of the townspeople, giving him the title of Tiamunyi. (Much later, he also became known as the cacique.) She gave him a staff of office, a wooden slat altar, and other insignia, filling his heart with her mind. He also became father of the Katsina because he was intermediary between the town and these rain-bringers, summoning them each time by burying four baskets of offerings.

The people began to build the first kiva, intended to represent ShipopU. An excavation was made and prayersticks and bits of different-colored turquoise were buried under the foundations at the four directions: yellow turquoise in the north, grue in the west, red in the south, and white in the east. Four posts set up in these positions held up the roof and represented the four evergreens planted at ShipopU. Under the entry ladder, representing the Rainbow, was the fireplace, called Bear. Around the interior wall was a bench, believed to be occupied by supernaturals during rituals and called the 'fog seat'.

The Hunters priesthood was created when U selected a man to lead it, providing him with songs, prayers, and a wooden slat altar. He became the Hunt Man, who made prayersticks and small hunting fetishes to be loaned to men when they went out hunting. The fetishes represent the Animal Hunters of the six directions: Cougar of the north, Wolf of the west, Lynx of the south, Wildcat of the east, Eagle of the zenith, and "something like a shrew" of the nadir. The Hunt Man set the rules for hunting, and directed the communal rabbit drives, seated beside an outdoor fire.

Whenever a hunter killed large game, such as a deer or bear, his family ritually welcomed it into their household. It was given a place of honor and decorated with textiles and jewelry. Other people came by to visit and welcome it into the town. Then, it was butchered and the skull given to the Hunt Man, who supervised members of the priesthood as they painted and decorated it. The skull was then left at a mountain shrine so the animal could be reborn.

Reviewing her labors, U became concerned that Tiamunyi would be overworked and so selected a man to be Outside ~ Country Priest. Thus, the duties of running the town were divided such that the Town Priest became concerned with internal, ritual affairs, while the Country Priest handled external, defensive concerns – ranging from patrol of the territory to matters of discipline and civil law within the town. The Tiamunyi could only deal with good things, keeping his mind untroubled for his ("her") real work of fasting, praying, and making offerings for the benefit of the community. The Outside Priest had to deal with disagreements and revenge, assisted by the war captains because of the enormity of these duties among a people dedicated to carefully balanced harmony.

Although some versions have the priesthoods created in the lower worlds, U seems to have given them final form and instruction at White House. Doctors and priests were taught to fast, pray, and cure at night, using special paraphernalia: painted slat altars, obsidian knives, sand paintings, fetishes, mittens of left bear paws, and eagle bone whistles. The fetishes represented the Animal Doctors of the six directions: Bear of the north, Cougar of the west, Badger of the south, Wolf of the east, Eagle of the above, and a rodent of the below (Lange 1968a: 230). Sometimes, animal doctors are distinguished vertically: Eagle of the sky, Bear of the earth, and Weasel of the underground.

Bear is always the leader of the Animal Doctors; that is why curing priests wear bear paws. Each doctor also has a fetish made from a perfect ear of corn, finely decorated. When U made the first one, she hollowed out the core and blew some of her heart-breath inside, along with some honey "because it comes from all kinds of plants and it therefore symbolizes all plant food" (Stirling 1942: 32). During four day retreats in their own chamber, doctors practiced sexual abstinence to keep their minds pure and revitalize the power of themselves and their fetishes.

The managing priesthoods were founded by the creation of Koshari, wearing horizontal bands of black and white (like convict stripes) and a hairdo of two spikes wrapped in cornhusks, and Kwirena, who wore different colors on the right and left sides of his body and had sparrow hawk feathers in his hair. Little is said of Kwirena, who is overshadowed by the more boisterous Koshari. As soon as he came into existence, Koshari was a bossy know-it-all. On his way to help the first medicine priesthood, he blithely broke several taboos. Toward the end of the mythic age, Koshari and Kwirena left the people to go and live in the middle of the east side of the world. Their *iyaanyi*, however, still resides in the priesthoods bearing their names, helping people and coordinating all rituals.

As with the clans, the exact sequence of the creation of the priesthoods, together with their personifications as Man or Woman, varies with the town recounting the saga.

At White House, women and men argued violently for four days about which made the most important contribution to survival. Each sex met in different kivas, where they decided that henceforth they would live apart. Men moved across the river. When their sons were old enough, the women sent them across, too. The men lived on meat and thrived, but the women lived on plants and began to lose weight and weaken. After four years of hardship, the women begged the men to return. They did so and, after four days, the women completely revived on the meat provided by their kinsmen.

But all was not well. During the separation, women had children without the help of males and these grew rapidly into giant cannibals, who caught and roasted many people. Other people were killed by giant animals who had also appeared while the men were off their guard.

People despaired until the Sun took pity. He appeared on earth as a handsome young man and gave two pinyon nuts to a virgin girl. Twelve days later, she gave birth to male twins, Masewi and Oyoyewi, who grew up quickly. As they came to know their surroundings, they asked after their father. Once informed, over their mother's objections, they resolved to visit him, aided in this quest by "Grandmother Spider," her only son, and her many daughters.

They reached the home of the Sun in the sky, where he tested them, to make sure they were indeed his sons, by sealing them in a hot oven, which merely made them full grown and very handsome. Then, he placed them in six different rooms, one for each direction, filled with a ferocious species. Each time, when the Sun looked in, the boys were playing with those animals. Satisfied, the Sun gave them special weapons to kill the giant Wolf of the east, Cougar of the north, Bear of the west, and Eagle of the south. In lieu of destroying Antelope, they made it into the harmless creatures of today. The twins also killed the parthenogenetic cannibals.

They forced people to live correctly. Before visiting one town, they coated themselves with honey to look poor and dirty. Among the Keres, guests must be welcomed and fed. At this town, however, all but one couple refused them hospitality and food. Therefore, after the couple was spared, the spirits of the townspeople turned into canyon wrens, and their bodies and town changed into stone. Through these and other efforts, the twins turned hostility and unkindness to the good.

White House became characterized by constant solemnity and fasting. To provide periodic relief, U suggested to the Outside Chief that he invent social dances and kickstick races. Men also devised gambling, becoming so obsessed with it that disaster followed. Young men made up gambling songs mocking U, the Katsina, and women. Angry, U left for ShipopU, but promised to continue as their mother. So her children could return to her, U introduced death, which also kept the earth from becoming overcrowded (Benedict 1931: 5). Just before she left, she taught the Country Chief to count "beginning with the little finger on the left hand" (Stirling 1942: 47). Because of the mockery, the Katsina refused to bring rain to the Keres, causing drought and famine.

Conditions worsened. Finally, a virtuous and industrious young man, living with his mother, began to dance alone in a plaza upon the advice of a priest. He danced for a day with all sincerity and, thus, coaxed back the Katsina to visit White House. The people prospered, but also began to gamble. During one game, someone verbally insulted the Katsina. Sitting unnoticed in the back of the room, a Katsina heard this and reported it to his fellows. Their leader tried to be plead for peace, but was unsuccessful. A swarm of angry Katsina followed their messenger, the Gomaiyawish, and attacked White House. The people were unprepared and many were killed. Hearing the battle, the twins rushed to arrive and carried the day for humans. Afterward, Masewi and Oyoyewi went around reviving the fallen Katsina, but they could do nothing for the dead humans. To punish the Gomaiyawish for leading the attack, the twins castrated him.

After two insults and the fight, the Katsina decided they could no longer visit the Keres in person. Instead, Heruta, the leader who had tried to remain neutral, decreed that he would initiate willing humans so they would be able to wear masks and costumes like the real Katsina, who would send rain and blessings in thanks for respectful petitions. Finally, the Katsina went home, dying again for a month. The Keres spent this month in disagreement. Those who did not want to be initiated left White House, never to be seen again. Those who remained were initiated in the summer, founding the Katsina cult.

The following winter, it was also decided that the Kopishtaiya should no longer visit in person and so they too began to be impersonated. People learned that when a dancer put on the mask of either a Katsina or a Kopishtaiya, its spirit entered that human for the duration of the rite. At the end, the mask was removed, and offerings were sent along with the departing spirit.

These cults allowed the people at White House to be content and successful again. All went smoothly until disease struck and many died. This was taken as a sign that it was now time to move further south in quest of the exact center of the world. At this time, U sent different languages to the people, who broke up into groups led by priesthoods, all of them guarded by the twins. Masewi and Oyoyewi became reckless, however, and began to kill enemies without provocation.

The deities became angry and sent a dead girl to haunt them. In some versions, she was one of their victims, who pursued them endlessly. She looked beautiful at a distance, but close up, she was a rotting corpse. At Laguna, she was very beautiful to the east, but ugly to the west (Boas 1928: 16). The twins began to panic, running everywhere to hide from her. Finally, at South Mountain, a spirit frightened her off with a blood-filled baby's head. This spirit then explained to the twins about their offense, lifting their punishment and instituting the Warrior (*Opi*) priesthood. Henceforth, the scalps of enemies were hung from poles and danced with by the people to welcome them into the town. In return, the scalps would send rain. The scalp taker went through a lengthy purification and fast, ending up as an Opi warrior. Eventually, the twins also left the people to live on a rocky promontory, either the Sandia Mountains or Acoma Mesa.

The saga of each town concludes with its arrival at its present location, always regarded as the center of the world. Each town site is selected by the Outside Priest and consecrated by burying baskets of prayersticks and offerings at the center of the main plaza (Stirling 1942: 79) and at the boundaries in the four horizontal directions. Then, the priesthoods lead the people into the space to begin building their houses. At Acoma, people moved from the base of the mesa to the top, after a splinter group continued on southward.

At Acoma and Laguna (Gunn 1917: 73), Pushani was an evil character who created itself early in the saga. Elsewhere, Poshaiyanyi was a helpful young man who visited all the modern towns before moving on to Mexico. He was a native Puebloan, born of a virgin, and equated with the Plumed Serpent, Quetzalcoatl, of Mexican religions. Before heading south, he taught the Sia to hunt communally by forming two lines converging on a center (Stevenson 1894: 65). These visits by Poshaiyanyi represent the border between Keresan and European history. Thereafter, each town mentions the Spanish *entradas*, the colonies in the Rio Grande, and the 1680 Pueblo Revolt, which forced the Hispanic survivors to flee to El Paso until the 1692 Reconquest. Since then, every Keres town has had a Spanish name, Catholic church ~ mission, patron saint, and feast day.

TOWN	SAINT	FEAST DAY
Cochiti	San Buenaventura	July 14
San Felipe	same name	May 1
Santo Domingo	same name	August 4
Santa Ana	same name	July 26
Sia	Nuestra Senora	August 15
Acoma	San Estevan	September 2
Laguna	San Jose	September 19

Santiago (San Diego, Saint James) and his wooden horse have become important supernaturals impersonated on feast days when the rooster pull (*gallo*) is held as an adjunct to the rain making ceremonies. The blood, scattered as the buried rooster is pulled from the ground by a man on horseback, is believed to produce rainfall. Now, the Christian God is offered prayersticks in the same way as other members of the Keres pantheon.

Still, people are initiated to wear masks for the Katsina and Kopishtaiya, or dress as Kwirena and Koshari. Kivas are built, used, and maintained according to the commands of U. Matriclans and priesthoods regulate the life of a individual and of the community. The Animal Opi survive in some towns, but American military activity entitled young Keres to revive the Opi, renewing another channel for bringing rain to their crops, thirsty animals, and the arid landscape.

Analysis

Analysis of Keres genesis begins with a general consideration of the patterns in the myth, before I turn to specific considerations of the Man/Woman categories as these pervade the saga. The data on sensory and cosmological features will be reserved for treatment in later sections.

The saga has two locations, ShipopU and White House. At the first, the sisters were guided by T, creating the modern world, and, more generally, instituting life. At the second, the twin brothers were guided by the Sun, fixing up the world, and, more generally, dealing with death. Both parts share the same system of dualistic priorities: vertical over horizontal, elder to younger, center to periphery, and man to woman.

Events in both begin along a vertical dimension before they move to a horizontal one. The sisters were created in ShipopU, the center of the lowest world, and grow up under the care of T. They may continue to grow as they move successively up into higher underworlds since they are not named, recognized as full adults, until facing the newly-created Sun of the last world. The eldest is named first, by precedence. The vertical is also represented by trees, reeds, and burrowing animals. At White House, the twins were born from the union of Sun and a virgin through the medium of pinyon nuts. Presumably, the Sun came down to earth and gathered them up where they had fallen, ripe and ready. The twins shot up quickly and visited their father in the sky before they are completely grown. The heat of his oven makes them tall, handsome, and mature – analogous to naming children in the heat of the first rays of the sun.

After final emergence, events occur largely along the horizontal plane, moving from periphery to center. All life begins and ends at the cosmic center called ShipopU, an ultimate nexus. The sisters bound the plane with four sacred mountains and populated these with plants and animals. Rodents and grasses sprout on the plain; larger animals and trees inhabit the mountains. Creatures of the air and water were created after those of the land. Since air and water are under the control of the Sky People, this horizontal plane is bound to the vertical one.

Born at White House, the twins moved out from this world center, preparing the way for the eventual move to the south after the epidemic. Visiting the Sun, they are sealed in rooms for each of the peripheral directions. Once their father gave them proper weapons, they killed monsters in the four directions. Yet, for all their wandering, they frequently returned to the center, which was more accessible when the world was new. When the fight with the Katsina began, the twins heard or sensed it though they were far away.

Many aspects of the saga seem contradictory because it is a sacred text relying on faith. The possibility of multiple centers becomes less confusing by reference to the Tewa belief in ordered centers linked by labyrinths.

> In addition to defending the center, the labyrinths also include some idea of purifying or consecrating it anew at critical points during the year ... it is equally obvious that the labyrinth itself is also a sacred center, for it represents ... a mode of access to the sacred underworld (Ortiz 1969: 161).

Another important opposition expressed in the saga is complete / incomplete. The heat of the Sun completed the sisters and the twins. The raw and soft earth had to be hardened and dried. At Sia, this was done by a bolt of lightning, extending the equation of completeness with cooking, as among the social ranks of Keres society. The number four also expressed completeness, as in the four levels of earth and of sky mentioned at Acoma. In ritual and myth, actions are attempted three times before being accomplished on the fourth try. While the sacred directions are sometimes augmented by above, below, and center, the cardinal four are always invoked. Thus, the full seven represent an integration of the horizontal four and the vertical two with their intersection.

The saga also asserts the priority of left over right. At Acoma, N is on the left, but the rays of the Sun are blocked by the left wing of Magpie. The Outside Priest learned to begin counting on his left hand. Keres doctors wear left bear paws over the left hand when curing. Keres men still wear bow guards on the left wrist to show that they are "real men, that they are sons of Masewi and Oyoyewi" (White 1942: 353). The section on The Ego considers such laterality and handedness in greater detail.

The quarrels, tests, and separation of U and N gave the Keres a focal deity and a distinct identity. By herself, U created the Katsina, Kopishtaiya, and, in some accounts, the priesthoods. She set up the patterns of reciprocity by which deities came from the edge of the world to the town center, exchanging services for offerings. The Inside and Outside Priests, sometimes also called chiefs, mediated between the people, the environment, and the supernaturals. When fully functioning, the circuitry of the Keres world became complete when U returned to ShipopU, instituting death to close the cycles. Multiple routes were created by building kivas to represent ShipopU. As the sisters formed the world, the twins passed judgement on it from White House, charged to do so by their Sun father above. The most serious problems they corrected had to do with breakdowns in this flow of exchanges.

In one important episode, women overvalued their economic importance and told the men to leave. Afterwards, the men thrived on meat, but the women wasted away on vegetables. Without male contact, women gave birth to monsters. Therefore, it is likely that N had healthy sons because water, at least as rain drops, is a male element. Further, the birth of giant monsters near White House is the reverse of the sisters enlivening tiny images from their baskets at ShipopU. The great ones caused death, but the little ones created life.

When men and women lived together properly, human children were born. A virtuous girl gave birth to the war twins after meeting the Sun and eating tiny nuts. Their healthy births vanquished the monstrous ones.[11] Later, men were at fault, undervaluing their economic roles by spending too much time gambling and mocking their benefactors. They were deserted by the supernaturals, until ready to reform and follow a virtuous man who danced to entice the Katsina back.

The second time gambling got out of hand, there was a disastrous breach between humans and Katsina, resulting in the fight where the twins defended the people. Afterwards, they were able to restore most of the decapitated Katsina to life. Because of the angry battle, only impersonations were allowed for the Katsina, Kopishtaiya, and twins. Thus, the growing difficulties of direct contact and exchange were alleviated by making them intangible and symbolic. In Acoma belief, once the reality of these beings was established, power could be derived from them. For example, when the first Kopishtaiya visited, U said "that they were real and that all went well so she told the people to believe in them" (Stirling 142: 28). Hence, the spirit and power of these supernaturals continues to

---

[11] The Navajo version of this gender battle has the women triumphing (Haile 1981).

inhabit their impersonators for as long as a mask is worn during ritual dances.

The twins were charged with correcting and restoring the patterns of exchange. When they visited unfriendly, unsharing towns, they turned everyone to stone, except for a hospitable couple. Their human souls, however, were changed into canyon wrens, presumably so they can still contribute to the flow of animate life in the world.

When the twins themselves tilted this balance, they too were punished and corrected. The blood-filled baby head that scared away the specter inverted the bloody decapitation of the Katsina during the fight (Stirling 1942: 53). The institution of the Opi Warriors, founded by the twins, gave explicit recognition to the fact that the Keres have to share the world with other people, including enemies. The Keres dead return to ShipopU and later are reborn as Keres infants, but the afterlife of these other people is unspecified. Part of them continues, especially if they were scalped.

Once ritually purified, these scalps serve Keres interests and help to bring rain. The scalp and Keres warrior form a reciprocal bond, extending to the community which danced to welcome it. This link between Keres and other beings involved a reciprocity extending beyond death that was, therefore, immortal.

Relationships are variously manipulated throughout the accounts, as exemplified by baskets and honey. In a version of the life of the twins at Acoma, their grandmother made bows for them out of the rim of a basket (Wick Miller 1965: 248). Later, seeking their father, Spider Grandmother transported them into the sky in a basket. We already know that the sisters carry images in baskets. Accordingly, men are associated with incomplete baskets and women with complete ones. Some reversals are spatial. When making the fetish of the perfect ear of corn, U put honey inside it; later, the twins put honey on the outside of their bodies to look filthy.

In addition to these ranked and altered relationships, the saga is pervaded, as is the rest of the culture, by a Man/Woman echo drawing an analogy between all life and human genders. Sun, Earth, animals, plants, and supernaturals are men, women, or both. Indeed, biological species wear a plant or animal outer skin to cloak their inner humanoid form. By extension, animals are associated with men and male tasks, as plants are with women. At Acoma, the manly creator turned a clot of his own blood into the womanly earth. At Laguna, land emerged from primordial water, perhaps the same as that which impregnated N to allow fertilization. Thus, as land is womanly, so water must be manly, a primal pair present at creation. Similarly, the images in the baskets were in gender pairs, as are the Katsina and Kopishtaiya. Each of the various priesthoods was originally created in the form of its Man or Woman patron. At White House, the virtuous girl produced the twins and an earnest man coaxed back the Katsina, each serving as a kind of parent.

Gender pervades the cosmos. Aside from married pairs, other spirits, such as those of the directions, can nonetheless be identified as Man or Woman. In addition, Keres also recognize a category, technically known as berdache, of intermediate gender, often filled by men who become women (White 1943: 324). The sisters were involved with life and the twin brothers with death. Under the Ego, we will learn that life is womanly and death is manly. Further, it is important that the sisters did not complete their task until N gave birth to her sons, who allowed the women to create humans and found the priesthoods. The twins left no direct heirs, only annual officials who take their names. This suggests that Woman is incomplete, while Man is not. The woman Spider doctor only partially firmed the earth, but the male one fully hardened it. Thus, womanly can be viewed as unmarked, generic, and inclusive; with manly marked, specific, and exclusive. The Woman category can include both men and women, but that of Man is limited only to men.

Running through the saga, there is also an association of men with asexuality and women with sexuality, especially reproduction. The creator made the world from a blood clot and T created the sisters from parcels, but the sisters worked only with gender pairs, espousing the coupled harmony of normal life. Nevertheless, the ability to procreate seems to reside with the Woman in and of herself. Without men, women produced offspring, although these were monsters. Impregnated by rain, N had proper, healthy children. This was not the case when she worked alone. When N tried to baffle U, she made a creature neither man nor woman, with crossed right and left legs. Thus, as long as manly and womanly elements are involved, even incest does not affect the wellbeing of the child. In legend, conception took place without direct or physical contact, since the twins were conceived, literally, from swallowed pinyon nuts given to their mother by the Sun. Even Spider Grandmother, whose many young children covered the walls of her house, specifically has only one son (Wick Miller 1965: 253). Moreover, as the Origin Saga progresses, new creations were produced from earlier unmarked forms, the specific from the generic. Thus, the Outside Chief was specifically instituted to lighten the burden of the Tiamunyi. On symbolic levels, the split between men and women might also represent the separation of the manly and womanly towns toward the end of the occupation of Chaco Canyon, with the manly towns relying more on priesthoods than clans in their government.

Asexuality, sometimes called ritual chastity, remains a crucial requirement of men, as wearers of Katsina masks and as members of priesthoods during retreats and cures. Men often spend time by themselves in kivas, secluded meetings, and on hunts. The most manly of the supernaturals are asexual in the extreme. The Kopishtaiya voluntarily gave up sex in order to win back the corpse of a dead girl from necrophilic witches. The Gomaiyawish were castrated after the fight. Unfortunately, we know little about these supernatural messengers, even though they are impersonated in four Keres towns. Town officials are also expected to practice occasional continence. Although of the Woman category, the Inside Priest is a married man and father of children. While praying and fasting in retreat, however, he avoids contact with his wife and other women. He thus has associations with sexuality and with asexuality in relation to his unofficial and official capacities. At Acoma, the Country Chief, more commonly the war captains in the other towns, must live apart from his wife and family for the year he holds office, keeping his mind on his official duties for the community.

As the relations between the genders set up the echoing tension of the culture, so "thought" supplies its mediation. During creation, the instructions from T were made via thought, and the first Town Priest was consecrated by contact with the mind of U. Like waves of power rippling through the universe, consciousness is a fundamental attribute of all animate life, deified by Keres as the apical T.

Tsityostiinako ("T") did not answer when the sisters asked if "it" were man or woman. Boas (1928: 228) was told this deity sometimes looks like a man and sometimes like a spider. The ending -nako occurs on the names of women. Therefore, White (1962: 113) translated this name as Prophesying Woman, because "it" knows, rather then deciding ~ determining, what will happen, and is ubiquitous, expressed in the thoughts of people. Gunn (1917: 89) called "it" personified reason. Davis (1964: 170, #455) listed /cidyustA/ as "to think, to worry." From all of these, it can be seen that none is an adequate translation. The first part of the name refers to conscious mental activity, like pondering ~ alert awareness, so I will refer to T as Consciousness Deity.

Other indications that mind ~ intelligence is accorded importance come from Keresan grammar: Spencer (1940: 74) lists "verbs of mental process" as a residual type. Further, a Keresan speaker must grammatically identify whether something being said was experienced personally or vicariously (Fox in Lange 1968a: 572). Among other things, this indicates the degree of mental awareness involved in any statement.

While Levi-Strauss has shown the universal human importance of Mind as the mediator between Nature and Culture, the Keres do him one better and deify these as Consciousness Deity, whose Nature is represented by the spider and Culture by primordial divinity. Spider in myth gives the most sage advice, often sitting behind the ear of a hero to do so (White 1942: 82, note 19).

In all, therefore, the web of Keres culture is revealed by this very creation. Now, we can proceed to isolate and analyze the details of Keres society provided in the published ethnography, rethinking the data to reveal more clearly the pervasive redundancy of the Man / Woman echo among the matrices.

#2 Chart

Keresan Ethnology

I. Keresan Ego

	Manly	Center	Womanly
person	guardian	mind	heart-breath
laterality	left	heart	right
colors	turquoise	pink	yellow
	white		black
shapes	square [	D	round)
words	sacred	thought	ordinary
groups	men only	priests	women + men

II. Keresan Social Contexts

	Center	Inside	Outside
Officials	Tiamunyi people	Captains town lands	Governor aliens

Priesthoods

		Womanly / Manly	
	Koshari	Flint / Fire	War
	Kwirena	Shikame / Insect	Hunt
	(Shrutzi)	Giant / Snake	

	Center	Inside	Outside
Kivas	Office	East Kiva	West Kiva
Animals (Woodrat)	Cougar	Doctors	Hunters
		Bear Deer	
Plants (Honey)	Maize Crops	Trees	
	Squash	Fir	

III. Keresan Towns

	Center	Inside	Outside
Manly (Katsina, clay people)	Cochiti	Felipe	Santo Domingo
Womanly (Katsina, Gomaiyawish, prayerstick)	Santa Ana	Sia / Acoma	Laguna

IV. Pueblos

KERES   Towa Hopi Zuni Tano Tiwa   Tewa

Chapter Three

ETHNOLOGY

Relying on the Keres mythic charter, we now consider more detailed aspects of the culture. Here, the gender echo will be explored in the ethnography of present towns. Next, its traces will be sought in the artifacts and architecture of the Southwestern archaeology, particularly Chaco Canyon.

The ethnographic evidence is considered, in widening domains, under the headings of the Ego, Social Ego, Towns, and Pueblos. The Ego is a sapient Keres individual involved in a series of sensory dualities. The Social Ego (*nawai*, central person) occupies the intersection or nexus of a concentric grouping with a center, inside, and outside. To distinguish these concentric units from other matrices, I have used the term "contexts" for them. While the Social Ego serves as Ego ~ nexus for the members of a context and so is constrained by a primary identification with that context, an Ego can choose to adopt, change, or modify his, her, or its religious affiliation, matriclan, or priesthood in accord with what Elsie Clews Parsons (1923: 169, note 3) called "freedom of choice among various fixed principles."

Later, the persistence of such Keres principles is examined in Southwestern, specifically Anasazi, archaeological reports in an attempt to establish patterns, distributions, and a relative time depth for the axiomatic place of gender among the Keres. Thus, while gender concepts were and are important among Puebloan and other native cultures, they have ultimate priority among the Keresans.

A synthesis of the Keres ethnographic record upholds their symbolic ideals because, as Ortiz (1969: 38) has already noted, there is a remarkably close fit between Pueblo culture and society, between what is said and what is done.

The Ego

The Ego is a normal Keres adult, possessing conscious awareness and functioning as a particular individual within the world. Children are excluded because their mental abilities are incomplete. They have yet to share in the wealth of esoteric knowledge giving increasing surety and insight about the cosmos. An Acoman once referred to his Katsina initiation as the time when "he was given the mind of an adult." Babies begin life with little consciousness but two personal patrons, a breath-heart and a guardian (White 1942: 173). The first seems to come from the mother and the second from the father, thus establishing the importance of gender from the moment of conception.

An Ego can use at least four pairs of metaphors to express the complementarity of Man and Woman: laterality, color, shape, and language.

The bilaterality of the human body serves as an immediate referent for many important symbolic considerations. Among the Keres, left is to right as Man is to Woman (Miller 1972a), as illustrated by the story of how the Cougar created the domestic cat.

> The mountain lion stood in the middle of a circle and all the oldest animals were smoking around him. He said "Now I am ready." He sneezed and out came a female cat from his right nostril. He sneezed again, and out of the left nostril came a male cat (Benedict 1931: 154).

In addition to aligning, by nostril, Man with left and Woman with right, this citation also indicates the function of a Social Ego, providing the focus at the center of a concentric arrangement and acting on behalf of all involved in it. For the Keres individual, the center of this context is the heart (Miller 1980), with the body heart-soul inside and the guardian outside.

Of the colors named by the Keres, four of them, two pairs, carry important symbolism: white and black, turquoise and yellow. On ceremonial occasions, men wear kilts woven of white cotton, rubbed immaculate with kaolin; while the _manta_ dresses of women dancers are black. In the cosmological order, however, turquoise (green-blue ~ grue) represents Man and yellow, like maize, is Woman. When the Flint priesthood puts up its altar at Santa Ana, prayersticks painted turquoise are deposited on the left side on behalf of the men and yellow ones are placed on the right for the women (White 1942: 335). The inclusive center of this context seems to be pink since White (1942: 97) noted an association between the cacique and this color.

Shapes are also used to express the gender dichotomy through angles = [, curves =), and bows = D. The linear, angular, or squarish are associated with Man; the circular or curving with Woman. Thus, the pottery medicine bowls important to the curing priesthoods have two shapes. The Koshari use a square one (Stirling 1942: 112) because he was the first man (1942: 33), while the Flint priesthood has a round one (White 1962: Plate 1) and their insignia is a Woman (1942: 115). In half of the Keres towns, the cacique is also head of the Flints. The inclosive shape is a D, combining "[" with ")" ~ [+) = D, as discussed in the section on archaeology.

Several scholars have noted that the Keres use two forms of the language, a colloquial ~ everyday one spoken by both men and women and a ceremonial one spoken only by men in ritual situations. The Keres say the ceremonial language is very ancient, regarding it as an "archaic" version of ordinary Keresic. White (1944) has given examples of it from Sia and Santa Ana, and Fox (in Lange 1968a: 558), discussing Cochiti, used the distinction between ceremonial and colloquial cited here. Hrdlicka (1903) published an interesting account of ceremonial terms from Laguna, where this language is called _Hamasija_. Colloquial Keres has been discussed by Boas (1928), Spencer (1940), Davis (1963, 1964), and Wick Miller (1965).

"Two varieties of Acoma Keresan can be distinguished. Archaic Keresan is more sophisticated and grammatically more complex; it is used in songs, prayers, oratory, philosophical discussions, and legends and mythology. Contemporary Keresan shows more influence from other languages and permits code-switching with English and the use of Spanish loan words." (Garcia-Mason 1979: 450)

The recognition of two languages should not be underestimated. As Money and others (1975: 335) noted "Establishment of one's gender role and orientation appears to have much in common with the establishment of one's native language." It is likely, therefore, that the identification of men with one, and of men and women with the other has strong bearing on the organization of the culture. The inclosive member of this matrix is thought, the means of communication from the very beginning of the universe.

Personal identity is also bound up with the type of group membership to which a person is entitled. Cohen (1964) refers to this process as the anchorage of a person within firmly bounded groups. Among the Keres, there are two such firm collectivities: one for men and one for men + women. Together and separately, these play vital roles in the Keres life cycle.

Children are born into the matriclan of their mother, which has both male and female members. At birth, the mother is assisted only by a woman or midwife. For a difficult delivery, a priestly doctor, generally a man belonging to the Giant priesthood, is summoned with an offering of ground shell and corn pollen held out in the right hand, associated with life and birth (Stevenson 1894: 132). In all, birth is on the side of Woman.

After parturition, the mother and child are secluded four days in a darkened room. On the fifth morning, the baby is presented to Father Sun and named by ceremonial god-parents, while the mother stays indoors. These ceremonial parents are usually a priest and his wife. Sometimes, the naming is done only by women, but one of them is a paternal relative of the baby. At the naming, an infant is given several names, one of which eventually predominates. Upon presentation to the Sun, the mother's clan and the baby's gender are specified, as illustrated by this formula from Cochiti.

There has been born a male (female) infant of clan _____. We offer him (her) to you, so that when he (she) grows up and begins to talk and asks good fortune of you, you may recognize him (her) by his (her) name. We give him (her) the name of _____. (Dumarest 1919: 144)

The naming is handled by a male + female group, explicitly or by intent involving both genders.

About the time of puberty, young Keres are initiated into the Katsina cult and told its secret. Responsible initiates were told that these beings left the world after the fight at White House, but gave humans permission to impersonate them so rains would come. Anyone who told the uninitiated about this masking was sentenced to death. Children learn the broad outlines of the Origin Saga of the town, which gives them a basis for future esoteric knowledge and provides them with the mind of an adult. The significance of three of the towns initiating only boys into the cult, while the other four induct both boys and girls, is considered below in terms of intertown relations.

While all Keresans now belong to both a clan and kiva, in prehistoric times the complement of the matriclan, for men, was the priesthood, sometimes called a male fraternity ~ society. A man joined a priesthood as the result of kinship obligations, a personal vow, being cured by its members and thus learning some of its ritual, or being trapped or caught by it under special circumstances. Women might help the doctors, but they "never doctor; they brew medicines and they make yucca suds to simulate clouds or to wash the head ritually, all functions close to their ordinary economic ones" (Parsons 1939: 132). Some priesthoods go so far as to forbid women to associate with them in any capacity. These different kinds of priesthoods are discussed in a later section. The medicine ~ curing priests treat diseases caused either by natural phenomena or by witches.

Other types of cures are performed by the clans – if the illness is more emotional or psychological, affecting women more often than men. The cure consists of adopting the patient into another clan so that she will have the benefit of more relatives, maternal support, and nurturing regard, all mystically bound up with clan membership (Fox 1967: 194).

The most obvious example of the men-only group occurs when males leave women in the town and journey into the mountains to hunt, practice dances and rituals, or, in the past, to fight battles.

When a Keres dies, a priesthood supervises the burial, not the clan. Members are summoned to the corpse with an offering of corn meal held out in the left hand, routinely associated with the dead (Stevenson 1894, 143). The body is washed by kinswomen, and dressed by kinsmen, who also bury it. Four days after burial, the priesthood handling the funeral returns to the deceased's home to send the breath-heart back to Iatiku (Corn Mother), an alter ego of both U and T, at ShipopU (White 1962: 307). Death is called the birth into ShipopU (Stevenson 1894: 143). In all, death has manly associations through the left hand, priesthoods, and set rituals.

Matriclans and priesthoods occur in every Keres town, although given differential emphasis according to reflections of the echo at the level of the towns. Each exemplifies what Cohen (1969: 108) calls a firmly bounded social system, the notable characteristics of which are role transposability, undifferentiated internal networks, differentiation from external networks, and consensus or inability to tolerate sustained or outspoken dissent.

The men + women group displays transposability and undifferentiation in that – while some are better at these tasks than others – all men are farmers, kinsmen, and ritualists; all women are housekeepers, kinswomen, and ritual adjuncts. Group consensus is maintained by gossip, ridicule, and, ultimately, witchcraft accusations and punishment (Hoebel 1968: 129).

Within the men-only group, all are hunters, warriors, or doctors, excluded from women. On lengthy expeditions, therefore, a few men are appointed to do the cooking. While the men are away, they put consensus to the test:

The hunters sit around the fire after supper telling stories and singing hunting songs. They tell stories about their love affairs,

about their sweethearts and mistresses, their conquests in love ...
But it not infrequently happens that a man tells a story of a love
affair with another hunter's sister, daughter, or wife ... Feelings are
likely to be hurt by this, but before the party returns to the town, the
elder war captain tells them all to forget everything that they have
heard or said (White 1942: 289).

Alone and as a member of a group, the Ego affects and is affected by
the world around him or her, yet makes it conform to cultural expectations
through the use of laterality, colors, and shapes. He or she is affected by it
as a member of a social group, firmly or loosely bounded, and as a speaker
of ritual or of ordinary Keresic. Group activities, however, are directed by a
leader, functioning as a Social Ego.

The Social Ego

Symbolically, the Social Ego stands at the center of a context, a matrix
with a focal point of three components: center, inside, and outside. For a
manly context, all of the items in the matrix have associations with Man,
while for a womanly one the members are mixed. In general, the center is
inclosive, the inside inclusive, and the outside exclusive among the Keres.
Placed at the center of a context, a Social Ego expresses the importance of
Mind as the redundant mediator of Keres culture, at its crux.

For example, a Keres farmer places an offering of deer meat and
bread crumbs, together with corn meal and pollen, at the center of his field
before beginning to plant (Parsons 1939: 301). This placement of the
offering serves to center his thoughts and those of the deities on the field.
Thinking of good crops, he plants from the outside edge, spiralling inward
to the center (Lange 1968a: 94). Also, in the Keres judicial system, official
statements are called 'inside' and unofficial opinions or talk is 'outside'
(Hoebel 1968: 128). Indeed, it is law that best characterizes the importance
of the Keresan centralized theocracy in each town.

As a system of tribal law, the Keresan Pueblo type is probably
unique. It is totally centralized and spectacularly concentrated on
societal maintenance and unyielding commitment to a specific set of
cultural and jural postulates ... The comparative counterpart is the
totalitarian oligarchy, whether secular or theocratic, and its use of
repressive authority to maintain order and conformity of belief and
action in societies based on dogmatic ideology ... Unanimous effort

of body and mind is not only a key value, but it is enforced ... Any action, whether physical or verbal, which is construed by Pueblo authorities to be contrary to group concerns and unanimous will of the village is promptly and severely punished (Hoebel 1969: 115-6, 98).

For each town, the center is the open plaza, the inside is the houses, and the outside is the fields. The inside is womanly and the outside manly, but the entire town belongs to the Woman category. Crops in the fields are "owned" by men, but once inside the house, they "belong" to the women (Lange 1968a: 74) The center of the town is womanly, marked by the buried basket holding offerings and clay figurines, representing the townspeople as the children of Iatiku (Ellis 1959: 335).

Individual Keres think only in terms of their own town, not of all the Keres. This cohesion is a task for the priests, who are concerned with interconnections and holism. Within each town, the occupants form a context whose Social Ego is the theocracy, headed by the Tiamunyi.

Town Officers

The most important town officer is the Town Priest ~ cacique. After "his" initiation in bridal costume or women's ceremonial dress, "she" is believed to be nurturing, womanly, and the human embodiment of Mother Iatiku (White 1962: 127). "Her" duties are to pray and to fast for the good of all and to conduct rituals on schedule. "She" now occupies the center of the context.

The "Cacique is the object of much reverence, is freed from physical labor, and is supported by the produce of certain fields that are communally cultivated on his behalf under the orders of the first war captain. Communal deer and rabbit hunts provide him with meat. He holds surpluses for ceremonial feasts and for dispersal to the needy. He invests the 'annual officers,' who in the modern situation are his executive officers. He is thus not ordinarily directly involved in the administration of legal or governmental affairs, for he should concentrate all his thoughts in a positive way, 'willing' the well-being of Zia. Quarrels and mundane affairs spoil his good thoughts" (Hoebel 1979: 415).

The inside segment, when not associated with the Town Priest, is now filled by the present war captains and their messengers, collectively called the Outside Chiefs (White 1942: 102), whose position shifted with the arrival of the Spanish. The former outside officials moved "inside" to handle native affairs, while officers imposed by the Spanish took their place on the outside to deal with Europeans, those foreign aliens who were truly outsiders.[12]

The war captains, named for Masewi and Oyoyewi, manage ceremonies, guard the priesthoods during retreats and fasts, and punish witches. They are solely responsible for the area between the boundaries of the territory and the outer edge of the fields. They are annually selected from the members of each kiva in alternation. One year Masewi, the elder, is drawn from the East kiva and Oyoyewi from the West kiva; the next year recruitment is reversed. As the earthly representatives of the war twins, these officers are consummately manly.

As just noted, at present, the outside is occupied by the so-called Spanish officials, instituted by royal decree of the King of Spain about 1620 (Ortiz 1969: 61). The governor (_gobernador_) and his staff deal with non-native foreigners, usually representatives of the American and Catholic bureaucracy. These officials are also selected annually from the kivas in turn, as described in considerable detail for Sia (White 1962: 123). The Spanish officials seem to be womanly since many of their activities deal with the Catholic saints, Jesus, and Mary: a rich texture involving men and women.

Priesthoods ~ _chaianyi_

Within each town, the priesthoods themselves form a context that is particularly complex, based on their control of power rather than numbers. "When one thinks of the structural and ideological power of the religious societies at Zia, it comes as a shock to learn how few members are involved. In 1960 the all-powerful Flints had but 8 members, the Giants 9, and the Fire Society 10" (Hoebel 1979: 415).

Goldfrank (1927) referred to those of the center as managing fraternities ~ priesthoods: the Koshari and Kwirena sacred clowns. They are directly involved in all rituals and dances, whether in the plaza, kivas,

---

[12] An alternative analysis would place the Tiamunyi inside and the War Priest outside, before the Spanish arrived, leaving the center for the theocrats at Chaco.

or chambers; the unquestioned leaders of esoteric rites and full knowledge. The head of the Koshari serves as the Social Ego because his prototype was created first, before the Kwirena (White 1962: 115), whose patrons include Hododo, Wikori, and Kwirena (1962: 168).

In general, the Koshari are associated with winter and the Kwirena with summer (Fox 1967: 64). In three towns, the leader of the Koshari also heads the Flint priesthood and serves as Tiamunyi. As though by deliberate intent, Tewa towns have the same managing priesthoods (called Kossa and Kwirana), but reverse their seasonal associations (Ortiz 1969: 144).

Only Cochiti also has a third managing groups, the Shrutzi, responsible for the Katsina cult. Since its activities are more limited and popular, I suspect it controls lesser esoteric lore and ranks below the other two managers. The supernatural patrons of the Shrutzi are the Katsina (Lange 1968a: 284), forming the outside of a managing priesthood context with Koshari at the center and Hododo, Wikori, and Kwirena inside.

Overall, for priesthoods, the inside is occupied by the medicine ~ curing priesthoods, each maintaining an official kiva-like chamber within the town. Internally, they are divided on the basis of their cures and memberships. Stevenson (1894: 72) learned "Disease came either from witches or the anger of animals, usually insects." Those treating witchcraft cure internally by sucking, while angry animal diseases are external ~ cutaneous, usually taking the form of rashes or skin eruptions, cured by brushing (Stevenson 1894: 75).

Further, witches can be women or men, while the angry animals belong entirely to the male domain. Accordingly, those priesthoods curing witchcraft are womanly and allow women to act as auxiliaries or helpers, while those of the so-called Beast patrons are manly and permit only men to participate. Among the curing priesthoods, important womanly examples are Flint, Shikame, and Giant; important manly ones are Fire, Snake, and Insect (Ant-Spider-Eagle). As shown by the chart below, each town has at least one womanly and one manly medicine priesthood.

The supernatural patrons of the curing priests are the Kopishtaiya, led by Dziukiri and K'okiri (White 1932a: 86), noted for being celibate and implacable foes to witches (White 1932a: 65). The Animal Doctors of the six directions are also likely patrons of the manly priests, although all priesthoods acknowledge Bear as the greatest curer (White 1962: 144) and all curers wear a bear paw on the left hand (Paytiamo 1932: 120).

Curing Priesthoods by Town

```
COCHITI (Lange 1968a: 263-272)
    womanly:  Flint, Shikame, Giant(?)
    manly:  Fire, Snake
SAN FELIPE (White 1932b: 40)
    womanly:  Flint, Shikame, Giant
    manly:  Snake
SANTO DOMINGO (White 1935: 60, 63)
    womanly: Flint, Shikame, Giant, Boyakya(Tano)
    manly: Spider, Toad, Snake
SANTA ANA (White 1942: 115)
    womanly:  Flint, two Shikame
    manly:  Fire, Spider, Snake
ACOMA (White 1932a: 107)
    womanly:  Flint, Shikame
    manly:  Fire, Spider, Snake
LAGUNA (Ellis 1959: 331)
    womanly:  Flint, Shikame, Giant-Ant
    manly:  Fire, Snake
SIA (see below)
```

The order given for these priesthoods is intended to represent their relative rank. Of the womanly ones, Flint is unquestionably the Social Ego. It was made first, as a Woman (White 1962: 146), and often shares its membership with the Koshari. While all Flint are usually Koshari, not all Koshari become Flint doctors. At Cochiti, San Felipe, and Santo Domingo, the Town Priest must be both a Flint and a Koshari, usually head of both (White 1932b: 12, note 23). The Shikame rank below the Flint, but similarly all Shikame are Kwirena, but not the reverse. Santa Ana alone has two Shikame (South, Southeast), each associated with a division of Kwirena (White 1942: 115-119). Lowest in rank is the Giant, protector of the 'raw' ~ common people, having knowledge more exoteric than esoteric, suitable for treating such practical concerns as childbirth. Only at Cochiti does Giant have a bond with another group, the singular Shrutzi (Lange 1968a: 285).

Among the manly curers, Fire acts as Social Ego. At Acoma, it is the equal of Flint (White 1932a: 99), performing outdoor exhibitions that include fire walking, rolling in hot coals, and handling hot liquid (1932a: 114); implying the possession of esoteric lore. The Insect (variously called Spider, Ant, and Eagle) specializes in angry animal ~ Beast illness. At Sia, Spider ranks first because it was founded by T. Eagle is listed, possibly as a degree ~ order, because these birds are believed to eat insects and be powerful curers (White 1942: 117). Lowest ranking is Snake because it is often only an informal association of those who have been bitten by rattlesnakes and survived. At Sia, it has a more formal organization, however, probably because it is linked to the Insect priesthood (White 1962: 156). Nevertheless, the Snake priests are so distinctively Keresan that a similar cult probably existed in the Chaco.

Priestly Membership At Sia (White 1962:)

	Priesthood	Membership		Page
Managing	Koshari	both sexes	169	
	Kwirena	both		170
Curing	Flint	both	148	
	(Shikame)	(both)		
	Giant	both	149	
	Fire	both		154
	Insect	both		156
	Snake	both		165
Protecting	Warriors	men only		176
	Hunters	men		171

The Sia priesthoods have been reported in some detail so they will serve to illustrate the division in membership between the curing groups, although women were only adjuncts.

These memberships hold for the other Keres. The Shikame has lapsed at Sia, but elsewhere it draws members from both genders, as is the case at Santo Domingo (White 1935: 54). Women are never full members of these priesthoods; they are always distinctly called 'woman members' (Koshari goyawi, not Koshari) to distinguish them from the initiated men. They are also called 'outside' (White 1935: 63) and even non-members (Lange 1968a: 265).

The outside priesthoods are the Warriors and the Hunters, concerned with external activities. The Warriors (*Opi*) ranked highest because of the greater knowledge required of such man-killers and scalp-takers (White 1942: 316). Their patrons were the war twins, Masewi and Oyoyewi (1942: 304). The Hunters survive as a select group of meat providers, whose patrons are Hunt ~ Game Man and the Animal Hunters of the six directions: Cougar, Rohona (Jaguar ~ Young Cougar), Bobcat, Wolf, Eagle, and Shrew (White 1942: 283). Lange (1968a: 231) records another, less complete, list from Cochiti. At Santa Ana (White 1942: 118), these patrons only allowed the animals to be sighted; Father Sun gave the ability to kill them.

Kivas

The previous discussion leads directly to a consideration of kivas, particularly since academics have not agreed on the number and type of kivas in every Keres town. Most often, two kivas are reported, but Acoma has been said to have as many as six. There is order, however, in this diversity. Hawley (1950a) rightly insists that kivas be considered apart from the chambers of the priesthoods, although they may be architecturally very similar. By doing so, each Keresan town can be shown to have two kivas: East and West.

Indeed, Cochiti (Lange 1968a: 50), San Felipe (White 1932b: 15), Santo Domingo (White 1935: 48), and Santa Ana (White 1942: 142) explicitly have two kivas, called East (Turquoise) and West (Squash, Pumpkin). At Sia, there are two, one called Turquoise on the east side and another called Wren on the west (White 1962: 40).[13] Before the 1870 schism, Laguna had an East side kiva and a West side one (Parsons 1923: 237, 239). At Acoma, only two of the six religious buildings serve the entire community. When the Koshari supervise a dance, the Chief kiva and the Fire chamber are used. Further, the Chief kiva is associated with the townspeople of the east side and the Fire priesthood chamber with those of the west (White 1932a: 100). As confirmation, a town member reports that Acoma has "two main kivas ... comparable to the Eastern Pueblo's moieties, with two kiva groups in one moiety and three kivas in the other. There is one other kiva that remains independent" (Garcia-Mason 1979: 463).

The square shape of the Acoma buildings has also been problematical. Elsewhere, kivas are round, associated with Mother Iatiku and ShipopU. As noted above, squares are manly and circles womanly, so Acoma kivas associate with the sky, as befits their location atop a solid rock mesa. Further, Kidder (1962: 192) noted that "It is evidently a strict requirement that kivas should be below the surface, and in essence all of them are merely holes in the ground lined with masonry" (my emphasis). Among the Keres, the kiva has a close association with female deities, and is sometimes equated with a womb.

At Acoma, the kivas could not be build into the rock without great

---

[13] The Wren kiva was burned to the ground in a factional dispute, about 1947 (White 1962: 51). Former Sia kivas were square, presumably because they were built above ground, like those at Acoma.

labor, so the kivas are built upon the mesa surface, and made square like the houses. This accords well with some other manly features contributed by Acoma within the context of womanly towns. The effort of building kivas into bedrock could have been managed, so Acoma was responding to other considerations. The Hopi, for instance, have built their square kivas into the bedrock. Moreover, when the Acomas lived at the base of the mesa, their kivas were built round and below the ground (Stirling 1942: 18).

Moreover, a kiva leader had an educational role. Each Keresan town ~ tribe

"also had a formal education system with kiva headmen as the traditionally recognized professional teachers. Their native school curriculum consisted of lectures on the care of human behavior, human spirit, and the human body, ethics, astrology, child psychology, oratory, history, music, and dancing. Theology was not only taught but also practiced as the most crucial substance of existence" (Garcia-Mason 1979: 460).

Before the kiva context can be fully explained, another kind of ceremonial building needs to be considered, different from kiva or chamber. This is the _hotcanitsa_, the office of the Town Priest where "she" fasts and prayers away from "his" family. The most sacred of the ceremonial paraphernalia are stored there, as are food supplies for the poor. Solar observations and calculations are also made from this landmark (White 1962: 49). Apparently, in the recent past, the town built a new office for each succeeding Tiamunyi.

Taken together, kivas and office provide a context in each town. The office is obviously at the center because of its use by the cacique, the Social Ego of the town, for the welfare of all. The East kiva is inside because it is used by the cacique and others for public rituals on behalf of the town. The West kiva is outside since it is associated with hunting, warfare, and other male-only activities under the care of the Outside ~ war captains.[14]

Biota

Two other important contexts relate to the realm of Nature, where

---

[14] Jessup (1985: 167) noted that Squash and Pumpkins were raised by women and maize by men, giving the West kiva a womanly association. In South America and elsewhere, however, gourds symbolize wombs and protective enclosures, which seems also to apply for the Keresans.

animals are equated with men and plants with women. At Sia, the split between men and women, meat and crops, left the men reasonably content and the women in hardship (Stevenson 1894: 41). Thus, men were able to survive alone, but women needed men.

In mythology, Cougar is the leader of the animals, acting as the Social Ego. He won this status by defeating Bear (Benedict 1931: 142). Thus, Bear is the inside member, probably joined by the other Animal Doctors. On the outside is Deer, prey of the Animal Hunters, described at Acoma as "made of sheets of clouds" (Paytiamo 1932: 74). Thus, when a slain deer fell to the ground, the hunter took a branch and brushed the body to remove the clouds to get at the meat. After he put a speck of yellow pollen in the deer's mouth, the hunter shifted the body so the head was toward the hunting camp, placed fetishes of the Animal Hunters on the body, and smoked a cornhusk cigarette while he talked to the deer. Later, the fetishes were returned to a pouch around the hunter's neck and the deer was butchered in ritual fashion. Kangaroo ~ Wood Rat, created from the heart of N, represents all wild animal foods.

For plants, the center and Social Ego is unquestionably maize ~ corn, the heart of Iatiku and the milk from her breasts (White 1942: 204). At the inside are other crops, herbs, and vegetables grown in kitchen gardens and fields. Of these, squash (pumpkin) figures most often in ritual. At the outside are trees, with Douglas Fir most prominent in myth and rituals (Lange 1968a: 146). Trees are manly. Men hunt and fast in the timber, set the logs for buildings, and decorate themselves with boughs during dances (Parsons 1939: 38, Lange 1968a: 329, 138). Honey represents this plant matrix overall.

There are many other triadic contexts among the Keres, but those just presented illustrate the general pattern, which, in all cases, conforms to the echo so that each member is identified as Man or Woman. Further, each can be fit into the matrix of relationships as inclusive or exclusive, also allowing for mediation by inclosive Mind. This applies to the person or group, as well as to the towns.

The Towns

Of the seven modern Keres towns, three are manly and four are womanly. The balance is so consistent, that I sought a fourth manly town, as discussed below. The best evidence that the towns form manly and womanly subcontexts relates to the alignments of kivas and Katsina cults.

Previously, kiva recruitment was regarded by scholars as highly variable. At Cochiti (Fox 1967: 62-63), San Felipe (White 1932b: 27), and Santo Domingo (White 1935: 101), children join through the paternal line. At Santa Ana (White 1942: 142) and Laguna (Parsons 1923: 220), kiva membership is a consequence of matriclan. At Sia (White 1962: 183) and Acoma (White 1932a: 99), kivas recruit on the basis of residence, a spatial division. At Sia, an imaginary east-west line runs through the middle of the town. Those north of the boundary belong to Wren kiva; those to the south belong to Turquoise. Because Sia is built on a north-south ridge, this line better divides up the population between the two kivas, which are, of course, West and East. At Acoma, during dances managed by Koshari, people attended kivas depending upon whether they live on the east or west sides of the town.

Hence, at Cochiti, San Felipe, and Santo Domingo, kivas are paternal and manly; for the others they are maternal and womanly. At Santa Ana and Laguna kiva membership follows clanship. At Sia and Acoma, it is more complicated. Keres matriclans are not localized, but Keres households are matrilocal. Therefore, any spatial division into east and west separates matrilines. Whether based on clan or residence, these towns essentially trace kiva membership through the mother. In the three manly towns, sisters, daughters, and wives are peripheral to their kivas, but in the womanly towns they often determine leadership among the males.

Further support for the town genders comes from community-wide alignments called kiva wings, fixed linkages between kivas, priesthoods, or matriclans. San Felipe (White 1932b: 41) and Santo Domingo (White 1935: 54) have a Flint-Koshari-East kiva wing and a Shikame-Kwirena-West kiva one. The Town Priest and elder captain are in the first and the younger captain is in the second. Cochiti (Lange 1968a: 457) has the same two wings, but adds a third of Giant-Shrutzi-Katsina. Because it has this third wing, structured for greater completeness, Cochiti ranks as the Social Ego for the manly towns.

Acoma (White 1932a: 99, 100) has a Fire-Koshari-West kiva wing and a Flint-(Sun)Koshari-East kiva one that also includes the Town Priest and "her" Antelope clan. Both the Antelope and Corn clans, which also uses the East kiva during its sponsored ceremonies, maintain clan houses. Laguna (Parsons 1923: 299, 231, note 3) had a Shikame-Kwirena-West wing and a Flint-Koshari-East one, probably including the Town Priest drawn from the Water Clan (Ellis 1959: 337). Santa Ana (White 1942: 142) has a South Shikame-Kwirena-West kiva wing and a Southeast Shikame-Kwirena-East kiva one. The Siyana Clan is somehow associated with the South Shikame (White 1942: 155).

Data from Sia are not clear, probably because its population was decimated while living at the site of Puname after Spanish arrival. The Kwirena use the West kiva (White 1962: 259), but there is no longer a Shikame priesthood (1962: 137). Flint and Koshari are not linked at Sia (1962: 147), although they do alternate in installing the Town Priest (1962: 127), after "she" is chosen from one of five matriclans. All together, therefore, it seems that Sia once had a Kwirena-(Shikame)-West kiva wing and another loosely relating the East kiva with Flint, Koshari, five matriclans, and the Inside Chief.

In addition, the womanly towns show a consistent link between the East kiva and Corn clan. At Santa Ana (White 1942: 142) and Laguna (Parsons 1923: 229), members of the Corn clan belong to the East kiva. At Acoma (White 1932a: 94), the Corn clan uses the East kiva every five years while sponsoring the ritual lighting of signal fires. At Sia (White 1962: 127), the Town Priest, linked with the East kiva, can be a Corn clan member.

According to their kiva wings, therefore, Cochiti, San Felipe, and Santo Domingo rely only on men drawn from priesthoods. At Santa Ana, Sia, Acoma, and Laguna, however, the kiva wings are womanly, involving both matriclans and priesthoods.

These town genders are also indicated by Katsina cult initiations, although only Elsie Clews Parsons (1939: 893) noted the significant fact that

> "Sia girls as well as boys are ~ were initiated into the Katsina cult as at Acoma and Laguna but excepting Santa Ana this is not the case in other Keres towns."

Moreover, to her further credit, Parsons (1939: 968) added that "The gomaiyawish are clowns of Acoma, Laguna, Santa Ana, Jemez [Towa], and Sia; not at Cochiti, Santo Domingo, or Felipe." Since, in the first four towns, the Gomaiyawish are linked with the Katsina, the manly towns of Cochiti, Felipe, and Domingo induct only boys, a sign of the exclusivity of Man, while these same four initiate both boys and girls and link together the Katsina and Gomaiyawish, indicating the inclusivity of Woman.[15]

Lastly, another dyad separates these towns on the basis of the background and insignia of the Town Priests. At Cochiti (Lange 1968a: 237), San Felipe (White 1932b: 12), and Domingo (White 1935: 36), the

---

[15] While they have some comic aspects, the Gomaiyawish, both red and white, are primarily messengers and scouts for the Katsinas, as described for Acoma in the final chapter.

cacique must belong both to the Koshari and Flint. At Acoma, "she" belongs to the Antelope clan (White 1932a: 43). At Sia, the office is filled from the Corn, Washpa, or Coyote clans (White 1962: 127). At Laguna, "she" once came from the Water clan (Ellis 1959: 337). At Santa Ana, White (1942: 97) had no clear report about requirements for the office.

At Cochiti (Lange 1968a: 145), San Felipe (White 1932b: 12), and Santo Domingo (White 1935: 35), the insignia of the position includes figurines of clay or stone representing the townspeople and other life forms. At Santa Ana (White 1942: 104), Sia (Stevenson 1894: 17), and Acoma-Laguna (Ellis 1959: 340), the insignia is a crooked prayerstick.

It seems the heads of the manly towns have a maternal reminder that they "stand for" U-Iatiku as mother (and father) of the Keres. The leaders of the womanly towns, however, have a reminder of the unity of the town represented by a vertical wooden staff bent back toward the earth.[16]

Of the manly towns, Cochiti is the center, with Felipe inside because of close links with Cochiti (Lange 1968a: 7, 228), and Santo Domingo outside, including influences from other Pueblos, such as the Boyakya priesthood, whose songs are in Tewa. While "the ancestors of San Felipe and Cochiti were one people who lived together at various successive villages" (Strong 1979: 392), Domingo residents have varied ancestry. According to the town map (Ortiz 1979: 380), neighboring house rows are named for Cochiti, Sia, Jemez, Santa Ana, and San Felipe.

After the context of womanly towns is discussed, we consider evidence for a missing fourth manly town.

Cochiti also preserves evidence for a Social Ego for all the manly towns called the _nahiya_ (Dumarest 1919: 198, Goldfrank 1927: 39, Parsons 1939: 901, Lange 1968a: 278). He was equal to or greater than the cacique, suggesting a glorified Outside Chief ~ Country Priest.

For the womanly towns, Santa Ana is the center, indicated by its women impersonating female Katsina, its double Shikames, and evidence for an extinct office that served as Social Ego for this womanly half of the towns. Because the Flint plays such a strong role in the running of the manly towns, the two Shikame of Santa Ana emphasize its own links with Woman. Also, Santa Ana recall an officer called the _naiya tsraikatsi_, who ranked above the cacique (White 1942: 87). The term is interesting because _naiya_ means mother and _tsraikatsi_ is one of the other names for the Town Priest at Santa Ana (White 1942: 142). As an uber "Mother" Inside Chief,

---

[16] Through the Americas, such crooks were a privilege of the elderly. At Sia, this prayerstick explicitly represented longevity (Stevenson 1894: 17). Vast numbers of prayersticks were preserved in intact rooms at Pueblo Bonito and other Chacoan sites.

this office would have been a womanly focus among all the towns.

Sia and Acoma are inside and closely related (White 1962: 83). Sia shares with Santa Ana tolerance of women wearing certain female Katsina masks. The manly peculiarities (square kivas and Country Chief) of Acoma become understandable in this context since they provide a needed manly element to the womanly towns. Some of these Acoma specialties are due to origins. "Until the thirteenth century culture in the Acoma area was reminiscent of that of contemporary Chaco Canyon but also of that of the Pinelawn Valley in the Reserve ares of the upper Gila. In other words, culture in the Acoma area was peripheral to that of both the nearby Anasazi and the Mogollon" (Ellis 1979: 439). Acomans today acknowledge four ancestral groups: original founders, Mesa Verdeans coming in the 1300s, and two groups from Cebollita Mesa region (Garcia-Mason 1979: 454).

Laguna is the outside womanly town, heavily influenced by Zuni and Hopi (Parsons 1920) before it was shattered by Christian factionalism and Americanization (Eggan 1950: 170). Like Domingo, it has been and is open to outsiders.[17]

The positions of Cochiti and Santa Ana as the central towns is supported by one parallel. These are the only towns to carry on a modern version of the Opi Warriors for men who kill a cougar, bear, or eagle (White 1942: 132). At Sia, the killers of a bear or cougar formed a lesser grouping.

Such parallelism among the Keres led me to seek evidence for a fourth manly town since, during the historic period, some towns of the Keres and other Pueblos became extinct (Schroeder 1979). A much more difficult question, of course, is why another manly town was not constituted to take its place, especially since the sacred objects and offices that constituted a separate town presumably already existed. The missing town would have been linked to Cochiti since it is the community that stands alone in terms of its dialect and triple kiva wings.

The best candidate, located in the Sandias east of the Rio Grande, would have been San Marcos (_yaa-tze_), which Hodge (1910: 44*) and Hackett (1942: xxxvii, #37) noted was occupied by about 600 Keres until the Pueblo Revolt and was not resettled. During the revolt, people from San Marcos, Cochiti, Domingo, and Felipe took refuge at La Cieneguilla near Santa Fe (White 1935: 14). White (1935: 28) thought that some of the

---

[17] Of related interest is the fame of several Laguna authors writing about their Pueblo. Leslie Marmon Silko (1977) began her important novel Ceremony with a poem about Thought Woman, the spider; while Paula Gunn Allen (1986: 15, 98, 223) overly emphasizes the role of Woman in Keres society, generalizing from Laguna and the womanly towns, at the expense of the gender balance of the Keresan intertown whole.

Marcenyos settled at Domingo, transferring the control of the Cerrillos turquoise mine, but there is also a close similarity between the native name of this town and that of the third Katsina group (*yashcha*) at San Felipe.[18]

Since San Marcos people did take refuge with the other manly towns, there is a slight chance that its religious and social identity continues within a modern town, much as the descendants of Pecos, who abandoned their town in 1838, maintain a distinct identity at Jemez, the only other Towa community. While Pecos people also went elsewhere, including one prominent family at Cochiti, the tribal identity remains at Jemez.

Further afield, a more provocative and controversial possibility was Awatobi, a town on Antelope (East ~ Fourth) Mesa among modern Hopi, which had a distinctly Keresan form of priestly leadership. Parsons (1936), amplifying the opinions of Fewkes and Hargrave, noted considerable influences from Keresan refugees at Hopi during both prehistoric droughts and the 1680 Revolt. Moreover, she called attention to an ancient Keres population on Antelope Mesa overlooking Jeddito Wash, the richest farmland near the Hopi. Hough (1903: 350) wrote of the ruins on this mesa:

> If there were no traditions among the Hopi relating to the five ruins mentioned, comparative methods would show that the bold symbolism on the pottery relates them to the Keres towns.

Of all the ruins, the largest was Awatobi, sacked by the Hopi in the autumn of AD 1700. After the 1680 Revolt and 1692 Reconquest, Awatobi reaccepted Catholicism and, in despair, its Town Priest, as the head of an ancient theocracy, asked the Hopi to destroy the town.

> When the Chief of Awatobi invited the Oraibi chief to destroy Awatobi, he displayed two clay figurines representing one, the townsmen, the other, the townswomen. Here, I have brought you my people, calmly he said (Parsons 1939: 336).

---

[18] "The *Yashcha* separated from the Turquoise group around 1900 ... For certain purposes, such as the annual feast day, Yashcha combines with Turquoise; for other purposes, such as Christmas dances, it operates separately" (Martin Murphy quoted in Strong 1979: 396). Presumably, this name is older than the splinter group itself.

Given that Awatobi was the biggest town on the mesa and that its Inside priest had a pair of figurines for the men and women, it suggests a fourth manly Keres town, since missing from the modern record because it was massacred, except for a few women survivors adopted into Hopi towns to perpetuate Awatobi rain-making rituals. Other Awatobis were buried below First Mesa in a mass grave (Turner and Morris 1970). While it seems remote, Hopi reports of Keresans living among them should not be discounted.[19]

The Pueblos

Within the general region, Keresans share a spatial and conceptual world with neighboring Pueblos of the Southwest, placing itself at the cosmic center. All are surrounded by the same six sacred directions and sacred mountains at the boundaries, but differ on their interrelationships. For the Keres, each mountain and direction is associated with particular supernatural colors, weather spirits, warriors, women, animals, birds, snakes, trees, and more. The Tewa associate them with other colors, corn maidens, mammals, birds, snakes, trees, shells, lakes, and so forth (Harrington 1916: 41-45). In lieu of examining all of these variations, the colors charted by Dozier (1970: 205, Table 7) will serve as an apt example.

	KERES	TEWA
north	yellow	blue
west	blue	yellow
south	red	red
east	white	white
above	(all colors) all colors	
below	black black	

While largely the same, the reversal of the north and west

---

[19] Scholars have argued with me that Awatobi was Hopi, particularly since modern Hopi claim it. Indeed, in the aftermath of massacre, women survivors were adopted by Hopi, mostly at Second Mesa, but all early scholarship agrees that these Fourth Mesa towns belonged to the Keresan tradition. Since the seep springs at the base of the Hopi Mesas have provided water during the worst droughts, refugees flocked there from throughout the Southwest. For hundreds of years, Hopis accepted other groups if they could provide an effective rain-bringing ritual. The ancestry of modern Hopis, therefore, is complex, rich, and varied. Initially though, as ancient near neighbors, Keres played a crucial role in converting these Great Basin Numics into Hopi Pueblos.

associations transforms each of these systems into different wholes.

Another example of varying relationships among Pueblos relates to the square/round opposition. Among the Keres, shapes express either Man, Woman, or both. Among the northern Tiwa at Taos, kivas are round inside the town wall, but square outside it (Smith 1969: 5, Figure 3). Among the Tewa, San Juan, Santa Clara, and Tesuque have square kivas, but San Ildefonso and Nambe have round ones (Stubbs 1950). While we know little of the symbolism involved, such variations express distinctive community sentiments. "Politically the Pueblos have never been united and each village ~ pueblo is an independent unit ... Language, appearance, ceremonials, anything that may be compared and evaluated is at its best in one's own pueblo" (Dozier 1970: 210, 209).

Yet, towns that are related linguistically and culturally share much in common, and such diversity may well be more apparent than real. Among the Keres towns, a unity exists beyond the diversity of kiva numbers and recruitment, of Katsina initiations, and of differential import given to matriclans or priesthoods. To better understand the Pueblos as a unit, I will now examine these same features among the Tewa, Tiwa, Towa, Tano, Zuni, and Hopi. While Parsons (1939: 940, 975) and others have been descriptive, treating each town pircemeal, here we seek the primacy of Keresan priesthoods on Pueblo cultures.

Each Tewa town has one large kiva (Hawley 1950:288, 291), which recruits for each moiety (Summer / Winter) through men, generally paternal relatives (Ortiz 1969: 44). The Tewa have no Katsina as such, but the Finishing is held for both boys and girls so they might know that adults wear masks of deities. Fundamental units of Tewa society are the Summer and Winter moieties, mediated by the Made People, the theocrats called "of the middle of the structure." Within this hierarchy, right has priority over left. Thus, the right hand assistant assumes a vacant position, and the left hand man moves up to become the right hand assistant (Dozier 1970, 198, Table 5). Tewa are cured by members of the Bear medicine priesthoods, which are explicitly said to derive from Keres (Laski 1959: 119).

Traditionally, the Tiwa had one large kiva per town (Hawley 1950: 387), recruiting for each moiety through both parents and initiating both boy and girls (Parsons 1939: 929, 933). In succession to offices, Tiwa gave priority to the right hand helper (Dozier 1970: 198, Table 5). Ellis (1964: 49) has Tiwa moieties divided between winter-males and summer-females, together with smaller constituents (corn groups) something like clans. At Isleta, at least, their medicine priesthoods acknowledge Keresan origins (Parsons 1939: 264).

Since they have lived among the First Mesa Hopi for almost three centuries, Tano ~ southern Tewa social organization has been colored by their matrilineal neighbors, within the limits allowed by the culture. Tano have two kivas that recruit through matriclans (Dozier 1967: 73, 42), and both boys and girls are inducted into the secret of the Katsina cult (1967: 59). The Tano also have a group of masked curers called the Sumakolih, which seem to be unique to them (1967: 78).

For Pecos and other Towa speakers at Jemez, two kivas recruit paternally (Ellis 1964: 37) and both boys and girls are initiated into the Katsina cult (1964: 34). Each of the priesthoods is linked to a particular matriclan, but at least some derive from the Keres (1964: 46). Of special note, succession within the priesthoods passed to the left hand man, then to the right hand one (1964: 16)

The Zuni have six kivas, one for each of the directions, but historical and cultural considerations may also be involved. About 1540, Zunis occupied six separate towns whose members later amalgamated into the single modern town (Eggan 1950: 176). In addition, the six kivas express a complex symbolism based on pairs. Linking the directional associations for the kivas supplied by Bunzel (1932: 877) with the discussion in Stevenson (1904: 63), for some purposes the North, South, and Above kivas act as elder brothers to the West, East, and Below kivas, who are younger brothers. On other occasions, North, West, and South are respectively paired with the East, Above, and Below kivas. Among other things, these cross pairings serve to integrate the various memberships at Zuni, as Kroeber (1917) aptly noted. Zuni kivas recruit through ceremonial fathers and only boys are initiated (Eggan 1950: 205). The primary social unit is the matri-household, with the more elite ones owning fetishes and holding official positions in the theocracy (Fox 1967: 36). The Zuni hierarchy includes eleven priesthoods, six of which acknowledge a Keresan source (Stevenson 1904: 424).

For the Hopi, three kinds of kivas are reported, but only the _Mung_ ~ Chief kiva serves the entire community. Kiva membership is traced through ceremonial fathers (Eggan 1950: 97), but the kivas per se are controlled by matriclans. The Katsina cult takes in both boys and girls (Titiev 1944: 107). Hopi society itself is firmly based in the matriclans, which loosely combine into phratries and towns to perpetuate ancient rites (1944: 104, Eggan 1950). Of the priesthoods at Hopi, at least the Snake and Antelope derive from the Keres (Parsons 1936).

As indicated by this brief review, the Keres have had a great impact throughout the Pueblo region. The most widely shared feature for all but the Tano is the priesthoods, which originated among the ancestral Keres as family specialties. For the Katsina initiations, all but Zuni share the practice of the womanly Keres, while Zuni matches the manly towns. Both the Tano and womanly towns recruit to the kivas through women, usually mothers. The Tiwa recruit via each parent in alternation, and the remaining Pueblos trace kiva membership through males, sometimes fictive kinsmen. The Keres, Towa, and Tano share a two kiva system, with the Zuni another possible member if their kivas were once more strongly paired. The Tewa, Tiwa, and Hopi emphasize one kiva per town.

Features, such as weaving and certain clans – other than those related to the priesthoods, and sand ~ dry painting, passed from the Keres to other Pueblos and neighbors like the Navaho and Apache. In terms of a relative scale for Keresan influence, closest to them are the Towa, geographically and culturally, as indicated by a shared left hand priority and recognition of the war chief as 'father' and the town chief as 'mother' (Ellis 1964: 25, 42). Next removed are the Hopi and Zuni, who share all traits except perhaps kiva numbers. In addition, the Hopi (Parsons 1939: 239 #2, 977) and Zuni (Stevenson 1904: 183, note A) believe that their ancestors spoke Keresic in the primordial underworld. The Tano share most features except priesthoods with the Keres, a curious lack unless the Boyakya at Santo Domingo is considered. Next are the Tiwa, who have priesthoods and supplementary features like the Town and War Chief distinction (Ellis 1964: 50), which were and are common throughout the tribes of the Americas. Furthest removed are the Tewa, close neighbors for several centuries, who obviously have reversed and transformed cultural traits to remain distinct from the Keres.

This degree of Pan-Pueblo influence indicates that the Keres were less a bridge and more a "Chacoan" hub in the dissemination of the Puebloan style, particularly among the Hopi. Keresic central location, unique language, and esteemed position facilitated their task. Even now other Pueblos cite Keres as the source for some of their more important esoteric lore and rites. Except at the extremes of Domingo and Laguna, however, the Keres do not return the favor.

Keresan Indicators in Archaeology

Manly	Center	Womanly
left	heart	right
kivas	priesthoods	clans
winter	solstice	summer
animals		plants
turquoise		corn (crops)
north, west	town	south, east
Gomaiyawish	(Katsina)	Shiwana
Kopishtaiya		Maiyanyi
Sun		Earth
San Juan	Chaco	Cibola

Chapter Four

ARCHAEOLOGY

The modern situation among Keresan towns, of course, represents only the most recent cultural solution for expressing their basic gender echo in a changing world. While the trappings and institutions of the culture have changed through time, a few pivotal relationships have guided these changes within a framework for continuity.

Over time, features of male/female activity have been influenced by newer innovations and older patterns have become consecrated to religious ~ ritual use, venerable because they reflect older traditions. Everything is infused with a religious sense, as Ellis (1983: xxxvi) noted:

"Each officer was the personal representative of a parallel member of the hierarchy of beings. A man took his responsibility and the power which implemented it directly from his supernatural counterpart."

Indeed, features reflecting the cosmic order, so important to the Keres theocracy, were treated in ways to render them valuable as precedents. It has been this impression of continuity which provided the recurrent pattern to trace Keres ancestry, especially in terms of increasing control of supernatural Power.

As "new" archaeology has rejected culture history in favor of predicting universal laws of human behavior, long-standing interests of Southwestern research have been abandoned. Thus, while this chapter examines the rich archaeological record for the region, it does so in terms of less popular theories about artifacts reflecting the symbolism of a culture. Indeed, missing from much of modern archaeology is any recognition that artifacts are both technological and semiotic statements, with the more diagnostic ones particularly sensitive to the restraints imposed by a culture. For much of the Southwest, this diagnostic artifact was and is pottery, both for academic archaeology and ethnology as well as for the native peoples themselves. In the distant past, however, this position may have been shared by the loom and textiles, providing models and fabrics mirroring the pattern of the universe, as was the case in many other areas of North and South America.

In general, an emphasis on economy has had more to do with the cultural concerns of white America than with cross-cultural research, that is, with the culture of the archaeologists rather than the archaeological culture being investigated. For example, Keres culture places greatest emphasis on the religious institution, which pervades all others. From this perspective, the Southwestern archaeological record will be reassessed in quest of Keres ancestry as seen through the evolution of their cultural pattern. From a Keres perspective, the most important aspect of this development has been the increasing access to and control of supernaturally powerful energy (*iyaanyi*) for the benefit of the entire community.

In lieu of predictive model building or testable hypotheses as such, we will study a kind of culture history, not in its discounted version of old, but rather in the light of a modern understanding of Keres culture as expressed by a Man / Woman echo resounding through examples of the context matrix. The aim, therefore, is to turn "ethnographic analogy" on its head and propose a kind of "archaeologic analogy" for the Keresan record.

Pueblo ruins and buildings themselves provide a telling example of this difference in interpretation. Instead of the rock and adobe piles viewed by archaeologists, pueblo towns were and are regarded by their inhabitants as living beings, with wood frames for skeletons and walls for skin. When finished, rooms were consecrated by priests with offerings of cornmeal, gems, and prayersticks. These rites and gifts made them alive. Indeed, "once a house was built or made, its fabric was considered living" and its strength came from the power "within the structure of the world and, ultimately, its creators" (Saile 1977: 79).

iyaanyi ~ Puwah ~ Cosmic Power

Men and women, in accordance with the gender duality so pervasive in all of Keres culture, have differential access and control of *iyaanyi*. Men are able to attract and direct "power," with adepts being able to concentrate power in ways proportional with their rank and grade in the priesthoods. Women, unless they act very much like men, are unable to attract, control, or concentrate power, presumably because their "natural" responsibilities to home and family distract them from the "cultural" life of prayer, meditation, and fasting that is necessary to maintain good relations with power. For example, at the solar rites to turn the sun, treated in the final chapter, men pray for their own access to power, while women pray that power come to their kinsmen, not to themselves. This does not mean, however, that women have absolutely no links to *iyaanyi*, because they indeed have a most vital one. While men are able to attract, direct, and control power, it remains actively kinetic: highly mobile and fluctuating. It pulsates with definite rhythms like music, a significance noted by White (1962: 114): "One of the most effective ways of obtaining and using supernatural power is by singing."

Song pulsates with power and allows humans to manipulate it. *Iyaanyi* is most like sun beams, radiating out from a center and moving in absolutely straight lines that can be angled but not curved by using reflective surfaces like quartz crystals or the sheen of shell, stone, or mica.

Therefore, power can only be concentrated, revived, and renewed by the cooperation of both men and women because *iyaanyi* is closely associated with life, functioning as a vital force whose source and summary is androgynous Consciousness Deity. As men and women are both necessary to the creation of life in its most viable forms, so they are also able to concentrate and renew power through their own respective abilities.

This renewal of power requires the cooperation and union of men and women in ways that are neither sexual nor extraordinary.[20] There is no Tantric or similar ritual among the Pueblos because these cultures emphasize restraint and a general incompatibility of biology and religion. Body fluids and natural acts seem to be abhorrent to supernaturals, with the exception of the all powerful Koshari, who signal their greater, if unrestrained, abilities by coming into contact with feces and urine, or simulating sex for comic effect at public rituals, representing the desired balance between the serious and the joyous to maximize blessings.

Thus, the sexual union is not invoked in these rituals of renewal, rather, it is the more nurturing and supportive parental behaviors that appear. Men act as protectors and teachers to instruct the power of their wishes, while women nurture and cuddle power or its representations to give it strength and support. In all, power is least influenced by anything associated with the reek of mortality (coitus, birth, or death) and most compelled by acts of kindness, support, and good intentions from the community and its leaders.[21]

Because power mirrors life, it is strongly associated with the immortals dwelling in the cosmos. According to the outline of the world discussed above, the directions are associated with particular deities who

---

[20] While Koshari and some Katsina sometimes simulate pelvic thrusts for comic effect, Underhill (1972: 211) learned at Hopi that the symbolic intent was for children to "understand that creating life is a sacred act."

[21] The sacred clowns, of course, in their guise as embodiments of the anti-social, do rely on sexual humor for much of their repetoire. Even more involved with biological functions are witches, the very essence of anti-social forces.

conform to manly or womanly categories.

Based on contemporary ethnography, the most important groups of immortals are the Katsina (and Gomaiyawish) of the West and the Kopishtaiya of the East. It is unlikely, however, that all these groups can be projected back into the prehistoric past because there is ample evidence that the Katsina Cult, as it is presently known, began in the Southwest with some Mesoamerican influence about AD 1300. This does not mean that the West direction lacked supernaturals before this time, only that they did not have the helmet-mask appearances of modern Katsina, who surely must have absorbed the prior deities of the West. In all likelihood, they were like the Katsina in being male and female immortals associated with farming and fertility. It is probably, given the extreme religious conservatism of all the Pueblos, however, that the Gomaiyawish were predecessors of these modern deities and survive in the present as less prominent scouts now overshadowed by the Katsina.

The Kopishtaiya of the East are more problematic, but, lacking archaeological evidence to the contrary, they seem to be older members of the Keres pantheon who entered the modern era in largely unchanged form.

Because duality is so fundamental to the Keres and other Pueblos, it seems probable that the present Katsina / Kopishtaiya pair was earlier represented by another one less obvious in the modern ethnography, but giving every indication of great antiquity. Such a likely pair among the modern Keres includes the beings called the Shiwana and the Maiyanyi.

As I understand the terms, the Shiwana are cloud spirits who bring moisture and fertility to the fields and who are now considered to be synonymous with the Katsina, primarily in their aspect of travelling through the sky from the West to visit parched fields. "Shiwana [is] a designation also used for spirits of the dead who were believed to have become supernatural cloud beings," along with people struck by lightning (Ellis 1979: 445).

As the Shiwana are associated with the sky, so the Maiyanyi are attached to the earth, and are most often mentioned in connection with the Spring ritual cleaning of the irrigation ditches. So strong is the link between the Maiyanyi and the earth that they must be carried to safety when the irrigation canals are unclogged. Sometimes, a priest can be seen lifting them out of the ditches and later returning them after the cleaning is done. While the Shiwana are believed to be men, women, and children, I have been unable to learn the gender, if any, of the Maiyanyi. Their close, intimate association with Mother Earth suggests that they are womanly, but there may be a reversal here since Father Sky is the context for the travel of the womanly Shiwana, although the permanent sky residents, particularly the Sun, are male in keeping with the exclusivity of Man among the Keres. Therefore, it may be that Mother Earth includes manly Maiyanyi as a aspect of the inclusive womanly gender.

Such reversals apparently have to do with the directing of powerful energy or deities. A telling example of this is the alignment of kivas within each town. As directions, East is manly and West is womanly, but, in terms of the kivas, the East (Town, Inside) Kiva is womanly and the West (Country, Outside) Kiva is manly. Apparently, this has to do with the flow of power, particularly that associated with the Sun, a very powerful, male immortal with a great concentration of *iyaanyi*. As the flow of power seems to be one way ~ unidirectional in a straight line (like a sunbeam) generally from East to West along the surface of the earth, this positioning of kivas provides a way to funnel power to the general before the specific, the inclusive to the exclusive. In addition, there seems to be another movement of power from the center to the periphery – presumably after it has been concentrated in a locale, item, or person – and back again. Indeed, the angles and straightness of the Chacoan roads suggests that they were primarily intended to harness the flow of power, presumably outward from the canyon where it had been concentrated in the vast storage rooms of the greathouses.

Therefore, power flowing in the wake of the Sun is brought into the East Kiva, concentrated and strengthened in this womanly environment, and then filtered into the West Kiva for use by this manly arena. Power can be pulled in for the duration of a ceremony when some of it is captured in various fetishes and the rest is sent to travel toward the West, like the Sun moving to the sunset. In its revitalized form, power then emerges in the East like the Sun at sunrise. Many of the major rituals, however, are held at night since this is the time that power is most available in these renewed concentrations. Further, since the primordial world was dark, power at night is particularly protean. Of course, this natural concentration of power emerging in the East every morning becomes further strengthened by human intervention during rituals in the East Kiva or in the chambers of the womanly priesthoods, who then use it and pass it on for the greater benefit of each Keres community.

This East-West flow of power also relates to the modern placement of Keres towns, with the manly ones to the East and the womanly ones to the West. While each of the towns concentrates power in its East kiva, it is the men who control and direct its use. Thus, it is always men, alone or as part of a womanly context, who have the most direct access to power.

Perhaps, before the 1700 destruction of Awatobi, manly towns might have been located on the eastern and western extremes, presumably to guard and protect all of the towns between them.

In sum, the manly towns are able to attract, direct, and control power in ways beneficial to all the Keres. The womanly towns, or rather, their priests, tap this flow along its route to the West and renew its strength and vitality before dispersing it.

Recognition of this flow also helps to explain the modern placement of Santo Domingo. As it is the only manly town, since San Marcos was abandoned, located on the eastern side of the Rio Grande, Santo Domingo might be thought to have greatest access to power, but, as we have already seen, its internal organization is not sufficient to properly harness power in the same manner as that of Cochiti with its three kiva wings. As Domingo had earlier village sites on the west side of the river, it may be that they relocated to be closer to the East to compensate for the loss of San Marcos, which controlled the Cerrillos turquoise mines, and for the bad luck that included the flooding of their older town. In consequence, Domingo came into closer contact with the Tiwa and Tewa villages on the eastern side, exposing themselves to greater outside influences.[22]

Such compensation to reset a balance must have been more frequent in the past when land was available and migrations a practical recourse. Interestingly, the Keres still recognize that the decision to undertake such a move was and is made by the War ~ Country ~ Outside Priest, as the community was venturing into the Outside and needed his protection against uncertainty. The Outside ~ Country Priest provides this protection by virtue of his ability to control pure, concentrated power as the ultimate manly official. As such he works with the cacique, who has access to renewed but diffuse womanly power.

This complementarity of men and women, as expressed in a wide range of artifacts and spatial arrangements, is, in fact, a hallmark of the Keres cultural tradition. It differs from that of the other Pueblos and other tribes in terms of the totality of relationships and representations emphasized. Many of the individual items and details are shared widely, so each alone cannot be considered diagnostic. Rather, a variety of items and relations must be used to show a pattern that is culturally specific. In other

---

22 Adolph Bandelier had the good fortune to arrive at Santo Domingo in 1880 while it was being built on the eastern bank, documenting how efficiently construction was done by family groups – Men doing the heavy labor and wives feeding them until the women applied the final plastering (Ellis 1983: xxxvi).

words, while summer / winter dominate Tewa ideology, where seasonal evidence best supports the axiom, the Keresan Man / Woman is more susceptible to examination because so much that men and women did and do becomes part of the archaeological record.

Those representations of Keres culture with greatest salience in the archaeological record are the West / East orientation so important for the flow of *iyaanyi* at the level of cosmic emanations, that between men / women at the interpersonal one, and those of line / curve and of hard / soft (stone / clay) at the sensory one. In addition, each of these oppositions has a central mediator, related to the concept of Mind, to fill the triple categories that constitute every Keres context.

Most of the mediators have been treated previously, but it is important just now to specify that for the sensory emanations, the mediators are the D-shape between line / curve and flexible objects sharing qualities with both the hard and soft. For example, in the distant past, as stone work was a male task and pottery making was a female one, so basketry, involving flexible materials bent and stretched, was done by both sexes such that plaiting in more lineal compositions, like wickerwork altars, was associated with men, while coiling in circular patterns was done by women. The consequences of these associations will be more fully explored when we look at archaeological details from Keres prehistory. Throughout, no single association is sufficient to identify ancestral Keres. Instead, it is the overall pattern, the combination of relations at a certain time and place, that is most telling.

Through the stages of the Pecos Classification, I once backtracked or upstreamed from the ethnography into the archaeology, but, beginning with modern Ceramic Pueblo V and moving backward to Pueblo I periods, then on to Basketmaker III and into the Archaic became too cumbersome and self-serving. Rather, since the overall model of Keres culture was presented in the first half, this chapter discusses its development from Archaic to modern times instead of its fading into a remote past.

Already, many Southwesternists have attempted to reconstruct the movements of people considered to be ancestral to modern Pueblos (Wendorf and Reed 1955, Ellis 1967b, Ford, Schroeder, and Peckham 1972). Such reconstructions have been general and impressionistic, based upon sequences of changing pottery types, some distinctive architectural features, and a personal sense of local archaeology derived from field experience and banter with other excavators. Here, however, the logic of certain forms and relationships, derived from the ethnography, will be emphasized to establish a pattern of Keresan prehistory, and to set it off against comparable developments in other regions of the Southwest where academic agreement has located other language groups, while also allowing for migrations over time and place.

The Archaic

Cynthia Irwin-Williams (1973), seeking to define Keres ancestry in the Archaic, designated their continuing tradition as the Oshara within the more general Picosa Desert Archaic at the start of the Anasazi (Puebloan) continuum, as defined by the Pecos Classification of techno-artifactual developments, divided into periods from Basketmaker I-III to Pueblo I-V.[23]

Research since then has identified an earlier Paleo-Indian occupation before 7,000 years ago, when these big-game hunters gradually moved east into the Great Plains. In succession, moving eastward from California, hunting and gathering Archaic peoples settled in the Southwest, elaborating their technology through the Basketmaker Lithic and the Pueblo Ceramic periods, when the economy shifted to intensive farming supplemented by natural harvests (Schoenwetter and Dittert 1968).

The Southwest branch of the Desert Archaic, the Picosa, includes the Pinto Basin (Pi-) found in areas of modern central and southern California, the Cochise (-co-) of southern Arizona, and the San Jose (-sa), a splinter group from the Pinto Basin who settled throughout the northern Southwest. A few centuries after the birth of Christ, the Ceramic complexes included pottery, farming, and settled village life. Thus, the Pinto Basin developed into the Hakatayan-Yumans of the Colorado River, the Cochise became the Hohokam-Pimans (with some influence from Mexico) in southern Arizona and the problematic Mogollon of the Arizona-New Mexico mountain ranges, while the San Jose became the Oshara-Keresans of the Anasazi. Mogollon migrants, ancestral to Tanoan speakers (Eddy 1966), a thousand years ago, moved up the Rio Grande Valley and into northwestern New Mexico, effectively encircling the Keresans and stimulating the cultural entrenchment or defensiveness that lead to Chaco Canyon. This migration resulted in a crossing over into the Anasazi tradition of these former Mogollon.[24]

---

[23] The alternative is the Gladwin Classification divided into roots, stems, branches, and phases.

[24] Early Southwestern archaeologists, having defined the Anasazi, assumed other traditions were variants or aberrations of it. Over time, however, archaeologists realized these were not variants but independent traditions. These four separate branches became known as the Anasazi, Mogollon, Hohokam, and the Hakatayan.

A separate, little known Archaic branch, related to the Frontera complex of northern Mexico – particularly in the states of Coahuila and eastern Chihuahua and the New Mexico-Texas border – probably represented ancestors of the Zuni.

This rough outline of ancestral languages and archaeological complexes refers not to whole populations, but rather to the elites who formulated later localized developments. Some have argued that such reconstructions are useless (Plog 1978), but this academic tradition of culture history has been an important focus in Southwestern research, tracing the developments of modern cultural and linguistic descendants by a full use of the archaeological record. The arid climate, allowing superb preservation of the full range of artifacts (wood, feathers, fur, and stone), and the monumental architecture, build under priestly authority, demand the kinds of rigorous analysis and synthesis that only the Southwest can contribute to the prehistory of North America.

Indeed, much of Southwestern prehistory is already known in broad outline. Of the different Pueblo linguistic clusters, we are relatively certain that the Hopi originated among Numic speakers of the Uto-Aztecan stock and founded the Kayenta branch of the Anasazi about AD 1100, if not earlier. They became Pueblos during close contact with ancestral Keresans living in the Four Corners area (where New Mexico, Arizona, Colorado, and Utah intersect). The Zuni probably originated in the Penutian stock along the Mexican border, arriving in west-central New Mexico about AD 1300 and interacting with resident Keres already there.

The various Tanoan pueblos have a long ancestry in New Mexico, first as members of the Mogollon and, after AD 1000, as migrants who diverged into the Tiwa along the Rio Grande, the Towa in the western highlands, and the Tewa near the Colorado border, particularly at Mesa Verde and the Chama basin.

According to chronologies worked out for Acoma by Alfred Dittert (1959) and for Sia by Cynthia Irwin-Williams, Keresan ancestry in the Southwest covers a period of at least 7000 years, when Pinto Basin migrants moved along northern Arizona and New Mexico to become the San Jose. Eventually, the ancestral Keres population clustered in the area bordered by rivers now called the San Juan, Little Colorado, and Rio Puerco of the East. Near the center of this area is Chaco Canyon, which developed into the theological center of the Keres before it was abandoned after AD 1100 for settlements that colonized the middle Rio Grande and its

---

Further, the Anasazi Archaic / Ceramic border actually occurred in Basketmaker III.

tributaries, where modern Keres remain, surrounded by other languages.

This, in outline, is the path of Keres development in terms of modern state and tribal locations. Irwin-Williams (1973) has called the distinct chronology leading into the modern Keres the Oshara, recognizing it as the branch of the Anasazi that did the most to define the tradition and become the disseminating hub of Puebloan culture.

This emphasis on a focus, nucleus, locus or nexus is also in keeping with the prehistoric adaptation of the Oshara, whose sites indicate a preference for centrally-located base camps near springs or other water sources so vital in this arid climate.

The Oshara tradition begins with the Jay Phase (BC 5500-4800), whose tool kit "suggests a mixed spectrum of subsistence activities, adapted to year-round exploitation of local resources, whose maximum concentration was accessible from permanent water localities" (Irwin-Williams 1973: 5).

In the Bajada Phase (BC 4800-3200), sites are more numerous, indicating a slight population increase, despite a deteriorating climate, with base camps located at canyon heads and secondary special activity sites on mesa slopes and canyon rims.

The San Jose Phase (BC 3200-1800) included a more favorable climate, "greatly increased effective moisture, dune stabilization, and soil formation" (1973: 7), helping "to increase the number and reliability of springs and to improve somewhat the character, quantity, and reliability of certain of the economically valuable flora and fauna ... Base camp debris is both more concentrated and more extensive than in the Bajada Phase" (1973: 8). The tool kit is more poorly made, but indicates the beginning of a full seasonal round of economic activities. "Important additions are shallow basined grinding slabs and simple hand stones made of cobbles, both of which permit more effective utilization of grass and other seeds (1973: 8).

Joseph Toulouse (Bryan and Toulouse 1948), who first identified the San Jose complex, told me that these habitation sites had a number of small hearth areas around a larger central hearth. Such a central fire provided the focus for communal activities and suggests that the important fire / water (heat / moisture) opposition so pervasive in Puebloan religion had its origins in such San Jose camps near water.

Also, the San Jose levels in Jemez Cave near Albuquerque, a floor filled with fragile remains, clearly indicated a sexual division of labor. Debris from male activities like stone working and hunting tasks was at the front ~ rim of the cave, while that from women was inside and near the rear. This spacing suggests that the important outside / inside symbolism associated with water / hearth, winter / summer, and men / women also received elaboration during the San Jose.

Of course, the sexual division of labor, which began long before the San Jose, has been a vital aspect of all primate and human adaptations. Rather, it is from the San Jose that we have the first confirmation both of the universal pattern and of its importance to Keresan ancestors. In short, the gender ideology of Keres culture was evident during the San Jose, in preparation for its institutional elaboration in the next phase.

The Armijo Phase (BC 1800-800) marked the addition of limited maize farming into the subsistence pattern. Not surprisingly, the maize seems to have been grown in canyons on narrow flood plains near the headlands where springs were located. While only a small contribution to the diet, maize held definite future promise as "a relatively concentrated, relatively reliable and seasonally abundant resource, which could for the first time provide a source of localized temporary seasonal surplus" (1973: 9-10). Features and scatter indicate patterned work areas, seasonal activities, and population concentrations, like that in the fall (harvest time) at Armijo Shelter, "a cliff base overhang located at a canyon head near the best of the seep springs" (1973: 10). This shelter also included evidence of early ceremonialism, most particularly a stone phallus suggestive of a thousand year continuity in Pueblo fertility rituals (Miller 1975).

The En Medio Phase (BC 800-400 AD) is a local variant of Basketmaker II, as the succeeding Trujillo Phase (400-600 AD) is a variant of early Basketmaker III. These phases reflect an increasing reliance on maize and a related population growth. "All of the cliff base sites produced evidence of intensive repeated occupation, although most are much smaller than Armijo [Shelter] ... Likewise none of the others produced as varied or extensive tool assemblages, nor any magico-religious objects. Much in evidence at all of these sites are well made, sometimes slab lined, storage pits ... The potential for lengthy occupation of these smaller sites was probably much increased by the development and growing importance of storage pits" (1973: 12). "Deep basined grinding slabs and cobble handstones are abundant throughout, while new flat and troughed grinding slabs and long flat handstones were introduced late" (1973: 13).

The brief Trujillo Phase reflected accommodations to an increased population, including the first evidence for bow and arrow use and for the manufacture of plainware pottery of the Lino Grey type. A new kind of seasonal site also occurs, located on north-south dune ridges cut from the gravel-capped uplands. These ridges afforded large concentrations of wild grasses, cacti, yucca, amaranth, chenopods, and juniper berries from April to September. Water was accessible to such sites from stream beds running parallel through the dunes. Despite such diversification reflective of a larger population, expanded seasonal round, and greater number of camps, Armijo Shelter remained the ritual nexus for the Arroyo Cuervo drainage.

The elaboration in technology following an increase in population indicates that Trujillo was the source of the distinctive artifact categories that carry us through the Keresan chronology: stonework and pottery, respectively associated with men or with women. As we will see, these categories also reflect the symbolic attributes of Man as exclusive and of Woman as inclusive.

Temporary shelters ~ habitations appear in the sites of this time period, but it is not until the later Basketmaker (BM) III and Pueblo (P) I periods that villages ~ settlements develop with clustered households.

For the Cuervo region, the Sky Village (AD 6-700, late Basketmaker III) and Loma Alta (AD 700-850, Pueblo I) Phases reflect the change "from a strongly seasonal mixed foraging-agricultural state to one of nearly full sedentarism ... complicated by the occurrence of a major climate change ... a brief but extreme period of desiccation and disastrous erosion which occurred between 600 AD and 700 AD." (1973: 15). In consequence, people congregated in the wide valley bottoms with farming potential, founding "pit houses, slab lined structures, or later, single above ground adobe or crude masonry rooms together with associated hearths" (1973: 1). Aiding the transition was the discovery that corn kept longer on the cob than shelled, so the cache pits for kernels of BM III were replaced by the cob storage rooms of P I (Sebastian 1992: 109).

With this last addition of above-ground masonry, the phases from Pueblo I to V fluctuate with regard to the type and degree of sedentarism for farming and ritual, especially in terms of large, preplanned architectural communities like those of Chaco, as distinct from villages in the pueblo apartment ~ condominium style. In the process of developing this multi-storied compound, pithouses gave way to surface rooms. The pit ~ subterranean houses were developed for shelter and dry storage, while storage pits gave way to storerooms built in arcs behind a pithouse. In time, these storage cists developed into habitable rooms which show evidence of occupation, such as internal hearths and household debris. The occupants were women and children since the pithouses continued to indicate male use as they were gradually converted into the underground ceremonial rooms now called "kivas" (Brew 1946, Bullard 1962). These buildings were not the modern, community, church-like town kivas, but rather, the fraternity ~ priesthood chambers which have a separate development from that of the two Inside / Outside ~ East / West kivas now so characteristic of Keres towns.

In all likelihood, the Inside ~ Town Kiva emerged from the ceremonial center ~ locus that began at least with the large hearth in some San Jose camps and developed through ritual centers like Armijo Shelter. Its distinctive character was achieved finally when, in contrast to the importance of pottery for women, stone slabs gained symbolic significance.
Slabs and sherds are contrasting features in Keres sites.

This opposition of slab / clay is probably the most distinctive attribute of Keres architecture after the appearance of sedentarism. It continues into the present, especially in ritual, a millennium after its practical beginnings. In a later section, we will consider evidence that the great kiva, the archaeological ancestor of the Keres town kiva, emerged from a ring of standing slabs to become the enormous masonry sanctuaries of Classic Pueblo III, especially at the pan-Keres center at Chaco Canyon. Other large slab rings, separate from shrines, are located in regional community centers that gave rise to some of the modern Keres towns.

Indications are that separate developments of the great kiva (also called a sanctuary) and priesthood chamber coincided with an increasing emphasis on East / West symbolism, especially evident in architecture, and presumably related to an even earlier association with the Sun as a source of supernatural power. As seen in the modern towns, the East Kiva is the inside one associated with men and women under the care of the Town Priest, while the West is the Outside one, associated with male activities under the authority of the Outside ~ Country ~ War Priest.

As these claims differ from the usual interpretations of the archaeological record from the Southwest, I will review evidence for the continuity of nexus-like fires, sacred sites, and great kivas; of religious beliefs as promulgated by a priestly theocratic class, and of gender symbolism using hearth / spring, summer / winter, adobe-clay / stone-slab, house / chamber, Inside / Outside, and so forth as representatives of, respectively, Woman / Man.

A full examination of Southwestern archaeology (McGregor 1941, Wormington 1964, Gladwin 1957) is beyond my scope, yet I will review sufficient data to make my argument compelling. Rather than survey the entire area, however, I will consider the best examples from different time periods to establish these continuities within a range of larger variations. Where possible, comparison will be made to another site from about the same time to show a contrasting cultural pattern to better highlight Keresan distinctiveness.

From the modern situation, we can see that the Keres and the Tewa, or the Tanoans more generally, emerged from similar Archaic adaptations to the same general region. Each, while evolving from a shared, common, pre-Pueblo conceptual framework, chose to emphasize an important aspect of the whole as a way of achieving a distinctive integration based on contrasting echos.

Given the generalized seasonal and sexual divisions of labor common to the Archaic, it is not surprising that the Keres and the Tewa have polarized their cultural differences by giving differential cultural emphasis either to the seasonal, as in the Tewa Summer / Winter moieties and hot / cold categories, or to gender, as in the Keres Man / Woman echo. In a similar way, they further polarized these symbols by reversing the basic definitions of each across their cultural boundaries (Miller 1972). This polarization is so systematic and consistent that it must be the handiwork of the priesthoods seeking to regularize such differences, especially since some of the fraternities diffused from the Keres to the Tewa, indicating the intensity of their close if diametrical relations.

Basketmakers

As generally understood, the Basketmaker Period extended to 700 AD in many areas, marking the development of farming, ceramics, and pithouse communities, often inspired by influences from Mexico. The type site for Basketmaker III is Shabik'eshchee Village in Chaco Canyon, excavated under the direction of Frank H.H. Roberts in the summer of 1927, the same year that the Southwestern Classification was formalized at the first Pecos Conference (Kidder 1927). This site was later dated in the AD 750s by Harold Gladwin's method of tree-ring analysis, making it much too late to be the source for Basketmaker III innovations. Yet the site otherwise suggested that it had played an important role during Basketmaker III. Hence, the site remained an anomaly until Alden Hayes (c1973) found two unexcavated pithouses (Y and Z) there, exposed wooden supports in them, and received more realistic dates from AD 550-600, if not earlier.

What first caught my attention at Shabik'eshchee was the 40 foot circle of sandstone slabs around an interior bench also faced with slabs. This was identified by Roberts (1929: 73) and, later, Vivian and Reiter (1965, 101) as an early great kiva. In comparison with the others I have identified, however, it seems to occupy an intermediary position between the earlier slab ring and the later masonry sanctuary.

Using the Vivian and Reiter (1965: 100-102) list, I added other examples from site reports, without being exhaustive, to determine three stages in the development of the modern town kiva. Rings of standing slabs occur at Broken Flute Cave along the northeastern Arizona border – with dates from AD 620-80 and a strong clustering of 620-30, at Site 1 in Cahone Canyon near Ackman, Colorado – with an impressive diameter of 81 feet, and at Whitewater Group 2 near Allantown, Arizona (Roberts 1939: 103, figure 25; 124-8), with a diameter of about 37 feet, but the dates are late (AD 840-60), confusing its interpretation. In keeping with its location on the northern periphery of the Anasazi, something of a backwater, the dates for the pithouses associated with the Cahone ring are equally late (AD 855-72). Another ring, as yet unpublished, stands on Sky Village or Helicopter Mesa in the Arroyo Cuervo region.

Rings with bench, both slab lined, and some interior features (fire box, ventilator, and post supports) suggesting the later masonry sanctuary, occur at Juniper Cove near Kayenta, Arizona and at Shabik'eshchee. A rectangular foundation with bench at Blue Mesa near Durango, Colorado (Vivian and Reiter 1964: 101) is clearly out of character with the others and thus is probably not ancestral to the Keres. As such, it is a logical prototype for the rectangular sanctuary of Fire Temple at Mesa Verde. In fact, these rectangular shapes suggest Tanoan usage since each represents a polarized opposite of the slab circle consistent with Keres development and thereby in keeping with the modern reversals between these two Anasazi complexes.

Another slab ring with bench, with a diameter of 43 feet, was found at Site 1 in Cahone Canyon, suggesting that it was the successor to the earlier ring. Also, there is a ring at Salt Point (Hibben and Dick 1944) near Chaco Canyon. A 63 foot slab ring with bench was found by Earl Morris at La Plata Site 33, with a date of 830.

Masonry great kivas, sometimes called sanctuaries to help distinguish them from all the other types of kivas (Leinau 1974), are well known from the Chaco region, where at least 10 have been excavated and others surveyed. Basically, they seem to be of two types, suggestive of increasing amounts of societal integration. Each of the great house ruins apparently had at least one sanctuary in its plaza or nearby. These were community kivas, presumably, and the ancestors of the modern East Kiva.

Moreover, isolated sanctuaries ~ great kivas, removed from any particular ruin, were strategically located to serve as the focus for a community scattered among Bc unit villages.[25]   Excavated examples of these are Kin Nahabas, appearing to date around AD 1000, and Casa Rinconada, better known and dating about AD 1100.

According to the most recent survey of Chaco, sanctuaries were more common in the canyon than previous research suggested:
Five isolated great kivas were recorded, each situated in the midst of a cluster of contemporary pueblos. Although all five were Pueblo II and III in age, we know from the old excavations at Shabik'eshchee, and from the 1973 excavations of 29 SJ 423 by the Chaco Center, that the great kiva was common in the canyon from Basketmaker III times. Tree-ring dates from the later site indicate an initial construction at about A.D. 500. Another 20 great kivas were counted at 15 pueblos ... It can be seen that almost everybody in the area during that stage lived within a mile of a great kiva (Hayes 1981: 40).

As an aside, Hayes (1981: 58) observed that

Great kivas had their origin in the distant past, but in Pueblo III, the circular firepit was pulled out of the floor and raised in the form of a rectangular masonry box, and the earlier subfloor pits that flanked it were built as masonry vaults above the floor.

His matter of fact account of this transition belies the important cultural attitudes revealed by these actions.[26] As we have already seen during the discussion of Acoma kivas, among Keres, buildings set into the ground were circular – in keeping with the consistent symbolism of Earth Mother, while those built above the ground were angular – appropriate for Father Sky and the manly Sun. Further, as sanctuaries were reflections of community solidarity, it was fitting that they have both manly (square

---

[25] Smaller hamlet or villages ruins are now called Bc units because in the initial surveys of the Southwest, A designated Arizona and C (capital letter) was Colorado, so New Mexico became B. Sites were then recorded with a regional designation like c (lower case letter) for the Chaco, hence Bc means a site in Chaco Canyon, New Mexico. There are hundreds of these Bc hamlets throughout the canyon so they became synonymous with it. Akins (1986: 11) describes the use of prior site designations for the Chaco.

[26] The opposition of round / square was and is important among all Pueblos. For example, in Arizona, among Hopi ancestors, "in most areas of the state, round belowground dwelling structures were replaced by rectangular aboveground ones between A.D. 700 and 1000" (Martin and Plog 1973: 34). Charles Adams (1991) argued that square kivas became important in connection with the spread of the Katsina cult after AD 1300.

vaults) and womanly attributes (round hearth) within an overall circular shape.

In some of the Chacoan great house ruins, there are both great kivas and tower kivas (circular great kivas built within a square room on an upper story of the building). I believe these different kivas were intended for the worship of and access to power associated with the earth spirits like the modern Maiyanyi in the case of sanctuaries and for that associated with sky ~ rain spirits (like the modern Shiwana) in the instance of tower kivas. This seems appropriate in terms of present Keres belief and practice. As such, this pattern is different from the kiva-tower combination in the Mesa Verde, which suggests that immortals were being drawn from the air into the kiva much as modern Tewa shrines are sometimes called "airports" for spirits (Ortiz 1969: 24).

In addition to the Chacoan sites, great kivas have also been found in the so-called Chacoan outliers, such as Aztec (Morris 1921-8), Salmon, and Lowry ruins to the north or at Nutria and Cebolleta Mesa to the south. Presumably, these reflect town ~ community integration on a seasonal basis, with the Chacoan ones used predominantly in the winter and the others during Spring and Fall farming. We will shortly consider this topic further in the discussion of Pueblo III in Chaco Canyon.

Regions	Slab Rings	Benches	Masonry
SW Colorado	Ackmen (81')	Cahone (43')	Lowry
NE Arizona	Brokn Flute	Juniper Cove	
Cibola (Zuni)	Whitewater (37')	Nutria	
Animas River		La Plata (63')	Aztec
Chaco		Shabik'eshcee (40')	
	Salt Point		

Now, we can return to the Basketmaker sites. There are clearly many more of these pithouse villages than have been identified because their antiquity has meant that they have been silted over, built upon, or utterly destroyed by nature or man. What sets them apart, however, is evidence for ceremonial centers associated with an emerging class of priests. This situation was earlier suggested by Vivian (1959: 85), whose "incipient theocracy" was an

> Inference from the specialization in ecclesiastical architecture, so to speak, ... whether disregarding or taking into consideration the possibility of external influences from the Meso-American region,

we see throughout the Chaco and Mesa Verde area that the basic, town-dwelling, agricultural pattern with its religious emphasis upon agriculture, had become well established.

Vivian (1959: 85) hedged, however, by arguing that "such a theocracy never developed into an identifiable, priestly ruling class; and that a priestly ruling class was not in evidence as such at the time of European contact." I infer from this that he had in mind Pueblos like the Hopi, who are usually regarded as egalitarian, although this is erroneous because their priestly rulers have been misunderstood by academics (Whitely 1988: 64-70). While the priestly control of knowledge still constitutes the basis for ranking among the Hopi, who were never centralized, the modern Keres give every indication of an earlier period with an intertown theocracy that can still be glimpsed among the modern towns. Further, this hierarchy was not noted by Europeans because religious persecution warned the Pueblos to keep their priesthoods a closely-guarded secret for their own protection. Until the consistent duality in Keres culture was recognized, the logical intertown organization of the Keres could not be appreciated.

It has long been held that the inspiration and details for much of Puebloan agriculture and ritual came from the south, particularly Mexico. While such influence cannot be denied, it is important to understand that the ancestral Keres probably met these influences not as pawns but as masters of their own fate. The internal consistency of Keres culture and its reflection in ancestral sites suggests that Mesoamerican features were integrated into the earlier patterns, rather than forcing a new one to be made of whole cloth. In short, the Keres as Oshara and later peoples controlled their own assimilation of foreign traits, rather than being dominated by them.

In the period before AD 1000, these traits filtered through the Mogollon, whose "great lodges" probably functioned as community buildings from AD 1 to 600. At its most distinctive, a great lodge was kidney (rounded D-) shaped with a stepped entry ramp (Wheat 1955: 58). Again, this form contrasts with the use of slab rings. Further, the ramp itself may have been reversed by the ancestral Keres to make it distinctively their own.

Unfortunately, the best example for this is Casa Rinconada, several hundred years later, where a buried walkway slopes up to emerge at the center of the floor. Assuming that this feature was a development from earlier examples during the intervening centuries, a comparison, therefore, can be drawn, especially in terms of the formalization of the belief in the

Maiyanyi earth spirits, who would have been enticed into the kivas at certain times. The possibility, hence, is that the sloped entry into some Keresan sanctuaries deliberately reversed the entrance ramp of some Mogollon great lodges. The sanctuary passage sloped upward into the center, while the lodge ramp rose toward the outer wall.

While each settlement probably had its religious leader(s) ~ family line of ritualists-curers, there were also large ceremonial gathering areas, the loci for various regional groups. Each of them had a slab enclosure that served to represent regional cohesion. As the symbolism of sky / earth, square / round, winter / summer, and fire / water served the interests of integration within the total environment, so that of stone / clay and West / East helped to capture the integral differences within the human community. All of these oppositions, of course, were reflections of paramount Man / Woman categories, as can be seen in the construction and arrangement of Keres pithouses.

In the early days of Southwestern archaeology, Alfred Kidder referred to such habitations as "slabhouses," and thought they were a distinct tradition. Such insight into diversity was unusual since Kidder and others of his time recognized only a single all-purpose Anasazi tradition. Here, inadvertently, he did identify a distinctive feature of ancestral Keres construction – the use of such sandstone slabs, as one side of an articulated contrast that included the use of adobe, clay, or mud. In the Basketmaker Period, such mud was usually mixed with wads of vegetable material, reaffirming its symbolic association with plants, women, and softness.

In short, the use of stone slabs was an aspect of manly contexts, while that of slabs and / or clay was associated with womanly ones. Hence, slab rings as religious buildings were associated with men, while houses of stone and adobe were linked with families, particularly women as housekeepers.

Indeed, concern with gender was a prominent feature of ancestral Keresan architecture. In contrast to the saucer depressions of Mogollon and later Navajo Reservoir pithouses of ancestral Tanoans, the deeper Oshara pithouses had low partitions, often of standing stone slabs, called wing walls ~ radials, separating the quadrant between the door and hearth from the rest of the floor. Since grinding tools have been found in this section, it was a female work area. In the rear of the house were stone-working debris and tools associated with men.

As the door often had an eastern exposure, women were located in the East and men in the West. Further, a hole is sometimes located in the west section of the floor. Known as the _sipapu_,[27] such an opening in modern kivas serves as a channel to the underworlds, the focus during rituals of offerings and prayers. Since pithouses became kiva chambers with this opening intact, direct continuity with the modern _sipapu_ is indicated.[28]

Domestic activities gradually moved to the arc of rooms behind the pithouses, developing from the rows of storage cists of an earlier period. At Ackmen-Lowry, these arcs indeed ran East and West in slab/ mud pairs, with the rooms entered through roof hatchways.

> The arrangement of these various kinds of rooms was as follows: a row of slab-lined rooms running East and West; to the south of them, a row of pole-and-mud-wall rooms; to the south of this double row of above-ground rooms, the pithouses (Martin 1939: 462).

Bullard (1962: 175) generalized from this and other sites to trace the evolution of pueblo multi-story architecture:

> The bringing together of slab lined storage rooms into arcs ~ rows behind the pithouses led to the development of surface architecture, so that by the end of Pueblo I true masonry multiroom surface structures were built. Increased use of surface structures as dwellings led to a gradual shift in pithouse function from domestic house to ceremonial ~ communal chamber.

Thus, by the end of Pueblo I, the earlier gender spaces divided by wing walls became separate buildings. Such a transition to surface apartments stands apart from that noted by F.H.H. Roberts (1930) for the Piedra district of Colorado, where pithouses with sloping walls were jammed together to form a connected block of rooms behind a single kiva. These domestic units, according to Cordell (1979: 100), provided private space that allowed hoarding and limited access to produce, setting the stage for distinctions based on inequality. Since Puebloan ranks were based on the control of knowledge, however, privacy was best achieved by leaving the community rather than retreating behind walls. Again, her

---

[27] SipapU or shipapu is one of the religious terms that the Hopi and other Pueblos borrowed from the Keresans.

[28] Variations in sipapu shapes have not been studied. Keresans made deep, tunnel-like holes, while Tewa made broader, more basin-like depressions, as appropriate for people who emerged from a lake.

argument is a European rather than a Puebloan one.

As Paul Martin mentioned, not all of the rooms at his site had slab walls. Some were made of jacal, again, in keeping with the inclusivity of Woman, especially within domestic spaces. This attribute of the womanly, having the qualities of both genders, also appears in the pithouses within some (or all?) of the ancestral Keres sites that seem to have been ceremonial centers. At these sites, at least, the roles of Inside and Outside Priests would have been passed down family lines, perhaps as stem kindreds or patrilines that stood in contrast to the localized matrilines in the households, linked into clans (Davenport 1959, Steward 1937, 1970, Service 1968). As each priesthood owned objects of great power, so too did important clans have fetishes handed down from its ancestors. Parsons (1968) regarded this fetish-house-clan linkage as a fundamental aspect of Puebloan society. When combined with the priesthoods, such a double descent system would be a logical beginning for the more elaborate one of the modern Keres.

As a consequence of this, pithouses, at sites with great kivas (as on the chart), appear to occur in pairs with one of them slab lined and the other plastered with adobe clay. Presumably, the first was the dwelling of the family of the Outside Priest and the latter that of the Inside Priest's wife and children. The actual situation was more complicated, of course, but at least this much can be glimpsed from early excavations. Future Basketmaker excavations, hopefully, will pay attention to this important but overlooked detail of intracommunity pithouse variation.

Unfortunately, if such variation was noticed, archaeologists typically assumed that it had only a practical function. Thus, Bullard (1962: 149-50) argued that slab lining served to reinforce weak walls or to hold back sandy soil. While this may have been the case occasionally, the consistent contrast between slab and clay as a feature of pithouse architecture belies such practicality.

At Shabik'eshchee, the twenty-odd pithouses seem to represent two separate occupations with a break between them. Roughly half of the houses have wing walls, while the others lack any dividers. Similarly, about half have slabs along the walls, although Roberts (1929: 16) thought that all of them had been slab lined before some had their linings removed for reuse elsewhere. This deconstruction seems unlikely, however, because some walls had only a coating of clay plaster and no evidence of slabs ~ slab imprints. While pairs of slab and adobe pithouses could be listed by comparable size, shape, orientation, and internal features,[29] such dualism would not be conclusive without better excavation records.

In one example, however, a definite pairing can be seen. This is Pithouse M, also called the double house (Roberts 1929: 49-52), since the structure had two hearths, two partitions, and two deflectors. It was oriented southeast-northwest, with a slab deflector and entry on the southeast. The walls were lined with slabs, with an adobe partition near the door, and a slab divider toward the west where a _sipapu_ was located just in front of it toward the center of the room. The firepit, south of the door, "had small stone slabs covered with plaster for its interior facing .... The one at the north had been lined with plaster" (1929: 51). Thus, the 19 x 16 foot room indicates a joint occupancy, with slab deflector, slab firepit, and adobe radials near the door; _sipapu_ toward the rear; and slab partitions and adobe hearth at the back. Each hearth group, therefore, combined slabs and adobe in different ways, with adobe given more prominence toward the East and slabs emphasized toward the West. Possibly, Pithouse M was built for expediency at the start of the reoccupation of the side.

Recently, at least two other canyon sites (724 at AD 760-820, 1360 at AD 850-1030, especially AD 950-1010) have also indicated occupation by paired ~ double families (Vivian 1990: 158), as I surmised from Shabik'eshchee Village. Since two women and three infants were buried on the floor of Pithouse B at Site 1360 (1990: 199-202), matrilocal residence seemed likely. "Most of the stone and bone tools were on the bench and 75% of the pottery was on the bench or behind the wing walls, leaving the central floor area for living and [food] processing. Pottery behind the southern partition was primarily large-volume containers used for storage, whereas most vessels stored on the bench were smaller. Based on the diversity and quantity of the pottery (24 vessels), the presence of paired sets of decorated bowls, pitchers, and ollas, almost equal sets of culinary vessels, and some spatial distribution of paired vessels within the house [Peter] McKenna postulated that at least two families had occupied the structure" (1990: 202).

At Broken Flute Cave, the pithouses had radials made of mud foundations with a horizontal log or vertical slabs set along them. The front of many of the houses had eroded away, so complete construction details were lost. Of note at this site are two features. First, on the eastern side,

---

[29] For example, Miller (1972: 48) pairs 16 of the pithouses dug by Roberts as Slabs: O, H, L, F-1, N, F, D / Adobe: I, E, K, B, Q, G, A, C, P). C and J were made of poles and branches. M is the double house discussed. Recently, two more pithouses (Y, Z) were excavated by Alden Hayes (c1973).

was a slab ring "constructed of a single row of sandstone slabs set upright" (Morris 1980: 40). Second, directly across from it on the west was Pithouse 9 (1980: 35) with walls coated with mud, a radial composed of mud and logs ending in slabs to the cliff edge, and a deflector of pine slabs. This deflector, a feature of modern kivas, indicates a ritual significance for Pithouse 9, as do the number of wood and clay figurines found in the fill.

Incidentally, the significance of the deflector as a sign of a religious building recalls an argument between Edgar L. Hewett (1943: 222, 289) and Jesse Walter Fewkes. Hewett argued that the so-called deflector and ventilator shaft were really an altar and passageway. Fewkes, whose opinion gained currency with the support of Neil Judd, held that the shaft merely brought fresh air into the kiva, while the slab deflected it away from the fire. The evidence from Broken Flute Cave, however, suggests that Hewett had the correct cultural explanation. Further, this interpretation has been confirmed by modern Keres priests who visited ruins and commented on these kiva features (Hoebel 1953).

Hewett spent his life in the Southwest paying careful attention to the natives of the past and the present. In keeping with my larger argument, I would like to note his observation that "the religion of the Pueblos, as of all their cultural relatives, rests on two basic ideas: namely, belief in the unity of life as manifested in all things, and in the dual principle in all existence, fundamentally, male and female" (Hewett 1943: 74). Clearly, Dr. Hewett had been listening to some Keres, most likely during his excavation of Tyuonyi (1943: 218-31, 1909), the important protohistoric Keres site in the Rito de las Frijoles now part of Bandelier National Monument.

In terms of the flow of power, the so-called ventilator shaft served to direct power down and through the kiva wall to the so-called deflector where they rested in this altar. As the different types of kivas developed, each performed a different function in terms of harnessing power.

For the Classic Pueblo III, two kiva types are well known. The so-called Chacoan kiva is round with a low, wide bench, a subfloor vent shaft, a slab deflector, and a roof of cribbed logs forming a dome. The subfloor vent probably relates to the inverted ramp of the sanctuary, as the slab deflector also implies strong continuity from the Oshara.

The Mesa Verdean kiva has a keyhole shape, six or more pilaster supports for the cribbed roof, a wall vent, and a layered masonry deflector. It is not as obviously a part of Keresan tradition and I suspect that it had another cultural source.

The best example for the use of slabs and plaster in paired pithouses is Whitewater Group 2 with its slab ring, slab lined cists, and six pithouses (numbered 12, 13a, 13b, 14, 15, 16). Based on details of size and layout and the superimposition of later buildings over earlier ones, there are three pairs of pithouses at this site. The earliest pair is 13a and 14 as both were small and built over. Pair 12 and 13b were close in placement, size, and orientation, although 12 was later remodelled by the addition of a bench, throwing into question its tree ring date of AD 844. Pithouse 13b was lined with slabs, but 12 had only a plastering of adobe. Pair 15 (with a date of AD 857) and 16 had nearby granaries, but those northwest of 15 were square and those beside 16 were oval. Appropriately, 15 had a facing of stone slabs covered with plaster (Roberts 1939: 135), but in 16 "The walls of the main pit were not lined with slabs; they were simply covered with a thick coating of plaster" (1939: 151). Thus, the squares and slabs of 15 were manly; the ovals and clay of 16 were womanly.

This pairing of pithouses around a ceremonial slab ring suggests communal cooperation among priestly leaders. As Fox (1967: 165-185) has reconstructed Keres kinship terminology, male relatives were distinguished by whether they were related through the father (-*mu* males) or through the mother (-*wa* males) (1967: 171). I surmise that such terminology arose under conditions where the paired pithouses and later block units were participating marriage alliances over several generations.

"Good" families would have passed particular curing techniques, sponsored by an animal spirit, down patrilines. Thus, men of certain families became famous for their abilities to perform ancestral treatments. Given the animal patrons of the six directions and the combinations of songs, medicines, and goals, a wide variety of shamanic techniques were available, providing the context for the development of the small kiva or chamber that became associated with particular priesthoods when these were formalized in settled villages and, later, institutionalized in the greathouses of Chaco canyon and the outliers. Over time, the ancient shamanism of the Americas became "professionalized" as the priesthoods of the modern Pueblos.

In keeping with the exclusive dimension of the manly, these finer distinctions separated out males related through the father (also with the Outside Priest) from those males related through the mother and having womanly associations with the Tiamunyi Inside Priest. In all, slabs relate to the male sphere of religion, spirits, warfare, and power, but slabs + plaster express community, economics, and children. Buildings of jacal and / or adobe plaster seem to reflect the womanly in some more restricted female sense. As the inclusive category, however, Woman had no reason to distinguish different degrees of involvement by the various genders.

Of all female activities, ceramics probably has had the greatest bearing on archaeological research because it is both durable over time and sensitive to cultural fluctuations. Here, too, the Oshara and ancestral Keresans set themselves apart from other contemporaries by the use of mineral and glaze paints and of the linebreak decorating the rim, both reflecting associations with women.

Again, this interpretation contradicts the previous view in Southwestern archaeology, where it is assumed that the darker, harder, and more lustrous mineral paint was always preferred, regardless of cultural preferences, so those people in areas without access to iron or lead had to make due with carbon paint, ignoring the possibility of trade to supply such minerals. In practice, the preparation was the same for both mineral and carbon paints (Hawley and Hawley 1938). A plant, often Rocky Mountain beeweed (tansy mustard at Hopi), is boiled down to a sludge to make the basic carbon paint. A pulverized ore, usually iron or manganese (lead for glazes), is added to the carbon base to make a mineral paint. Of the two, mineral paint more closely reflects the inclusive quality of Oshara-Keres womanhood, blending soft plant with hard ore. In the modern Keres Pueblos, the use of mineral paint was reinforced by the use of crushed stone as the tempering material. This addition was not consistent over time, however, because it was affected by regional trade.

For example, Santa Ana was making sand-tempered Puname Polychrome in Pueblo IV when Sia was making a basalt-tempered version. Both used a hard material for temper, but the difference between sand and basalt was more important for intra-Keres town expressions than for intercultural differences.

More confusing, perhaps, was the use of carbon paint on much of modern Cochiti pottery, a very manly town likely to underplay the female associations with pottery. The reason, however, was historic.

First, very few local painted ceramics were made in Cochiti in the period 1700 to 1800. Most were imported from San Ildefonso, or made at Cochiti by Tewa potters in completely typical Tewa style. Second, whatever pottery was made by the Cochiti themselves during this period remained distinctly different from the contemporary Tewa wares (Harlow 1973: 46).

These Tewa were living among the Cochiti as refugees and as affines, so their women continued their own ceramic traditions while also profiting from their economic specialization as the suppliers of pottery for the town.

Once aware that women of another cultural tradition were involved, the situation at Cochiti confirms the association of Keres women with mineral paint and Tanoans with carbon styles. Incidentally, it also serves as a warning against assuming that only one cultural group occupied a site. As we know from the present, members of different pueblos are often surprisingly friendly with each other, visiting back and forth or living away from home for years at a time. This pattern is in no way unique to the present.

Another feature of pottery made by Keres women through the centuries is the addition of a painted line around the lip of a vessel except for a small gap ~ linebreak left between the two ends. While often interpreted as a symbolic opening for the passage of spirits or an escape for any misfortune associated with the pot or potter, "Of historic groups, until recently the Hopi used it consistently, as did the Zuni. It was standard at Keresan Acoma, Laguna, Zia, Santa Ana, Santo Domingo, and Cochiti" (Bruce Ellis 1951: 265). Further, Ellis followed Morris and Burgh (1941) in linking the gap to an ancient fertility cult, centering around the Basketmaker II burden basket and intensifying during Pueblo II in the Chaco-Gallup area. He quotes Zuni data from Frank Cushing to the effect that a closed line would snuff out the subtle source of life.

> The potency of the completed circle as a trap or a prison is widely believed in today in the Southwest ... Among the Keres and southern Tiwa the stick-scratched or cornmeal-traced circle is used to capture recruits for Koshari or Kurena societies, to guard the corral during the hunt, to imprison witches or renegades against tribal custom. The belief is recorded that if a man puts his hand into the mouth of a cooking pot while on a hunt he will become lost, always walking about in a circle ... At Santa Ana, ... the break formerly was an intimate and personal affair to the potter, which had to do with the well-being of her family – its continuation and health (1951: 274, internal references omitted).

As these examples illustrate, the closed form was a manly one, associated with male activities of hunting, protection, ritual, and restraint. Actually, it is more often square than circular in this context. As the manly is a closed category, so the womanly is an open one, having its own characteristics, along with those of the manly to give it (her) completeness. It is in this sense, then, that the gap ~ linebreak is to be understood as a Keresan development. Once originated, however, like so much else that was Keres, it was adopted into other cultural traditions by the Hopi, Zuni, and Tanoans. Yet, like a word borrowed from another language but meaningful only in terms of its origins, the line break best makes sense for the Keres, who continue its use within their own logical system.

Thus far, I have indicated the long and sustained progress among the Oshara Keresan ancestors through a series of overlapping foci ~ nexi beginning with the central springs, larger hearths, and cavernous gathering places of the San Jose and continuing through the slab rings and masonry sanctuaries. Each nexus served to integrate a larger sense of community. In addition, there were a series of internal differentiations expressing the similarity and difference among humans as men and women, conceived of in the broadest possible terms within a humane universe. Among its expressions were the general oppositions of the seasons, winter and summer camps related to animal hunting and plant gathering, together with the more specific ones of slab / clay and of West / East.

In each case, West and slabs were more delimited, while East and adobe clay were more variable or mixed, often including male traits. The prime motivation was the increasing access to and control of power, now known as *iyaanyi*. Presumably this is why the Oshara began to inclose spaces with slab rings, divide off the male and female activity areas in the pithouses, and, later, move into small kiva chambers and surface room blocks, to intensify male access to power.

Kivas added ventilators and altar slabs to direct and retain some of the power attracted to them, together with clay and stone effigies kept there for the same purpose. Presumably, as sky or earth spirits, the Shiwana and the Maiyanyi were recognized as manly or womanly. Other strategies were devised for attracting their power into the plaza or a tower kiva. The chambers, derived from pithouses, served the specific purpose of housing ceremonies for the curing of internal and external diseases. These rites were family traditions passed down through sons, with those associated with the leading families including features of the others, much as Flint priests now must undergo initiations into other priesthoods in addition to their own so as to know "all the secrets." Pervading all of these relationships has been the reverberation of Man / Woman as the organizing principal of Keres culture, the echo that provided consistency, uniformity, and continuity.

The culmination of all of these facets of Keres culture, spanning the period from AD 850 to 1150, was Chaco Canyon, the pan-Keresan center and the glory of Southwestern prehistory (Hewett 1936, Jackson 1887, Gladwin 1945, Gillespie 1979, Gwinn Vivian 1990, Sebastian 1992).

The Chaco Phenomenon

Today, this isolated canyon consists of over a dozen greathouse ruins and hundreds of smaller Bc unit ruins scattered in an area set apart from other Anasazi population concentrations. During the occupation of Chaco Canyon, the major features of Keresan society were defined architecturally. Matrilineages occupied the smallhouses throughout the region, while the leaders of major clans occupied the greathouses, both at outliers near clan lands and, in the case of important clans, in the canyon itself, where public ceremonies like those sponsored by the Antelope or Corn clans at Acoma (see the last chapter) took place. Males, initiated into family priesthoods, used the small kivas as their chambers. Both clans and priesthoods, arranged into alignments of kiva wings, cooperated in the use of great kivas as the overall integrative mechanisms.

Near the center of distribution of Oshara sites, the canyon itself runs East and West, making it an ideal Keresan focus. For over two centuries, "the Chaco phenomenon" played an important role in the integration of the Keres and in the exchange of information and goods among all Anasazi groups and Mesoamerica. It is not accidental, therefore, that the large scale abandonment of the Chaco seems to coincide with the rise of the Mesamerican trade network centered at Casas Grandes in modern Chihuahua.

In his masterful survey, The Chacoan Prehistory of the San Juan Basin, R. Gwinn Vivian (1990) summarized the history and theories of prior research, particularly broader perspectives on the Chaco Basin region, before presenting his own theory of Chaco development in a final chapter. Yet, by drawing his boundaries in terms of geography, cultural differences were obscured.

His perspective was further limited by looking only at the Eastern Anasazi record, rather than the entire northern Southwest. Since Keresan speakers were settled among both Eastern and Western Anasazi, important aspects of prehistory were ignored. Moreover, while Vivian (1990: 437) quoted Robin Fox on Keresan links to the Chaco, together with "a shift from lineage-based "unit houses" to segmented villages composed of multiple sibs to unplanned towns incorporating matriclans and patrimoieites," the full articulation of Keresan society in terms of matriclans, priesthoods, and dual kiva wings, traced above, was ignored. Thereby lost was the equation of smallhouses with matrilineages, small kivas with priesthood chambers, greathouses with clan fetishes and leaders, and great kivas with integrative kiva wings.

Rather, Vivian was particularly concerned with issues of environment and climate in the basin, and, in terms of these survival issues, he contributed a great deal. As he noted, Chaco canyon was advantaged over other parts of the basin because of its size and access to rain runoff from both head and side drainages (1990: 2). The canyon itself was a divide between primarily marine sediments to the northeast and land deposits on the southwest (1990: 16).

In tracing the history of research in the canyon, Vivian observed that while there was an early tendency to focus only on the canyon greathouse ruins (the Chaco Core) and to regard them as cultural experiments or deviations from Northern Pueblo history, present researchers assume that the Chaco Phenomenon "was an indigenous development with roots in the late Archaic" (1990: 7, 13). Moreover, persistent attempts were made to link together central greathouses to define some sense of a larger Chacoan community. For example, Edgar L. Hewett, the neglected Chacoan theorist, considered Pueblo Bonito, Chetro Ketl, Pueblo del Arroyo, and Casa Rinconada as a single town (1990: 52). As early as 1881, Lewis Henry Morgan noted that the same town plan was used for Hungo Pavi in the canyon and for Aztec West along the Animas River. Indeed, recent surveys suggest that there may have been a low wall around the four Core sites of Pueblo Bonito, Chetro Ketl, Pueblo del Arroyo, and Pueblo Alto (1990: 447, 482).

While tracing the Chacoan development from the Archaic of AD 500, particularly in terms of the growth of the great kiva, Vivian nevertheless noted considerable experimentation or creativity within the canyon and basin as evidenced by architectural redesignings. In particular, the rectangular Northeast Foundation built to the southeast of Bonito in 1070-75 suggested an attempt to break from the D-shape that long dominated the ground plan of this central greathouse (1990: 56, 284).

Vivian was particularly concerned with tracing the increasing recognition by researchers that greathouses and smallhouses were occupied at the same time, both in the canyon and in the basin.

Past theories to explain difference between great and small houses, always emphasizing the latter, invoked immigrant colonists, Mexican traders (pochteca, trocaderos), turquoise trade, cultural progressives or conservatives, different languages, wealth differences, complex ecology, and levels within administrative hierarchies (1990: 395, 407).

Before excavations and surveys, the National Parks Service Chaco Center argued for a redistributive network centered on the Core, but, after excavations, pilgrimages into the Core for "consumption events" seemed more plausible, with the intimation "that compensation for ritual services was construction labor on great houses to enlarge accommodations for future pilgrims" (1990: 408). Smallhouse excavations also suggested that craft specializations, particularly in turquoise, by these farmers was used to trade for food from outside the canyon (1990: 415).

While Vivian recognized a common origin for both great and small houses going back to the Archaic, he saw their difference as primarily related to social organization. The smallhouses, which he attributed to the Cibola system, were each occupied by a localized lineage, presumably of women (1990: 446). "Cibola social relationships were embedded in the lineage and functioned through the lineage for the duration of the Chacoan presence in the Basin" (1990: 449). He noted for the greathouse, called San Juan, "that two systems were present in the Basin from at least 400 and that one of them, the San Juan, was organized on the basis of dualism which became a critical factor in the evolution of Chacoan-San Juan nucleated communities in the Chaco Core" (1990: 491).

Within recent decades, moreover, others have suggested that greathouses at Chacoan outliers were built and occupied by a "selectively male colony" which intermarried with local women (1990: 76). Over time, these outlier greathouses, whether ancestral (organic within the site cluster) or scion (added later), formed a Halo around the western two-thirds of the basin.

Unlike prior scholarship which noted a break between Paleoindian and Archaic occupations of the Southwest, some of the latter may have remained in the region and adapted to a foraging economy about 7500 years ago. By the Late Archaic of 5000 years ago, a pronounced seasonal round had developed (1990: 84), with some evidence of maize growing about 3000 years ago.

While Vivian did not consider Archaic (Picosa) variants outside the later Eastern Anasazi region, after the transition from the Archaic to Basketmaker II, he carefully considered subregional variants for each time period. Since the Archaic, these variants went from two to four examples, with a distinct overlap occurring in the canyon and leading to the flourishing of the Core. Since these complexes have already been considered in terms of the chronologies of Puebloan languages, such variants will not be discussed further, except to note that Vivian largely obscured the Oshara tradition of Keresan development from others of the same times and places.

With reliance on the farming of corn, beans, and squash about the time of the BC/AD shift, the foragers moved into the upland mountains and the farmers took over the floodplains and lower elevations (1990: 120). While the use of slab linings was traced from pithouses to surface rooms, no special attention was paid to their significance. At a Lupton site dated around AD 800, "Brownwares were primarily associated with D-shaped pit houses with benches, but most graywares were found in circular, benchless pit houses" (1990: 148), which suggests Mogollon inspiration for the D-shape that later became so important for indicating priestly or religious sites. In the north, great kivas were becoming more common.

With the elaboration of sites in the Canyon after AD 920, social mechanisms devised to balance population density with resource availability included "task diversification and specialization within and between settlements, variable settlement patterns, and exchange within established networks" (1990: 168).

Surveys found 50 or more outlier sites (1990: 234), both ancestral and scion, scattered around the basin, but only about half had great kivas (1990: 234, 243). Since each of the seven modern Keresan town has about a dozen clans (7 x 12 = 84), clan ownership of outliers seems possible. Only the most important clans, such as Corn and Antelope which sponsor major rites at Acoma (see last chapter), had greathouses in the canyon.

Within the canyon, three great kivas were located at Casa Rinconada, Kin Nahabas, and site 29 SJ 1642 east of Wijiji (1990: 249, 251). (Two others have been mentioned). Such great kivas served as the integrative mechanisms for district and regional communities.

Small ~ chamber kivas were distinguished as Chacoan (1990, Figure 6.15) or Mesa Verdean (1990: Figure 8.4), along with hybrid kivas, combining features of both, during the Late Bonito. The Chacoan had "low, wide benches, horizontal log pilasters, subfloor ventilator, slab deflector, and roofs laid directly on the wall top or in some cases cribbed, with cribbing beginning on the pilasters" (1990: 161). The Mesa Verdean had a keyhole shape and "were deep, had a ventilator and firepit arrangement, and roofs supported on masonry pilasters set on an encircling bench" (1990: 230). Tower kivas set into upper stories also became more common through time. In all, Vivian (1990: 289) diagramed five kiva types for Chaco and the Anasazi. Since modern Tewa believe the keyhole shape of their shrines, which probably developed from kivas, directed power into that space, the Mesa Verdean kivas seem to have been concerned with the upper world realm, as the Chacoan ones concentrated on the underearth and Shipop. Tower kivas, presumably, represented access to power and spirits from the sky.

As the population grew in the canyon, resource use fluctuated, depending on supply, particularly in terms of varieties of game animals and lithics (1990: 215-7, 314-18, 378-91).

In his own research, Vivian (1990: 307-313) found evidence of water control systems in seventeen of twenty-eight drainages leading into the canyon. In addition, waffle fields and other special gardens were noted. While water supply was a crucial concern of life in the canyon, the symbolic importance of such fields should not be ignored. To this day, the quality of a native priest among the Pueblos is measured as much by the success of his cures as the bounty of his crops. A "good" priest must also be a good farmer to prove the virtue of his links with spirits and the land.

A singular contribution by Vivian (1990: 169) was his revision of the Bonito Phase (1080-1225) into Early (920-1020), Classic (1020-1120), and Late (1120-1220) to argue against McElmo as separate or intrusive settlers in the canyon. Instead, the McElmo sites like Kin Kletso were seen as a logical development out of the experimentation characteristic of Chacoan leaders. Though "It is assumed as well that the building of great houses was rooted in cultural precepts that were expressed conceptually in architectural plan and form" (1990: 265), Vivian did not suggest what those precepts were.

While builders had a master plan in mind, that plan changed over time. During the Early Bonito Phase, the basic unit was the suite of living and storage rooms, which then shifted to be the roomblock, and finally, by Late Bonito, became the entire ruin (1990: 269, 365). According to Stephen Lekson, who computed four stages for building episodes on the basis of the number of persons and the length of time needed, a 30 person crew could build Bonito in 21 months, although a third of that time was devoted to felling and transporting the timbers, probably in the late spring and early summer when "labor could be pooled from several great houses" (1990: 273), unlike the model of Lynne Sebastian (discussed below) which presumes that each greathouse acted alone. The Acoma clan-sponsored rites (see last chapter) suggest how such pooling or recruitment was possible by initiation godparents.

The typical building sequence began with an arc of central rooms which was then doubled in size by adding first an east wing and then a west one to define a plaza area (1990: 278, 280, 291). This series supports the argument that the orientation of the east side was the community and that of the west one was male specialized.

Continuing a practice as old as the shift from pithouse to kiva and to surface room, Late Bonitos moved functions "into separate buildings, where previously they were undertaken in different portions of a single structure" (1990: 296). This transition can be seen in the construction (1990: 285, 374) of Pueblo del Arroyo (1065-75) and Wijiji (1100-15) before the final sites (1100-15), when "Ceramic imports were more noticeable during the Late Bonito phase as a result of the appearance of Chaco-McElmo Black-on-white, a carbon paint type that contrasted sharply with earlier mineral paint types not only in the pigment used but in design style and rim decoration" (1990: 381).

"Several Chacoan growth models purport that the Late Bonito variant became more complex during the first half of the 12th century. According to these models, this process involved a concentration of energy in the Chaco Core, where population was massed in settlements with more restricted and precisely defined boundaries" (1990: 487)

The most distinctive addition to Late Bonito architecture was the Pueblo del Arroyo tri-wall with a central kiva and a double ring of six inner rooms and ten outer ones, dated from the early 1100s and suggesting the later office rooms of the Tiamunyi.

The appearance of block towns and carbon painted wares in the canyon indicated the outcome of the increasing priestly isolation or retreat noted by Lynne Sebastian and can be traced in a similar progression from plaza greathouses to block units found in Manuelito Canyon (see below).

The loss of the bracketed or enclosed plaza meant that public functions were curtailed. The core of the community and the template for the modern Keresan towns was defined in the McElmo or Late Bonito as a block of rooms with paired kivas, like those of the modern East and West town kivas. Later, except for important religious centers with a circular plan as at Tyuonyi, the aggregation of people during Pueblo IV was marked by towns arranged as a series of these housing blocks divided by street or open-ended plazas, like the modern Keresan communities.

After four decades of Chaco apogee,

"System disintegration rather than collapse may most aptly describe the process involved during the twelfth century if the term is understood to represent a change in composition through separation into constituent elements and not the complete loss of cultural and system identity. There is no reason to suppose that the basic social elements that served as building blocks for Chacoan culture did not survive in subsequent modified forms of Puebloan culture. If this was the case, the task becomes one of identifying those elements in the twelfth century forms" (1990: 333-34).

The last Puebloan occupation of the canyon, before Navajo arrival, was indicated by a Zuni glaze site dated to AD 1300-50 (1990: 389).

Because of its age, complexity, and richness, the Chaco has received considerable attention, although not as a religious center. Trade and tribute dominate interpretations, rather than a proper appreciation for respect, reverence, and ritual. Only Fritz (1978) has paid close attention to hints about the ideological system manifested in the ruins. As a healthy relief from testable and material aspects of prehistory, he reminds us that culture plays the vital role of providing "conceptual memory" in adaptation systems, serving as an organizational framework and control over content during long-term information processing, ranging from rules for private behavior and public conduct to elaborate symbolism relating forms to meanings.

Fritz's point is well taken, although it has been little heeded. Looking specifically at Chacoan architecture as a iconic code or grammar of design elements reflecting important cultural concerns, he sought an ideal order. In its own terms, devoid of any ethnographic analysis or comparisons, he found that Chacoan world view consisted of a cosmos with differentiated elements "dynamic yet bounded and restrained" (1978: 41). These patterns are expressed as symmetrical and asymmetrical relations that crosscut each other, with symmetry involving phenomena which were "located in the east and west and were defined by axes aligned roughly north-south," while asymmetry involved those oriented north and south "defined by axes aligned roughly east-west" (1978: 41).

For example, of the central greathouse ruins, Wijiji, Una Vida, Hungo Pavi, and Chetro Ketl are to the East, while Pueblo Bonito, Pueblo del Arroyo, Casa Chiquita, and Penasco Blanco are to the West. In all, he posits a balance of 4:4, if Kin Kletso is ignored and Pueblo Alto is substituted for Casa Chiquita of Late Bonito date. There is ample justification for these substitutions since the McElmo construction and dating put Kletso and Chiquita after the heyday of the canyon (Vivian and Mathews 1964).

Asymmetry was also characteristic of the canyon and of its ruins, together or separately. For example, the greathouses were built on the north side of Chaco Wash, but most of the smallhouse or Bc units are on the south side.

Asymmetry also applies in terms of a center / periphery opposition in that towns in the canyon bottom have more kivas and complexity than those above the rim or further away. In addition, there are distant outliers, presumably associated with regional great kivas and seasonal concentrations, connected with the Chaco by straight sections of roadways that will be discussed below.

In all, the placement of Chacoan ruins most suggests a Keres context of center \ inside / outside in terms of Bonito, Chetro Ketl at the center \ Pueblo Alto, Tsin Kletzin at the rim/ nearby outliers along the Chaco Halo. Certainly, demography and lapses in the transmission of esoteric theological knowledge make problematic such direct continuity between all Chaco ruins and all modern towns.[30] At its height, Chaco was the elite center of a theocracy, not just a marketplace, however egalitarian. In particular, except for the grand pilgrimages during the year, the greathouses were more like monasteries because of the ceremonial chastity required during fasts and retreats. Chacoan priests did live with their families, however, when not engaged in rituals in their chambers.

Fritz interpreted other reasons for these differentially balanced relations. He decided symmetry represents a society based on equality within a "closed system of balanced duality" (1978: 50). Citing the work by Dee Hudson on measurement systems at Bonito, he argued for different social groups, like moieties, on the West and East, in part because the basic unit of measurement at Bonito was equivalent to 20 inches on the West and 29 inches on the East. Significantly, the eastern measure was the larger, making it more inclusive. The row of rooms down the middle of the ruin used both sets of measurement, suggesting its integrative character.

Fritz related asymmetry more plausibly to "control within a hierarchically organized social system" (1978: 51), with managers on the north side at the locus of sacred power and the managed on the south. Yet his own data indicated that both the north and the east were loci of ritual attention. For example, the east side of Pueblo Bonito had most of the kivas by a ratio of almost 2:1.

For the sanctuary called Casa Rinconada, he noted that the north / south orientation correlated with one of darkness / light and moisture / heat, but he stated these as a sacred / mundane association that seems inappropriate for a great kiva at Chaco, rather like misidentifying a chapel as a parlor in the Vatican.

While he linked the underground ramp at Rinconada with rituals of

---

[30] In Miller (1972), I drew detailed parallels between these ruins and the modern Keres Towns, but, to judge from reader comments, my intentions were misunderstood. Rather than tracing direct continuity from Chaco and regional towns to specific modern towns, I was seeking evidence of the overall town context itself.

origin and return, I suspect from modern Keres data that it was intended for the Maiyanyi and that it may have actually been used only once at the consecration of the building to draw spirits and power into the structure before that passage was sealed over to keep them inside.

This explanation is probable because the subfloor feature was not found until a year after the excavation was finished. Students later visiting the site noted its outline in cracks on the settling floor. Yet, as currently seen, this feature is shown to tourists as part of the functioning kiva, despite the fully plastered floor that hid it from its contemporary users and archaeologists for so long.[31] Ellis (1952) provides another ethnographic parallel for this argument from Jemez where a similar passage into each kiva is blocked up after its consecration.

As I have learned from other native groups, particularly the Tsimshian, the effectiveness of ceremonials relied in large part on the absence of many of the townspeople for part of the year. During this free time, priests (and their helpers sworn to secrecy) devoted much time, labor, thought, and attention to designing and building the equipment (Vivian, Dodgen, and Hartman 1978) needed to amaze an audience during rituals and displays, helping to assure continued devotion. Given the size and complexity of the Chaco, together with a period of dispersed summer farming on plots scattered throughout the San Juan Basin, a similar separation and conjoining by season probably effected the canyon.

Moreover, Altschul (1978) has considered the wider context of this so-called Chacoan phenomenon by looking at it in terms of the larger San Juan River drainage. The area north of the river is cut up into many plateaus and mesa fingerings, with a deep water table, many springs, and heavy summer thunderstorms allowing for floodwater farming. The area to the south is more dry, less bountiful, and more divided into planes of plateaus, cliffs, and deep valleys that are broader than those in the north. Within the Chaco, the south side with the Bc units parallels the general pattern of growth and construction for the entire San Juan region, while the north half shows "areal consolidation in a few large centers" (1978: 116). In the process, two features became closely involved in this consolidation: great kivas (sanctuaries) and waterworks.

Most researchers have argued for the beginning of the great kiva about AD 900 as part of the increasing social control suggested by the size and complexity of the early greathouse ruins. Once, great kivas were thought to be a uniquely Chacoan development, but excavations near Zuni,

---

[31] Similarly, the wall niches now exposed were plastered over to hide their offerings while Rinconada was in use.

New Mexico; Allentown, Arizona; and Lowry, Colorado also revealed sanctuaries. As I argued above, such sanctuaries are probably a Keres innovation, reflecting the community focus for both regional populations outside the canyon and of ritual congregations within it. Since there were Keresans over a wide area of the Southwest, with Chaco as their heart, it is not surprising that sanctuaries are found throughout the area, but most heavily concentrated in the canyon.

Recently, archaeologists argued that the great kiva served as a redistributive center, a store and supply house for entrenching political leaders. As a cross-cultural generality, such a statement has merit, depending on the way the terms are defined, but it does not consider its long development from the central hearths and springs of the Oshara. The likelihood, then, is that the sanctuary was built to attract and retain large reservoirs of power for the benefit of an extensive community. It may be that food and other supplies were stored in adjoining rooms, but this was probably to further sanctify it.

Following the hydraulic theory of Karl Wittfogel, many have argued that the motivation for strengthening the priesthood in the Chaco was the need to regulate the waterworks in the canyon. While some features of this network have long been recognized, it has been the work of Gwinn Vivian (1990) which has revealed much of its elaboration.

Throughout the San Juan, water control systems are concerned with either the conservation of rainfall and other water sources, or with the diversion of rain runoff. Conservation was used in the northern region, requiring little management. Diversion, on the other hand, was characteristic of the Chaco, requiring a coordinated management effort to use effectively a network of ditch laterals and switches. It was in the interests of such diversion, then, that the Chacoan priesthoods had the means to increase their authority.

Wittfogel and Goldfrank (1943) have discussed the modern Pueblos as representative (if minor) hydraulic societies, so continuity has already been indicated for this prehistoric pattern. For the Keres, however, priesthoods ~ fraternities have little to do with the control of irrigation systems, except for their annual cooperation during the Spring ditch cleanings. In the modern towns, the official in charge of irrigation is called the _mayordomo_, a Spanish title although the role is clearly aboriginal.

Rather than supporting a common pan-Keres use of the Chaco catchment system, each Keres town now has its own official. The evidence for anything like a central official occurs only at Santa Ana where a native priest has the role that the mayordomo has in all the other communities

(White 1942: 106). This man is appointed annually by the Town Priest to manage the irrigation system, but he does not have the ability to penalize. His distinctive insignia is a fine meal ground up from white beans, used while he prays. In short, he is a special priest with a unique insignia, all of which suggests a respectable antiquity that could stretch back to the Chaco.

The location of the Chaco at the heart of Keresan population density – reflected by the sanctuaries in other areas and its trade relations to the East for Cerrillos turquoise and to the West for trachyte (sanidine basalt) tempered pottery from the Chuska Mountains (Harris, Schoenwetter, and Warren 1967, Windes 1977a) and other ceramic styles from the Little Colorado region – was facilitated by a system of roads now mapped (Hayes 1981: 45). "There are no sweeping curves or lazy bends in the Anasazi roads. They are straight for long stretches. When it is necessary to change direction, it was done with an angle" (1981: 46). As these roads deal with the Outside, it was fitting from a Keres sense that they be angular and lineal, as appropriate for their manly associations and the beam-like character of the power they harnessed.

Outlying ~ satellite ruins surround the Chaco in all directions, again indicating that it was the heart of Keres territory. Over time, however, as centralized authority was entrenched in the Chaco, I have the impression that communities on the fringe, at Lowry in the north and others to the south, moved closer toward the canyon and road terminals. It is in this light that the later towns at Aztec and Salmon in the north and in the Nutria valley to the south should be viewed as relocated districts.

Moreover, some people may have been settling in the canyon itself, founding Bc units. As is clear from the surveys of the San Juan and larger Anasazi region, these smallhouses were consistent over the entire area, representing the organic growth of local populations. The greathouses, by contrast, can be traced back to the ceremonial centers like the paired pithouses with associated ring. These would be occupied by family lines whose men filled priestly offices, which increased in number and authority as part of larger demographic trends. The moiety-like characteristics of the greathouses with East and West wings, therefore, derived from these earlier pairings of leading families.

The smallhouses and the greathouses were contemporaneous in the canyon. Gladwin (1945: 123) once argued that they only dated from the same time because timbers from the small units, his Hosta Butte Phase, were removed and reused in the large ruins, his Bonito Phase. His feisty claims to a novel interpretation of the Chaco have not, however, proved correct. Hosta Butte and Bonito existed side by side, but with very different densities of occupation. "The Hosta Butte pueblos averaged 10 rooms. The Bonito Phase pueblos averaged 288" (Hayes 1981: 32).

Gwinn Vivian (1970) examined a number of hypotheses applied to the Chaco and found two particularly plausible ones: 1) the Hosta Butte units were occupied by localized lineages and the Bonito ruins by moieties, or 2) Chaco was a ranked society with the Haves in the great pueblos and the Have-Nots in the small ones. Paul Grebinger (1972, 1975) has pursued the latter theory, arguing for a pristine rank society in the canyon with the greathouses located on the best farmland until deforestation, changes in rainfall pattern, and over population led to a collapse.

While these general arguments have comparative merit, I think it important to push the ethnographic analogy with the Keres since it provides added depth and complexity to the interpretation. Also, Keres patterns closely approximate many features of Chacoan society, encouraging the position that Chaco was a Keresan climax. Analogy has the added advantage of being more culturally relative, lacking the obvious ethnocentrism of American culture so rife in recent academic theory. Chaco was a likely Keres focus for several centuries, as is indicated by analogies between major features and lesser details, as we shall see, particularly in the final chapter.

Like most of my predecessors, my earlier work on Chaco concentrated almost entirely on the more spectacular greathouses, which are indeed impressive. Now, in hindsight, I realize that the presence of both the Bc units and the great houses adds strength to the argument that they were occupied by ancestral Keres. After all, a culture so fundamentally dualistic as the Keres should be expected to produce two distinct ruin plans. As clusters of rooms, the Bc units would have been lineage family homes, with little religious symbolism, while the D-shaped, clan-owned greathouses with curved outer walls would be womanly, combining manly lineals with a womanly curve.

Further examination reveals, however, that most later greathouses began as a row with side wings, a bracket [shape, which only later had the outer curved wall added. Yet, the four earliest greathouses began as room arcs in a C-shape, with an outer wall added later. Peñasco Blanco, the first, became an oval; while Bonito was planned and built, after at least one false start, as an integrated D-shape. Significantly, the earliest masonry consists of sandstone slabs laid flat between masses of adobe mud, giving yet another expression to the slab / clay opposition. Later still, the masonry gained greater strength when sandstone bands were built as a veneer around an adobe rubble core, stone on the outside and adobe inside.

Four greathouses were built between AD 860-940. Three are well known, but the fourth at the East Community between Bonito and Pueblo Pintado is a recent discovery.[32]

The Chacoans situated the three large buildings at key locations where major side drainages enter the canyon; Una Vida, across from Fajada Butte and around the corner from Gallo Wash; Bonito, across from South Gap; and Penasco Blanco, on the bluffs overlooking the confluence of the Chaco and Escavada Washes (Frazier 1986: 175).

The next major construction, from 1020 to 1050, was at Pueblo Alto, Chetro Ketl, and Pueblo Bonito (additions). The architectural forms begun in the 900s were continued (1986: 176).

These construction phases and later developments suggest an ancestry for the pan-Keresan context. Within the canyon, paired towns were built, a manly and a womanly one, while on the rim of the canyon was built an outside town. Bonito is the only one within the canyon to be consistently male during the entire occupation. Initially, the inside womanly town seems to have been Una Vida, then Chetro Ketl located beside Bonito. Peñasco Blanco occupies a special place as an outside and circular town with a very long occupation and spectacular views in all directions.

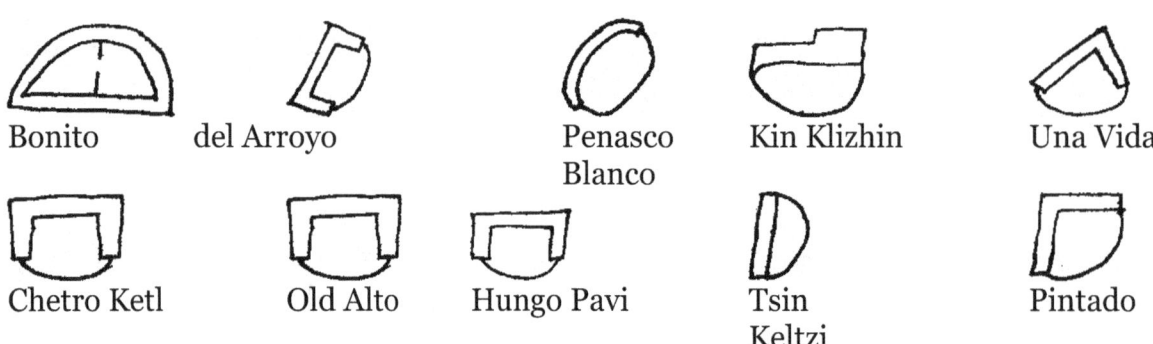

| Bonito | del Arroyo | Penasco Blanco | Kin Klizhin | Una Vida |

| Chetro Ketl | Old Alto | Hungo Pavi | Tsin Keltzi | Pintado |

Except for the later Bonito and Chetro Ketl mating, the other greathouses seem to have been passing through a developmental sequence from C to D, depending on the amount of power, position, and priestly leaders residing therein. During the 1050s, towns were planned as an

---

[32] Four, rather than three, earliest towns, of course, fits with Keresan, and Puebloan, number symbolism. U had charge of four towns in the four directions after coming into this upper world, before people moved to White House. The East Chaco Community greathouse was discovered by Tom Windes, who provided me with timely information. It is known as 29 Mc 560, its Navajo name is "the house next to the place where red ants have gone" = _Kin doo walachii yoo iina_.

angular [that finalized as a D. In all, the directional orientation, date, and placement of the ruin within the canyon should reveal its position within the Man / Woman context. For example, as a northern half circle, Bonito would be manly; as a southern half, Chetro Ketl would be womanly. Likely associated clans would be Sun for Bonito and Corn for Chetro Ketl because of their importance among all the Keresans.

While the greathouses were undoubtedly Keres, not all of the Bc ones were. Since a population was indigenous to the area and others were moving in from the periphery, some mixing occurred. For example, Leyit Kin (Dutton 1938) does not seem Keresan because of its predominance of carbon paint and Mesa Verde styles, suggesting ties with the north through kinship, trade, and immigration. At least some of the units were occupied by ancestral Towa, since modern Jemez elders have legendary accounts of the Pe'lush, whom Ellis (1953: 163) suspected were ancient Chacoans.

Further, while each of the towns had at least one great kiva, or perhaps, a sanctuary at each of its two seasonal locations, Pueblo Bonito and Chetro Ketl seem to have had two in use at the same time, with the remains of a third also reported from each. The likelihood, then, is that both were occupied year around, while the others had only their priestly hierarchy as permanent residents. As a representation of the Inside and inclusive, the East sanctuary served the town, attracting and renewing power, while the West one was Outside, exclusive, and concerned with regional manly activities. Over time, I see people drawing away from the canyon for more of the year, staying in their farming locations, and eventually fragmenting from the Chacoan center.

As yet missing from the discussion is any reference to the hotcanitsa, the office of the modern Town Priest and the heart of every Keres town. Basically, I trace its origin to the plastered pithouse closely linked with the slab ring at the late Basketmaker centers. In the masonry pueblos, it was a site centrally located for solar and astronomical observations along the skyline, such as the room row down the middle of Bonito. Later, it achieved independent existence as the triwall structures noted at Pueblo del Arroyo, Aztec, and elsewhere along the San Juan River.[33] One proposal is del Arroyo was built by a group who left Bonito after a disagreement.

This schism seems plausible, especially since del Arroyo has the earliest dated triwall (Vivian 1959: 84). To this day, the work of the Town Priest is to pray, meditate, and fast for the good, peace, and wellbeing of "her" townspeople. At council meetings, no anger or bitterness can be

---

[33] Tri-walls are clearly a feature of the San Juan River and the northern basin, where they are fully integrated into the regional site plans.

shown because this would disrupt the good thoughts of the cacique. If hostilities erupt, "she" must leave the proceedings. If the people founding del Arroyo did so after an angry departure, it would be very fitting for them to build a triwall office for their cacique, outside the town walls, as a calm haven from strife. At Cochiti, a new office was built whenever a Tiamunyi was installed, for "her" use, thereby allowing changes of style and design to influence the development of this building.

One of the major tasks of the priesthoods is to keep things running as smoothly as possible. The sense is that any anger, insult, or malice will cause bad thoughts, which will linger in the nooks and crannies of the village to eventually cause harm and upset. The greathouses with full D-shapes must have become great containers of power, where every thought and action had to be monitored carefully. Feuding would have offset this highly delicate balance with the cosmos.

The triwall with central kiva and double ring of rooms, an inner and an outer one, is an apt form for representing the entire community in the care of the Town Priest and, as such, logically conforms to the requirements of a *hotcanitsa*. As a further indication of the stress that the late occupation of the Chaco was undergoing, triwalls were located outside of their towns. Over time, however, they became reintegrated into the community as the modern office of the cacique. When times were bad and the cosmos was not cooperating, community relations must have suffered and the Town Priest needed his special building away from the community so as to better concentrate on a return to better relations with cosmic forces.

Neil Judd felt that the greathouses with their enclosing walls were built to be defensive, but there are few indications of warfare at this time. Rather, the greathouses were defensive only in the sense that they represented a Keresan unity in the face of encroachment by speakers of other languages. That greathouses were built as religious preserves makes sense in terms of the all-pervading importance of religion in Puebloan societies. Each greathouse was probably built to be an eventual repository of power, accumulated over time through its priests and rituals, until the outer curved wall was finally added to retain this amassed power. In the process, the town took its place in the context of the overarching hierarchy headed by Bonito and Chetro Ketl.

Recently, the massive surveys, excavations, and analyses by the Chaco Center of the National Park Service have added more information to our understanding of the workings of the Chaco phenomenon. All of these contributions, of course, are unabashedly materialist, concerned with artifacts, economy, and politics in ways that are meaningful to a Euro-American audience.

After a hopeful beginning, multi-culturalism, including alternative symbolism, has been largely shunted aside in Southwestern archaeology. Even while seeking only universal, albeit academic, laws about the development of human societies in response to internal and external criteria, the Puebloan archaeological record can also serve to explain how modern Pueblos emerged over thousands of years. Archaeology and ethnography can be mutually informative, despite comments such as

"The situation at Chaco is remarkable for a number of reasons, the most significant being that there are no analogs for Chaco among the modern Pueblos, and perhaps none in any contemporary society, that the tremendous growth of Chaco was so short-lived, and that the amount of labor invested in nonessentials such as beautifully decorated masonry veneers [probably plastered over] must have been enormous" (Cordell 1979: 149).

In the case of Chaco and the Keres, we can explore what has long baffled scholarly understanding: their particular blend of matrilineages and clans, based on the mother-child bond, of priesthoods, based on that of father-son, and of town kivas, based on a combination of these bonds with other choices and spiritual linkages.

Theories guiding the renewed research in the canyon and beyond sought materialist explanations based in the economic, trade, and political sectors. The grandeur of the greathouses and the dense scatter of other ruins bespoke a complex society that was probably a chiefdom held together by redistribution in which goods and services went up the ranks while decisions and gifts came downward.

But the theory fell apart in the aftermath of excavation because findings were not simple. Pueblo Alto, sampled as a representative greathouse and the end of the Great North and other roads, indicated intermittent occupation or population concentrations in the canyon. Since rooms were bare, except for a few connecting rooms ~ suites with hearths for cooking and warmth, the population estimates were seriously reduced. Two of these household suites had

stone- and adobe-lined hearths, storage pits, mealing bins for grinding corn and special niches for food. ... pollen and burned seeds from food plants indicated that food was processed and eaten in those rooms. The floors ... had been replaced many times, [and] were badly worn – presumably as the result of heavy domestic use (Lekson, Windes, Stein and Judge 1988: 104).

Further, the estimated 100 people who lived at Alto left 150,000 pots in the trash mounds over a sixty year period. At 250 pots per person a year, this figure is astounding. Yet these pottery sherds were not scattered evenly throughout the trash. Rather, they occurred in layers as though every so often people gathered together to smash pottery, probably as part of the feasting and ritual of a world renewal ceremony.[34]

Chaco, instead of being the political hub of a vast chiefdom, now seemed more like a center for pilgrimages. What held it together was a network of exchanges bringing in food, goods, and services in return for ritual uplift and blessings. These services were sometimes substantial, including the quarrying of sandstone slabs for walls and carrying trees for beams 60 miles from the Chuska Mountains.

This network was in place before the Chacoan florescence of AD 900-1130. The "great kivas, non-local [traded in] ceramics, minerals, and lithics" begin in Basketmaker III and continue because Chaco was a "cultural response ... to adapt effectively to a stressed, semiarid ecosystem of low productivity and low predictability" (Schelberg 1982: 2, 278). Three levels were involved: villages – basic producers of food or goods, outlier greathouses – arranging their transfer, and central greathouses (like Pueblo Bonito) – coordinating and receiving these materials but not dominating this trade.

Lynne Sebastian (1991, 1992) looked at Chacoan leadership, curiously disembodied, as an aspect of this regional exchange of goods, services, and information. The system grew, for her, as interactions increased, due to food exchanges, periodic aggregations, and cooperative building projects which occurred during times of drought and increased stress. Scholars find this amazing because, usually, during environmental crisis and food failures, people share less or not at all. Given the strong communal ethic of Pueblos, however, such sharing and cooperation was and is expected, reinforced by the threatened accusations of witchcraft for hoarding or being selfish. Indeed, while recognizing that Pueblo leadership, now and in the past, was based on the ownership of ritual knowledge, Sebastian is remarkably silent about the obligations of a leader to his or her community.

---

[34] Some aspects of this wholesale destruction of old items and their replacement by new ones, reflecting an annual renewal of the Pueblo world, appear in the Zuni Shalako ceremony. More direct Keresan parallels are treated in the final chapter.

Her study of leadership complexity, rather than leaders themselves, relied on five criteria: settlement pattern, site hierarchy, differential distribution of artifacts, burials, and water control devices. Based on size and attention, Chacoans were divided among the greathouses ~ Bonito ruins; the Bc ~ Hosta Butte smallhouses; the outliers, both home-grown or imposed (called ancestral ~ scion), copying greathouses on a smaller scale; and the later McElmo block units. Interlinking these were the formal roadways, line-of-sight signal stations, earthen mounds, and a network of masonry shrines. Everyday items like pottery and stone were shared evenly by Chacoans, but not luxury goods – since turquoise, shell, copper bells, macaws, inlays, jewelry, and more varied foods predominated in the greathouses, often associated with prestigious burials. Instead of irrigation channels, water control in the Chaco captured and distributed runoff from infrequent rains though a series of check dams, diversions, and stairways to slow the flow. To be effective, this network needed a centralized authority to marshall labor quickly when it rained.

Because the environment was harsh, she argued, mobility and flexibility were better adaptations than developing complexity. Previous archaeologists argued that complexity allowed redistribution, leveling out regional resource fluctuations for the benefit of all Chacoans, especially the elite. Yet the periodic "consumption events" when many pots were smashed discredited any smooth evening out, although movements of goods and services up the ranks continues to be cited as an initial motivation for the Chacoan system. Yet, seen variously as a form of social insurance or of welfare, Sebastian noted that moving people around was easier than transporting goods throughout the San Juan.

In the interest of increase production, according to Sebastian (1992: 100), Chacoans could use either of two strategies: land extensive or labor intensive. In the canyon, the latter was used, relying on building water channels to capture and direct rain runoff. While not an irrigation system, successful use required a central authority to quickly coordinate human efforts during a rain storm. The land extensive pattern relied on using a variety of fields in many locations to maximize harvest potentials.

Indeed, the greatest influence on Chacoan development was fluctuating rainfall patterns. Chaco building began during a drought, then construction resumed during a time of above-average moisture, and was abandoned after sustained drought. Each greathouse, therefore, expressed leadership success at recruiting followers while assuring legitimate succession to "his" position by acting as father or mother's brother.

While the first greathouses (Peñasco Blanco, Pueblo Bonito, Una

Vida, and East Community) began during decreased rain, all others were built when the climate was favorable. Finally, early in the 1100s before the abandonment, construction was limited to "arcs of rooms enclosing the plazas at these sites" (Sebastian 1991: 128) – which can be interpreted (see above on power) as "finishing off" the town by holding *iyaanyi* there, although Sebastian saw a closing up and looking inward at each site.

Overall, she saw a shift, about AD 700, from foraging mobility to settlements to allow for the overproduction and storage of crops as a backup against crop failures. During the 900s, Chaco began because regional hardships allowed canyon residents owning productive land to use generosity to become regional leaders, with followers laboring to build specific greathouses. Because Chaco Canyon was surrounded by desert, the population concentrated along the bottomlands. After this burst of building activity, however, most greathouses stayed the same for a century.

Such concentration was significant because "Pueblo III outside the San Juan drainage was a time of population expansion and growth" (Cordell 1979: 144), suggesting that the Keresans were being further hemmed in.

After AD 1040, building resumed during better 1050-80 rainfall, providing leaders with new appeal, perhaps in terms of competing cults based in the priesthoods and larger ethnic identity. Former greathouses were renovated with repeated, massive additions, and new ones were built, but usually with only one story, as at Pueblo Alto and Arroyo. During AD 1050-70, great kivas, both integral and isolated, were built and renovations concentrated on "rear-row rooms, upper stories over existing rear-row rooms, and massed blocks with many interior and few exterior rooms" (Sebastian 1992: 122, 123).

Distinctive core and veneer masonry of finely banded slabs of sandstone suggests the public work projects of modern Pueblos, but the outcome of the Chacoan style was so architecturally sophisticated that another, now lost, procedure must have been involved. Though this banded masonry required some skill, these buildings match the characteristics of most public architecture: labor intensive, able to be built in stages, and impressive enough so that every worker could feel a sense of pride (1992: 126).

We do not know where the workers lived while building the greathouses and outliers, but locating their homes should be instructive. In terms of modern Pueblo logic, such large construction projects would have required a religious and communal inspiration. If, as suggested above, the wearing of masks and execution of dramatic rituals (Vivian, Dodgen, and

Hartmann 1978; Geertz and Lomatuway'ma 1987) required a special or privileged initiation, unlike the more general ones now held for the Katsina cult, the training of young men for such a Keresan cult may have involved labor for greathouses, roads, and other public projects. Keeping these boys together and busy served the community and enhanced the fame of Chaco.

After AD 1100, before the catastrophic drought of 1130-80, "activities at the great houses seem to have turned inward, with the plazas being inclosed, the trash mounds falling into disuse, and the space within the structures being more heavily used for domestic activities" (Sebastian 1991). From 1100 to 1130, "trash deposition shifted from extramural mounds to abandoned rooms and kivas; that the source of imported black-on-white decorated ceramics changed, as indicated by the shift from mineral-painted to carbon-painted types; and that faunal procurement shifted from an emphasis on deer to an emphasis on small mammals and turkeys" (1992: 132). Outside the canyon, however, among distant members of the community, construction projects continued.

During the 1200s, people moved back to the canyon, but they lacked the complexity indicated by greathouse and great kivas. Since the McElmo blockhouses are now thought to have overlapped with the end of the original occupation, rather than occur during this later century, their use as storage bastions seems likely.

Looking at the entire span, Nancy Akins (1986) tackled the sensitive issue of burials in the canyon. When the estimates for the number of Chacoans ranged from 5,000 to 10,000 people, concern was expressed that only about 200 burials had been found. Reviewing excavation and catalogue records, however, she found reference to 663 burials, with evidence for 464. Now that the estimates range between 2000 and 5000, this number seems more appropriate. Given that the Keresans were scattered throughout the San Juan, however, those who died while visiting the Chaco may well have been taken home for burial.

Akins found that Chacoans were not a well nourished population, although both men and women buried in rooms at Pueblo Bonito, the central Great House, were taller – suggesting they were better fed than those buried in the Bc ruins. Moreover, greathouse burials were formalized, more elaborate, and better supplied with luxuries, indicating that they outranked ordinary people. While bones indicated dietary stress and some malnutrition, the possibility of fasting rather than food shortages was never considered.

A fascinating study of parasites (Akins 1986, Appendix E, Reinhard and Clary) also confirmed a dense and untidy population in the canyon, but, again, ceremonial requirements to fast and avoid washing may also help to explain these findings.

Of particular note for the Keresan association of men and death with the left was Bonito burial 14,[35] surrounded by thousands of turquoise beads and other jewelry that emphasized the left over the right side. For example, while his right wrist was wrapped with 617 beads and 168 pendants, his left had 2384 beads and 194 pendants. Similarly, the right ankle held 322 beads and 5 pendants, but the left one had 434 beads and 8 pendants. In all, Room 33 with a dozen burials included 24,932 beads, 512 pendants, 451 mosaics, 15 effigies, and 1,052 fragments (Akins 1968: 115). It is no wonder that most archaeologists believe that Chaco rose to greatness by controlling the manufacture and trade of turquoise throughout the Southwest and into Mexico, although they fiercely debate the extent of the Mesoamerica connection.

Since turquoise continues to have great spiritual and practical value among the modern Pueblos and the Keres still name one of their kivas after it, the final word should be that of Gwinn Vivian (1990: 490), a preeminent scholar who was raised in the canyon, "The Chaco system did not collapse, it simply readjusted."

In hindsight, therefore, Keresan matrilineages resided in the Bc (Hosta Butte) villages, town wings aligning clans and priesthoods were focused on the great kivas, both inside and outside the canyon, and coordinating priesthoods in the clan-owned Bonito greathouses managed relations between humans, spirits, animals, and the environment. Since modern caciques can never leave their towns without doing spiritual harm, high priests were probably also fixed to the canyon. The general population, however, remained mobile, farming town lands away from Chaco, presumably with manly towns to the north in the San Juan and womanly ones to the south in the Cibola. The modern two kiva system, thus, developed from the double seasonal and geographical locations of the same town. The East ~ Turquoise Kiva was located at the greathouse in Chaco canyon; while the West ~ Squash Kiva was at the farming site. When people stopped going to the Chaco, these kivas were joined together at the regional town. The building of a great house, therefore, did not represent the success of a leader ~ leading family, but, instead, indicated that the prosperity of a clan region was being shared within the canyon.[36] Since

---

[35] Since 14's skull had a fresh gash on the right parietal and his left femur had cuts or chops, he died violently (Akins 1968: 116-17).

[36] My analogy here is overseas Chinese sending money back to Hong Kong to renovate the family temple lavishly. Another component was the devotion European towns gave

clans owned land, each greathouse was under the nominal authority of the elite women and men of the clan providing agricultural produce.

The crux of this system and of Keresan genius was the evolution of the priesthoods, their gift to the Southwest. Beginning as family specialties centered in the religious chambers ~ small kivas that developed from the pithouse, Chaco provided the means to systematize and coordinate these specialties into an overall cosmology. In the process, men with the best memories were trained in the details of esoteric lore and learned, by pooling information, about the resources near the localities of their respective farming towns.

These same priests made pilgrimages to ancient sites to visit shrines and leave offerings, adding time depth to their knowledge. Hence, in all, Keresan priesthoods, which thrived in the Chaco and still maintain the Keresans, were the secret to their cultural success since they embodied the collective memory deified as the head and heart of the Keresan pantheon.

In all, then, Chaco Canyon was the fulfillment of Keres development and the mold that created the modern situation. Aspects of Chacoan invention can still be found among the Keres, particularly at Cochiti and Santa Ana, in addition to the other towns. Among the most significant of these traces are the possible relay points for fire signals strategically located along the rim of Chaco canyon. These call to mind the ritual reported only for Acoma called "Shuratsha Lights The Fire" (White 1932: 94), held every five years under the sponsorship of the Corn (Maize) clan, as described in the next chapter. Features of the ceremony are comparable with Zuni rituals of the Boy Fire God and may have ancient Mesoamerican parallels.

The link between clans and rituals among the womanly Keres towns probably goes back to Chacoan greathouses. The importance of religion, even in the domain of kinship, cannot be overemphasized. It is in this strong light that the Chaco must be understood, not in terms of the amassing of goods and position, but rather in the acquisition and controlled sharing of power. For example, Keres ancestors may have been convinced to build the elaborate network of roads in order to draw the enhanced power from the greathouses into their regional communities.

While Gladwin (1945: 65) noted practical reasons for the continued use of the pithouse as kiva, he slighted the religious considerations when he wrote of the Red Mesa Phase that

It would be very easy to say that the people lived in surface rooms all

---

to the building of their Gothic cathedrals.

of the time and that pit-houses had now become kivas, but the question at once arises as to why a family (and the houses were rarely large enough to shelter more than a family) should want a kiva all to itself any more than a modern family should want a chapel next to the living room. To a people who had only recently emerged from subterranean dwellings, the old pit-houses (protokivas?) must have had a good deal to offer in the way of coziness and warmth on cold, stormy nights in winter.

In a culture where religion pervaded everything, the sacred / domestic dichotomy implied by Gladwin, just like the sacred / mundane one of Fritz, is not useful. Rather, the functional situation probably involved women and children occupying the rooms and men spending most of their time in the kiva chambers, as reported in the early Spanish records and corroborated by the practice of separate male and female housing for much of Western America. In terms of modern America, the question of why a family would want a chapel nearby is of the same order as asking why a white family would want a bank account, since both store accumulations needed for continued wellbeing. In short, aspects of gender and culture explain the Chacoan situation much better than do appeals to Euro-American concerns. Food and goods were accumulated, not for their own sake, but as an outward manifestation of spiritual success, as with the Christian concept of grace. Further, Gladwin (1945: 152) argued that the Chaco collapsed because too much time may have been devoted to gilding the lilies of architecture and not enough to the production of food. To carry this idea further, it may be that the elaborations of the Great Kivas imply a top-heavy priesthood with more dependence on prayers and ceremonies than hard work to assure good crop returns.

Yet this distinction is meaningless in Pueblo culture since people are quite sure that both ritual and hard work are needed to bring in a good crop, but that hard work alone is bound to fail. Control of knowledge gave access to power and thereby assured success. Since power, knowledge, and life were equated, if not synonymous, these were the determining factors that allowed talent and ability to be successful.

Post-Chaco

In the light of a Chacoan readjustment rather than a collapse, an orderly withdrawal best fits with the evidence of continuity into the modern Keres. Indeed, there is the distinct possibility that Keresans, having built up the canyon and enclosed the major ruins as D-shapes, assumed that the Chaco would continue to serve as a huge transformer ~ power relay station for their continued wellbeing.

Towns ~ smaller kin groups seem to have left by two routes. The womanly towns appear to have gone south and east, following the modern course of highway 66, as noted by Ellis (1950). The migrations of Santa Ana were particularly complicated, according to oral tradition (Ellis 1967: 41). They moved near Santa Fe and the Galisteo Basin before coming into the Rio Grande and noting the farming potential of the Bernalillo area, where they are now. The migrants split up, however, some settling Paako in the Sandias and others living first near Sias, and then Acomas. In time, these wanders came back to the east, joined with those from Paako, and founded Tamaya, along with farming colonies along the Rio Grande.

The manly towns went north across the San Juan River to the Animas River near Aztec Ruin, before clustering around Tyuonyi in the Rito de las Frijoles, still claimed by Cochiti and its neighbors as an ancestral site.

The Rito duplicates the Chaco in that it also is a canyon running East and West, filled with both smallhouse ruins and the great circular village of Tyuonyi, occupied between 1350-1450 (Hewett 1943: 218-31, Smiley, Stubbs, and Bannister 1953). The shape of Tyuonyi as a circle, together with six similar ruins near Zuni (Spier 1917: 323-4, Table XI) and Tebugkihu (Fire House) near Hopi (Mindeleff 1891: 57) suggest that priests leaving the Chaco revised their town plans. Perhaps these circles represent the womanliness of the town, but I think it more plausible that these ruins were deliberately made as closed circles in an attempt to retain as much *iyaanyi* in their new locations as possible, analogous to the use of slab rings and sanctuary kivas. Significantly, Tyuonyi had only a long passageway through the East side to gain entrance to the plaza, allowing power to enter but not leave again because the western side was closed.

The suggestion is that the Oshara-Keres returned to their earlier pattern of having religious leaders reside within the lay community, not separately as they seem to have done in the Chaco. It is at this time that intracommunity secrecy, so common today, must have emerged or become strongly entrenched. Each priesthood had its separate chamber removed from the bustle of daily life, with the town oriented around its Inside and Outside Priests and East and West kivas, together with the off-limits office of the Inside Priest where esoteric rites were conducted in regular series for the benefit of all.

It was in this situation of priest and people sharing the same community that the laity came into their own with the adoption of the

Katsina cult, influenced by Mesoamerican prototypes.   Priesthoods continued the rituals of old, conducted in the seclusion of their chambers with an occasional night of public performance or curing in the kivas, while the laity had the more visible and public Katsina impersonations held in the plaza during the summer farming season and, perhaps, similar rites held in the community kivas during the winter.   In time, the Katsina eclipsed or blended with the Shiwanna cloud spirits of the sky, while the Maiyanyi earth spirits, if they included the Animal Deities as well, were retained by the priesthoods for their special regard.

The story of the fight with the Katsina at White House may represent a consecration of this period.   It is important that the fight ended with a compromise that allowed men to impersonate the Katsina by wearing masks.   If the Katsina cult reflects Mesoamerican stimulus, as seems likely, than the Katsina could represent professional (pochteca) traders and other visitors.   As the legend makes clear, however, the Keres met them on their own terms and from a position of relative strength.   As Keres once pilgrimaged to Chaco for rituals, now the Katsina spirits came to them from the West.

Settlement in the Rio Grande drainage brought a return of prosperity and a relaxation from environmental stress so that the old preplanned communities with outer walls were abandoned for the modern lineal houseblocks built around open-ended plazas.   Part of the impetus for this must have been some anxiety on the part of the priests that they could not maintain the close regulation of thoughts, actions, and sexual restraint required of laity and priests if rituals were to be effective.   Hence, they focused their concern on discrete ritual enclosures, rather than on the unmanageable community at large.

When the Spanish arrived to stay in 1540, this pattern of internal secrecy and special chambers became accentuated by the continuous repression of Catholic clergy and Spanish soldiers.   The traditions of the past moved, therefore, into less public circumstances.   By the time of Spanish _entradas_, all of the Keres towns were in their present locations, including Awatobi among the Hopi.

Only Laguna has been debated, since one reading of the Spanish documents suggests it was founded by Rio Grande Keres refugees in 1699, but this is impossible because their language dialect is close to Acoma Keresic (not a mixed amalgamation), Ellis (1959) has shown its in-place archaeological development, and Fox (1967) has indicated the town's organizational stability.   My earlier discussion of the town context also supports Laguna integrity from ancient times.   In all, then, the Catholic church at Laguna may have been founded in 1699, but the rest of the town had long been there.

In Pueblo IV, the Keres shifted from mineral paint to glaze, following its development in the Little Colorado, among Keresan (possibly Awatobi) ancestors, where the Katsina cult was also emerging. For several centuries, the Rio Grande Keres made and used glaze ware, but this mixture of stone (lead ore) and plant sludge was only a variation of Keresan paint styles. The East-West orientation continued in use, at least for ruins associated with town priests.

Near Cochiti, the Alfred Herrera site (LA 6455), occupied between 1400-1500 and using glaze wares, was built in two sections with adobe walls laid on cobble foundations. The east sector included a large kiva and the west one had two small, deep kivas, but there is no indication whether they were used at the same time or if one replaced the other (Lange 1968b: 73-110). Appropriately enough, the site was named for a recent Cochiti leader, since the implications are that this site was a ceremonial center for a more dispersed ancestral Cochiti population.

The combination of stone / adobe continues in the walls of modern Keres homes built in the old style. Men still do the stone work and place the heavy timbers before the women build the adobe walls and plaster them (Parsons 1939: 38). At Cochiti, the lower portion of each wall is stone and the upper half is adobe (Lange 1968: 65), continuing a tradition several millennia old.

Conclusions

This, then, is a short summary of Oshara and Keres archaeology within the Anasazi tradition. As migrants from the Hokan area of eastern California, the Oshara entered the northern Southwest as strangers and (I suspect) their linguistic peculiarity set them off from the beginning, encouraging them to act defensively by instituting a more centralized organization than their neighbors. Initially, this was a leading family who had responsibility for the largest hearth in a San Jose community, and for group rituals in the largest available shelter.

Eventually, population increase coincided with farming and greater sedentarism. Leaders emerged as priests and natural sacred places were augmented by slab enclosures. Multiple ritual nexi ~ loci developed until those in the centrally located Chaco took precedence. Here, the full import of Man / Woman symbolism became expressed in terms of slab / clay, stone / plant, winter / summer, lineal / curved, and West / East pairs.

Chaco functioned as a sacred reserve, with the laity visiting for major winter ceremonials and / or as members of spring and fall work parties assisting the resident priests and novices with construction projects and elaborate rituals. During the summer, most people were living at their farming plots all over the basin.

After Chaco, aspects of its ritual society were reestablished at various circular ruins in the larger region. Eventually, once power was again accessible and predictable, the community lost its outer perimeter as priests localized their concerns within manageable areas. Meanwhile, the laity joined in the ceremonialism by elaborating the Katsina cult and rephrasing the role of ancient deities.

This was the situation when Europeans arrived and it continues in a similar fashion into the present, with a marked increase in the need for self-protection through secrecy and exclusion.

For those readers, particularly archaeologists, disconcerted by my presentation, I ask them to bear in mind that I am addressing Keres culture as it is reflected in the Oshara and later configurations, a patterned totality that is much more than a random assortment of traits and details at various times and places. The decision to regard a site as Keresan rests on the same sorts of decisions as those for determining if a date is acceptable for a particular level or site. If a tree-ring, carbon 14, or archaeomagnetic date from a site is inconsistent with what is known about its pottery, architecture, or lithics, as dated at other sites, that date will be rejected unless other reasons are found for its inconsistency. A date of 800 for a Classic Pueblo III ruin is impossible, unless the source for the date was a reused timber or a slabhouse beneath the room.

Hence, the total configuration has to be considered, not just the date, or only the pottery, or only the style of architecture. In the preceding discussion, I have outlined those developments in artifacts that I have found consistent with the evolution of Keres culture, not as radical changes through time, but as permutations of the tension of Man / Woman so crucial for this culture and its member towns. If culture allows a steady course through time, than the Keres can lay claim to a respectable antiquity, a sanctified memory filtered through their culture history.

A consistent aspect of this development has been a centering of the culture in terms of an overlapping series of relationships which express a paramount concern with gender. The centralized authority fully realized in the Chaco continues into the present as the theological control of each town, while the network of intertown relations seems to survive in ritual interaction and initiations, despite the lack of an overall polity. This

126

modern centralization appears most clearly not in the rituals or social structure, partially because data on them remain slim, but rather in the study of law, as Hoebel (1969: 115-6, 98) has distinctly indicated.

Keres influence beyond their own towns is reflected among other Pueblos and neighbors like the Navaho, Ute, and Apache. Yet other Pueblos also had climaxes of their own. After Chaco, the next zone of cultural flowering was Mesa Verde in Colorado, which lacks Keresan diagnostics, although some Keres may have been living there as affines or ritualists. Mesa Verde was probably the Tewa center, favored by moisture and terrain for a few centuries, before its inhabitants moved down the Chama River into the Rio Grande.

After this, the next peak was in the Kayenta among some Hopi ancestors, influenced by resident and refugee Keres who later became connected with Awatobi. People were drawn to the lower Black Mesa area because its seep springs guaranteed a water supply during the most arid years, allowing the Hopi to develop their dry farming techniques. The Hopi accepted all migrants into their area provided each could first prove they had a ritual for bringing rainfall. Once again, the basic explanation for all acts among the Pueblos, as elsewhere in Native America, was a paramount concern with religion, expressed through power. All else was tangential to this (Hewett 1943: xiii, 24):

"Reviewing the literature of the Southwest, one is impressed with the substantial scientific and historical reports of the latter part of the last century, the more analytical though less convincing technical studies of recent times" [are, however, flawed because they failed to appreciate for Native America that] "The life thus evolved was preeminently aesthetic and religious, though these activities were so intimately organized with the industrial life and the social order that the result was a completely integrated culture."

#4 End

Chapter Five

CHACO CANYON AS
KASHKACHRUTYA ~ WHITE HOUSE

While the Keresan Origin Saga is a complex statement about their existence, it also includes a certain historical sense that increases throughout the narrative. Beginning in ShipopU and the underworlds, people emerge and set about ordering life after the founding of White House. With ShipopU as precedent, the sequence of events in White House,[37] continuously fluctuating between prosperity and disaster, roughly correlates with the improved archaeological record from Chaco Canyon ~ mythic White House. Similarly, a coordinating dual leadership is suggested by John Gunn (1917) of Inside (*Hochaiyanyi*) and Outside (*Sahte Hochaiyanyi*) Priests, also called *naiya tsraikatsi* and *nahiya*.

Keresan religion, their premier institution, was bound up with the observance of particular natural cycles, such as those of stars, animals, crops, and the span of human life. Overarching all these cycles, however, was the command to keep "'the universe moving' – the general and typical Pueblo concept of relatedness in the universe and reciprocity between man and nature," as Edward Dozier (1970: 153), Santa Clara anthropologist, expressed it so well.

While hunting, farming, curing, and life cycle rites are held when needed but involve only concerned segments of the population, momentum rites, by their very nature, involved the entire community in its most formalized guise under the control of its full complement of priesthoods, as will be discussed below.

According to the saga, the institutions begun at White House constituted a series of sacred centers from which the customs built outward. First off, a kiva was built to remind everyone of ShipopU. Then the Town Priest ~ Tiamunyi was installed as a man in the guise of a woman. From this moment, more and more authority and power passed to males, from generic to specific. A Hunt Chief was put in charge of the larger

---

[37] Simon Ortiz (1994: 65, 72), Acoma poet, spells it *kashkahtruutih, and adds* "And at Chaco, I've realized there is no past and no present ... To the Acoma people and other Native Americans, time and place are linked, a sacred continuum in which human consciousness is inter dependent with creation and its process. From the beginning to the present, nothing is left out because the Pueblos insist the purpose of knowledge is to clarify and to demystify."

domain, then the Country ~ Outside Priest took office to guard the boundary between town and territory.

The priesthoods received their final form and took command of society while espousing the outward forms of prayer, fasting, and nocturnal cures. The Koshari and Kwirena coordinated all of the public social activities, along with a covert desire to prevent selfishness, greed, or other forms of witchcraft.

Men ultimately concentrated their authority after quarrelling with the women, whose positions had become seriously eroded. By phrasing the argument in terms of the relative merits of crops versus meat, attention was deflected from the greater concern with cosmic harmony and momentum and, instead, deflected to plant or animal cycles. That women retained great power is indicated by the monstrous offspring they continued to produce. That men successfully usurped power is shown by the birth and triumphs of the war twins, who reset the balance of the world in terms of an asymmetry of genders in which Woman is unmarked and Man is marked. Since men and women met in different kivas, the implication is that there were paired great kivas or, alternatively, men met in a kiva in a greathouse, while women met in a chamber in one of the small ruins. On the whole, paired great kivas seem more likely.

Of note, after the quarrel, the men moved "across the river," perhaps the Chaco River itself, to thrive by themselves with sustenance from animals. If Chaco canyon was White House, its ruins interlinked into a pan-Keresan network, then the idiom of the separation of men from women may mark the beginning of the greathouses as priestly retreats sustained not only by the meat of game animals but also by the transfers of power enabled by the animal patrons of these organizations. Another interpretation of the split between men and women is that it also marked the independence of the manly towns, separating clans from priesthoods, as distinct from an earlier shared womanly pattern attributing priestly offices to particular clans.

The return of the women represented the reintegration of the larger network to include seasonal and gender-related aspects. Town lands beyond Chaco canyon were now a link between a priestly greathouse and a local administrative outlier, associated with women, domestic space, and clan fields.

This integration was the context for the "constant solemnity and fasting" that characterized life at White House when the twin brothers were vanquishing the monsters. Needless to say, such discipline probably coincided with the rise of a militaristic stance represented by the war twins, who eventually had their excesses curbed for the benefit of all. By implication, defensive efforts increased in the interest of protecting trade goods and routes, along with an increasingly coercive centralization by the priests. Indeed, the renovation and expansion of Chacoan greathouses, a century after their founding, seem to correlate with the twin brothers half of the saga. The Chacoan phenomenon was now set, including the final arrangement of monuments, both in the canyon and at outliers, along with roads, formal stairways, mounds, ramps, and other earthworks (Sebastian 1992: 33). The addition of upper stories and sheer-sided outer walls as facades implied, also, an "elevation" in sanctity of the buildings.

Prosperous and content, the priests then suggested a release for the people in fun dances, games, and, most decisively, gambling. The Katsina were mocked not once, but twice, sending droughts both times. Such episodes directly related to the rainfall fluctuations so typical of the canyon, providing a mystical connection between Keres behavior, moisture, crops, and deities.

As suggested by Sebastian's computer simulation (1992: 28, 30), four PI communities (near West Mesa, South Gap, Fajada Gap, and upper Chaco Wash) began building the first greathouses (Peñasco Blanco, Pueblo Bonito, Una Vida, East Community) during a time of drought as a special plea for divine assistance. Their success with above average moisture patterns led to the renovations a century later, along with the additions of Alto and Pueblo del Arroyo. Indeed, then as now, the amount of rainfall at a pueblo spoke to its moral condition.

After the first mockery, U left, creating death, accelerated by drought and famine, so that people could rejoin her in ShipopU. After the second mockery, battle ensued and the decision was made to impersonate the Katsina and Kopishtaiya with special masks.

Since Keresans were initiated into these masked cults during the summer, while the momentum rites occurred during the winter, seasonal activity probably increased in Chaco canyon during the cold period.

Though never stated, it is important to realize that Katsina and other masks exist in two varieties, ordinary ones reassembled and repainted for each use, and priest masks which remain intact between uses, although refurbished when necessary. Thus, even among the deities, priestly leaders preceded other members. It is likely, therefore, that Keresan deities of great antiquity, older than the Mexican inspired Katsina cult, survive among these priestly masked beings. Not all Keresans agreed to initiation. These dissenters left White House and went south, presumably into Mexico, at least according to legend.

In this way the carefully managed centralized unity of the Keresan began to crumble. Since everyone no longer "shared the same mind," the priesthoods had to be on their guard to enforce general goodwill. But this very concentration and centralization doomed White House because it exposed everyone to the epidemic that scattered the survivors. This final disease, its cause unstated, disorganized White House and forced everyone to resume their migrations in search of the center of their world, where each town now resides.

The last of the special orders or priesthoods to be established was also the most human since the Opi earned the right to be initiated by slaying an enemy. For it was then, at the end of their separate development as Keresans, that the former Chacoans had frequent and unregulated contact with other humans. Admittedly Chaco was the center of a vast trade system, but goods and services were exchanged on Keresan terms. Now, with the collapse of Chaco, Keresans met other Southwestern communities on a variety of terms.

During the early 1100s, part of the Chacoan theocracy seems to have shifted north to the vicinity of the Aztec ruin complex along the north side of the San Juan River, the trunk into which Chaco Canyon drains. What is intriguing about this relocation is that it probably involved the manly towns and so represents another aspect of the split between men and women. Since this authority probably moved on to Tyuonyi in Frijoles Canyon, this prosperity and unity of the manly towns stands in marked contrast to the lesser coherence among the womanly towns.

While David Shaul (ms.) noted evidence of word borrowings by Hopi, Zuni, and Pimans from Keresans, those terms referred to trade items and religious concepts, such as the term 'Katsina,' provided by the Keres. After Chaco, such contacts became more polymorphous, extending beyond the possible hostilities.

Moving out of their extensive homeland, Keresans moved east into the Rio Grande where Tanoans had long been resident. Complex interactions took place, not all of them peaceful. In other instances, however, Keres towns simply limited their movements to their outlying domain, abandoning their seasonal pattern of visits to or residence in a Chaco greathouse.

As with the various classes of masks, fascinating complexities in seasonal residence diversity are taken for granted by Keres and therefore remain oblivious to outsiders. During P II, at least, there was an increase in number of "fieldhouses," implying "a shift to a pattern of dual residence, with families or farmers occupying fieldside structures for part of the agricultural year and rejoining the rest of the family or group of families at larger, more substantial house sites for the rest of the year" (Sebastian 1992: 29). While this pattern continues into the present, the additional winter occupation or pilgrimaging to a greathouse in the Chaco was a feature unique to the time of the Chacoan phenomenon, providing an overarching unity for the Keres.

Indeed, while Sebastian argued inappropriately for either/or situations, the Keres genius did her one better by using all of the options. Thus, while she argued that mobility and flexibility were better adaptations to the arid Southwest than the social complexity developed at Chaco, the Keresans were probably using both strategies. Moving among fieldhouses, small houses, outliers, and greathouses – seasonally and spatially, the Keres remained mobile while integrating themselves into an overarching theological framework that offered practical solutions to their economic and political difficulties during environmental stresses.

Similarly, these multiple residences allowed Keresans to take advantage of two watering strategies to increase production, either land extensive or labor intensive. The former mode involves "planting in numerous physiographic settings to take advantage of natural water collection, water retention, and frost-protection features," while the later utilized "construction, maintenance, monitoring, and manipulation of facilities designed to capture and distribute runoff" (Sebastian 1992: 100). This labor intensive system, more centralized and providing more surplus, dominated in the Chaco, while both systems were used among the outliers, which were themselves positioned to be land extensive and provide supplies to the canyon towns.

Lastly, by keeping their population moving throughout their domain, with some people resident at each locale all year long, the Keres asserted ownership and control of their extensive territory, fostering their further unity because Keresans interacted almost exclusively with each other.

This is not to imply that there were no external contacts, far from it. While, however, the extent of Mesoamerican influence remains a contested aspect of Southwest prehistory, much indirect evidence indicates that such Mexican trade played an important role at Chaco. Although the Kellys (1975) overstated the case by suggesting that the population concentrations of Basketmaker III and Pueblo III were encouraged by resident pochteca (trading specialists), LeBlanc (1983: 161) has correlated the demise of the Mimbres and Chaco with the 1130-50 rise of Casas Grandes, the trading center in northern Chihuahua.

Indeed, such far flung connections were well within the context played by Chaco as a Keresan cosmological center and it is to their ritual requirement for keeping the universe moving, particularly, the sun, that we now turn.

Turning the Sun

While the annual cycle marking the growth and harvesting of corn did and does play a central role in Puebloan religion, the esoteric rites of the priesthoods always took precedence. Of all these rituals and retreats, the most important ones were celebrated to turn the sun in November and February, before the sunrise reached the extremes of its movement along the horizon. Presumably these solar momentum rites were once at the heart of the Chacoan system even as they remain the most crucial in modern Keresan towns.

These rites are held at two levels, an esoteric one involving all of the priesthoods in seclusion at the same time, and a public one involving all the other townspeople.

While these rites have been treated in general for each town, the most detailed account comes from Santo Domingo and will be summarized here (White 1935: 132-141). Unlike the other versions, however, that from Domingo all but ignores the central role played by the Tiamunyi and "her" office (*hotcanitsa*) in the planning and performance of these events. Later, the Acoma version, along with other rites, will be considered to expand the discussion.

The timing for celebrations is based on solar observations, usually made by the cacique, to trace the movement of the sunrise along the horizon to the far "corners" of the eastern edge, according to the Keresan view of the world as a cube. Goldfrank (1927: 60) best described these observations in terms of the cacique at Cochiti, who watched Nipple Mountain (presumably Tetilla Peak near Santa Fe).[38] The associations of cardinal directions with sides of the body, defined when the sisters were first named (facing east), is confirmed by her report that the sun reached the right side of the peak before summer and the left side before winter. Since south is to the right and north to the left, the image of a human facing east provided the model for this association.

The November rite, the most elaborate, is called Southeast Corner (*Haniko* = hani- = east, -ko = south; *Shuk'o* = corner) to move the sun from

---

[38] Curiously, Lange (1969a: 249) reported only that the cacique made "her" observations using holes through the wall of the hotcanitsa. When sunbeams touched certain places on the opposite wall or floor, rituals were scheduled.

its southern limit at the December 21 solstice, sending it northward. The February version is called Northeast Corner (*Hanikikya* = hani = east, kikya = north; Shuk'o) and pulls the sun northward toward the solstice extreme of June 21. Since the role of humans is to keep the world functioning smoothly, these rites occur before the actual solstices so that the sun can have time to respond properly to these human petitions.

November at the Southeast Corner

The greater emphasis given to the Southeast Corner probably relates to its role as the empty cell (with the sisters in the north squares and T in the southwest one) that was filled with all the life forms at creation. A Sia priest revealed that at the time of the Southeast rite, the sisters (called Mothers) and all their creations were meeting together at *mawakana gashdiyats kai* (underground(?) rainbow house), a giant cave at the southeastern corner of the world, which some elders equate, not surprisingly, with Carlsbad Caverns. Interestingly, this rite can not be held until the harvest is done and stored away, implying a connection between underground caves, storehouses, and the special chambers of each priesthood.

At Domingo, the heads of the four priesthoods (Flint, Shikame, Boyakya, Giant) meet to coordinate their activities. In other towns, the head priests meet with the Tiamunyi in his office to schedule the event and to receive from "her" pieces of fresh deer meat, provided by the war captains, to be cooked for the feast held in each chamber. To prepare, the doctors must purify daily with emetics. Meeting in their separate chambers, for four mornings, all members vomit. Non-members also come to the chamber to purge, but they only stay briefly. At Cochiti, two fasting women assisted each priesthood during its retreat, foaming water to represent rain clouds.

After the fourth morning, each head priest (*nawai*) made the priesthood's dry painting in the middle rear of the chamber. During the afternoon, the purging non-members brought turkey feathers to the chamber. All the priests were busy making miniature items to offer to the Sun. Weapons, animals, plants, crops, and other wished-for items were carved of wood and placed in front of the sand painting. Each carving was a prayer for that item and its welfare. Anything could be represented. For example, a silversmith made a tiny hammer so he would produce attractive jewelry and have good sales. Lots of prayer feathers were also made, incorporating the turkey plumes brought earlier.

When the area in front of the painting was filled with miniatures, the priests began assembling the bundle called the Sun (_oshatsh_). A big Navaho rug was placed on the floor, a large buckskin was spread over it and covered with a fluffy layer of native unspun cotton. All of the tiny offerings were arranged on this cotton cloud, itself a prayer for rain. This cotton was shaped into a bag, wrapped with cord, a prayerstick was stuck into the top opening, and the entire Sun was placed at the end of the line of cornmeal connecting the painting to the doorway. Then the priests swept up all the refuse, placed it in a basket, and gave it to a girl to put ino the river.

Women auxiliaries of the priesthoods brought in food for the members and everyone feasted. Non-members left, women going directly home and men bathing in the river along the way.

When only priests were present, each chamber set up its slat altar and identifying sand painting. That evening, non-members returned to the chamber to find a large cloth sheet or animal hide blocking the view of the altar. Women sat behind this sheet, out of view. Men brought bows and arrows to the doctors, who placed them in piles on each side of the painting. Food was brought and everyone feasted.

Then the priests sat in a line behind the altar and the head priest, in the middle, talked about the importance of what they were doing to move the sun. Then the priests sang. The nawai divided men and boys into two groups on either side of the meal road and allowed them to sing along. After several songs, men and boys retrieved their bows and arrows to dance standing up. Girls came from behind the sheet to take up the Sun and dance, holding it like a baby. Jokes were told to make the Sun happy.

After the songs and dancing, two priests took the Sun outside and deposited it as an offering. Though unreported, it seems likely that each of the four Suns was placed in a shrine for one of the cardinal directions. Like a prayerstick, it was probably "planted" (buried in the ground), sanctifying the entire world.

After the two doctors returned, the nawai talked about the coming year and its benefits. Then everyone was sent home.

To prepare for the duplicate rite performed by the "raw" ~ ordinary men of the town, Masewi called a meeting in one of the kivas, scheduling the rite for the next evening. After men left, he met with the priesthoods.

All the next day, Turquoise men gathered in one house, Squash men in another, to practice songs, while the priests met in the hotcanitsa. In the afternoon, Masewi went to the practice houses to select "raw" men to play the parts of eight priests and four officers. These appointments had the added advantage of trying out a man in an office to which he might actually be selected a month later.

Something of a burlesque, as well as recalling the status inversions that were such an aspect of the Medieval Feast of Fools, the raw version also served as an exorcism of the town.

A separate house was used by the impersonators to "dress up" for their roles, using substitute materials such as corn husks for bear claws and rags for fur. At the same time, the real priests were dressing in the *hotcanitsa*.

About 8pm, everyone gathered in one of the kivas. Turquoise and Squash members sat separately with an open central aisle for dancers; Turquoise on east, Squash on west, with men and women sitting apart. The substitute Masewi talked about what the ceremony enabled. Turquoise members sang a song or two, followed by Squash doing the same.

Then Turquoise sang in the procession of the "real" priests, summoning the animal patrons of the six directions: Bear, Cougar, Wolf, Wild Cat, Eagle, and Shrew. These men formed two lines down the aisle, one led by Masewi and the head Shikame and the other by Oyoyewi and the Flint nawai. They all growled like bears and wore a breech clout, an Opi kilt painted with a horned serpent, bear paws on their forearms, and black face paint.[39] They danced while Squash sang for them. Using eagle wing feathers, they brushed away harmful influences, sometimes slashing the feathers around like sabers. Squash sang again as the priests filed outside and moved around the plaza to purify it. That done, they returned to the cacique's office, changed clothes, and returned to the kiva to help sing and pray with everyone else.

By this time, special dancers, who had a lifetime obligation to perform this role, had entered the kiva, surrounded by "raw" teenagers who served as their attendants. Known as *Shpinyinyi* (referring to popped corn), these dancers wore a pointed wooden (tablita) frame atop the head, a black woven shirt with an elaborate "butterfly" made of flapping sticks and yarn on the back, a dancing kilt, and white moccasins.[40] Each kiva had a set of these dancers, sung for, in alternation, until midnight.

At that time, together as one, the kivas sang in the priest impersonators, who danced down the aisle in two lines. The "raw" *nawai* ~ head priest made a speech about the intent of the ceremony, followed by a similar talk from the "raw" Masewi. Then the Squash sang these men out so they could change clothes.

---

[39] The warrior aspects of their dress added strength to their efforts while exorcising the town.

[40] Cf. drawings (White 1935: 131, 137).

Though unstated, the appearance of these impersonating priests and officers, after the real priests had exorcised the town, suggests that they were a kind of decoy to lure any lingering malevolence into the open so that the community could be made truly clean.

In the kiva, after these "raw" priests had left, Turquoise and Squash alternated singing while their dancers had the floor. They used only ancient songs described as simple, monotonous, and filled with archaic (esoteric) words. At sunrise, the two drums used by the kivas were brought together at the middle of the kiva while ten songs were sung.

The Tiamunyi gave a final address about the good they had all done, then the head Shikame and Masewi repeated the same message. Led by the dancers and drummers, everyone left the kiva, washed in the river, went home, and ate lunch since it was now about noon.

February at the Northeast Corner

For the Northeast ceremony, the four priesthoods again held simultaneous retreats in their chambers, after four mornings of purging. Sand paintings, prayersticks, and prayer feather bunches were made, but no tiny images. No "Sun" was assembled. Members and interested non-members feasted together at noon. The nawai never left his chamber, but everyone else washed in the river. Women washed their hair at home. That evening, people gathered in the four chambers to sing and dance until midnight. Then two priests took the prayer offerings outside and deposited them. After they returned to the chamber, everyone was given a drink of water from a pottery medicine bowl. The priests drank last. The nawai gave a final speech and everyone went home, except the doctors who had to clean and tidy the chamber before they could leave.

For the "raw" Northeast rite, Masewi called a meeting of all the men in one of the kivas to schedule the ceremony either for the next night or for four days hence. Immediately afterward, Masewi met with the priests in the same kiva to ask their participation. The next day, the priests assembled in the hotcanitsa to make offerings, and the wife of Masewi brought them food.

In the evening, the priests went into the kiva first and sat, as was their privilege, with their backs against the front of the "fog bench." Then everyone else entered, Turquoise on east and Squash on west, men and women sitting separately.

Turquoise sang first, then Squash. When Turquoise sang again, the priests stood and danced in place. While Squash sang, the priests sat down.

When Turquoise sang, their special dancers entered, dancing back and forth down the aisle. Then Squash sang for their dancers. The kivas alternated singing and dancing for some time. At midnight, while Turquoise sang, everyone stood and danced in place. Then Squash sang while everyone continued dancing. Finally, the two drums were brought together in the center while everyone sang the same song.

At sunrise, dancing ended and Masewi talked about the sun and its motions and what they had done to keep these in balanced movement. Led by the dancers, followed by the drummers, everyone left the kiva, washed hands and faces in the river, and went home.

Implications for Chaco

These double (or quadruple) rites to turn the sun can suggest the cosmological role played by Chaco Canyon in Keresan unity. As both private and public rites sustaining the world order, every Keresan would have been vitally concerned in their success. Since the four original greathouses began during a time of environmental stress, challenging both religion and economy because of the role of corn and farming in Pueblo cosmology, these public monuments, like Gothic cathedrals, concentrated the wishes, hopes, and prayers of the Keres at locales where the theocracy could better control their own efforts and public response to them.

The practicality of this religious fervor was proclaimed by the succeeding years of better than average moisture, leading to the renovation of the older greathouses and the addition of others to the canyon and outliers to the hinterland. Roads, directing the flow of power, encouraged these improvements.

The solemn retreats of the priesthoods in the small kivas ~ chambers would have consecrated the greathouses anew before the public "raw" rites drew everyone into the canyon and the greathouses brimmed with people dancing, feasting, praying, and renewing the world as they knew it. The joking to please the Sun at the priestly rite broadened into the burlesque of priestly actions during the public rite. Humor must balance solemnity in the Pueblo view, much as sacred clowns of today will sometimes buffoon the Catholic mass, not in mockery but from a concern about preventing monolithic attitudes.

Purging, washing, and drinking medicine water aided this renewal, from the person outward to the limits of the cosmos. Commonly known in native religions as "going to water," these acts both flushed the system and sustained it for regrowth, like watering crops.

Coming just after the harvest, the November rite was the more important and drew the largest crowd of pilgrims. The February one, with the weather more uncertain, was more modest and probably less well attended, although many men may have wintered over in the greathouses, fasting and praying. While the summer became the time for farming rites and masked dances, the winter, then as now, was a time for more quiet but intense reflection and planning to keep the sun on track and the world in order. Yet, then as now, each town accomplished these feats in its own particular way, as illustrated by the elaborations at Acoma.

Periodic Rituals at Acoma

Estimates of 250 smashed pots per person every year for 60 years at Pueblo Alto bespeak the enormous size and/or numbers of the "consumption events" in Chaco Canyon. Clearly, the solar momentum rituals, even held from two to four times a year, may not explain all of these broken vessels. Yet, looking again at the record adds to the complexity of these events, particularly at Acoma where elaborate and dramatic rites (White 1932a: 84-96) accompanied the Southeast solar rite, the battle with the Katsina, and the fire and water pilgrimage.

Southeast Corner

Eight days before the Southeast turning, the Tiamunyi announced the rite, and everyone purged during the initial four days. On the fifth day, all made prayersticks, while abstaining from salt, meat, and sex, and the priesthoods went into a four day retreat. On the sixth day, men planted their prayersticks in the fields and women threw theirs off the east edge of the mesa. Newly made moccasins, seeds, shrubs, and live rabbits were collected. The seventh day, men who were to wear the masks of the Kopishtaiya made "bravery" prayersticks to strengthen themselves.

Boys, particularly if sickly, who had already been initiated into the secret of the Katsina, prepared to take part in the coming ceremony. A father signaled this intention by taking a handful of corn meal to the head of his kiva, asking that a man be selected to "look out" for his son during the next morning. The boy visited that man, soon to wear a Kopishtaiya mask, to be instructed.

During the pre-dawn hours of the next day, these boys were taken outside and hidden in depressions and cracks along the east edge of the mesa. The boys were nude except for a flap of rabbit skin around the genitals and some feathers glued to the body. In the dark, each sat on a sheep pelt wrapped in a blanket, waiting.

When the boys were settled, the men who became Kopishtaiya painted their bodies and carried their masks away from the town to the east. As a group, they prayed, planted their prayersticks, and put on the masks before scattering in pairs, singing war songs. Just before dawn, they turned and headed west toward Acoma.

Meanwhile, the Outside Priest roused the town to gather on the eastern edge to greet the visitors, who could be seen coming in two lines. By the time they were atop the mesa, each figure had a small fox skin bag filled with seeds, cattail fuzz, tiny trees, shrubs, cacti, and other natural objects. Along the edge, each man passed the spot where the boy he looked after was hidden. With a flourish, the man cast tule fluff at the ground and reached down to extract a naked boy. Sometimes, they threw fluff and had live rabbits bound off from that spot. People who were sick, old, or weak came to the dancers to be fortified by having the afflicted place touched with the tip of a lightning stick.[41]

At dawn, all faced the east and made a prayer offering of corn meal. The Kopishtaiya wedged shrubs and plants into rock cracks, and passed out seeds to be added by the family to those planted in the spring. When the east side was transformed into a bountiful land, the dancers went to their own kivas, one of five, where they unmasked. The Tiamunyi invited all the dancers to the main ~ East kiva for a breakfast of rabbit stew. Then everyone went back to the other kivas, staying for four nights and days.

On the morning of the arrival, the cacique, captains, and priests gathered at the place on the mesa called Sun's House which marked the southernmost limit of the sunrise along the horizon. The priests were fully dressed in bear paws, carrying flints blades and eagle plumes. The Tiamunyi buried a tiny suit of clothes (shirt, pantaloons, moccasins) for the Sun at this shrine.[42]

During the four day visit, the masks rested on the kiva floor, where they were fed and smoked three times a day. Every night, the masked men danced in the main kiva, sometimes also visiting the chambers of the priesthoods. Occasionally, the kiva groups danced in the plaza, joined by

---

[41]   A lightning stick stretches and collapses like an accordian. One of these important items of ritual was found at Chetro Ketl (Vivian, Dodgen, and Hartmann 1978: 110).

[42]   At Sia, the sun's clothing was deerskin shirt, leggings, and kilt, decorated with a painted snake, and moccasins embroidered with yellow, red, and turquoise beads. He had a bow, arrows, cougar skin quiver, and a huge mask that hid his body (Stevenson 1894: 35).

other masked figures.

After four nights, the Outside Priest reminded the dancers that it was time to go home. The dancers gathered at the eastern edge of the mesa, wearing the raised masks slanted along the top of the head, above the face. All of the plants left standing along the edge were thrown over the side, clearing the area. The masks were removed, held in both hands and pushed upward and forward four times, releasing the spirit. All of the food fed to the masks, twelve times in five kivas, was also thrown away over the cliff. Each man drew four lines on the ground with a flint knife between the mask and himself, sealing off the return passage of the spirit.

The masks were taken back to the kivas, where each headman placed them into a tiny room and plastered over the door for another year. The men who wore masks slept apart from their wives for the next 18 days. By then, life had returned to a normal routine.

As a low estimate, ten bowls of food at each meal (10 bowls x 3 meals x 4 days x 5 kivas) would produce 600 broken vessels, three each for 100 people at Pueblo Alto, and that was just one phase of a major ceremony. Assuming several hundred pilgrims at the greathouse, the concentrated ceramic scatter can be accounted for by a single ritual of major importance lasting several days. In addition, other rites were held at longer intervals.[43]

Katsina Battle

Every five years or so, usually early in the Spring, Acoma was ritually defended by the Antelope clan from an attack by the Katsina, supposedly as a reminder of the fight between humans and Katsina at White House. Unlike that battle, however, at Acoma it was only the Katsina who were killed, not humans. Presumably, this blood letting was another prayer for rain, saturating the ground. Conducted with great solemnity and ritual, the drama was dangerous because of the abundant weapons and the anonymity

---

[43] Comparison with other Pueblos also suggests dramatic incidents that might have attracted Chacoan pilgrims. At the Isleta solstice rite in December, the sun itself was twice "pulled down" into the kiva (Parsons 1932: 292). It was described as round, white, and blindingly bright while opening and closing, Cf. Painting 41 (Parsons 1962: 95).

of the masked participants sometimes provided an arena for covert murder and personal revenge, according to White's (1932a: 88-94) sources.

Of note, the ceremony of the Antelope clan contrasts with another periodic event sponsored by the Corn clan. Also held every five years, this ceremony of lighting signal fires by Shuratsha, discussed below, compliments the Katsina fight. In addition to the contrasting emphasis on meat or crops, the rituals emphasize the protective role of men or the nurturing tasks of women. Both involve set stops within the town, at barricade or bonfire, with Katsina present to threaten or entertain. As a result of both, the pueblo is renewed and fortified.

Before the ritual attack, the Inside and Outside priests met with the kiva heads in the town kiva, announcing the enactment and asking each kiva to provide participants. Each kiva then met with its members to recruit young men to personify the Katsinas. Meanwhile the Antelopes expanded their ranks by recruiting young men and women to join them whom they had sponsored at Katsina initiations, acting as ritual godfathers for the young initiates. Some men must choose whether they will be Katsinas or Antelopes during the rite.[44]

The next morning, the Outside ~ War priest announced a Katsina dance in eight days. Only those already recruited knew that this will not be a typical occasion.

During the preparations, the intended Katsinas practiced running and jumping early in the morning and late in the evening, vomiting before each exercise. The fifth morning, each man made eight prayersticks in his own kiva. Meanwhile, one at a time, each intended Katsina entered a side room where the leader selected the mask to be worn. The man put it to the side and covered it with an identifying cloth so no one would know what mask he would wear.

The sixth day, every Katsina killed a sheep (anciently, a deer), saving the blood in a bowl, mixing it with tallow and corn meal, and boiling it with the head to be eaten the next day. The blood from the heart sack was put into a length of intestines, to be worn under his mask around the neck. The mutton was used for the final feast.

The *Opi* warriors prayed every morning and night to the directions and at each kiva niche. The Antelopes prepared the defenses of the town. The governor appointed eight men to keep outsiders away from Acoma during the rite, a pair guarding the road in each direction.

---

[44] By implication, a host clan could therefore recruit widely to perform its rituals, thus explaining how Chacoan greathouses "owned" by a clan could attract many diverse pilgrims.

At midnight leading into the eighth day, Katsinas left the town, bidding good-bye to their wives and mothers in case they never returned. Every man stopped at his own kiva to retrieve a covered mask and went down the mesa toward the west, carrying a pair of new moccasins to wear with the mask, further obscuring his identity except, by mutual agreement, to brothers ~ trusted friends. Three miles from Acoma, they awaited daylight.

First to visit Acoma were two red Gomaiyawish and several friendly Katsina, who warned the war priest of the coming attack. Masewi and Oyoyewi, personified by Flint priests, also arrived in anticipation of the battle. The twins called a meeting of officials in the town kiva. Then each brother, with a flint blade in the right hand and a bow in the left one, pressed these against the house corners to fortify the walls. Some Katsina did the same, while others gave children an herbal drink to calm them.

Two white Gomaiyawish scouts arrived to pretend that a normal dance would be held. Red and white scouts argued and scuffled about what really would happen until white scouts fled, putting the town on full alert.

Soon, these white Gomaiyawish returned again as spies, but were run off. Meanwhile, six men with this hereditary duty passed from father to son, set up a barricade, fourteen feet long and twelve feet high, on the west edge of the mesa. The barricade was called by the same term as the wooden slat altar of a priesthood.

The white scouts came for the third time and the red ones reported their threatening message that every Acoman would be killed. The red Gomaiyawish attacked the white ones and took their moccasins. Fleeing back to Wenimatsa (Katsina home), they hurled many dire threats.

Now all the Acomans prepared for battle. Antelopes painted their bodies pink and faces reddish brown with micaceous highlights. Women painted their bodies and faces with yellow corn pollen. The _Opi_ painted their faces like Masewi, white below the mouth and black over the face, and took up flint knives.

Away from the mesa, the third return of the white scouts signaled final preparations among the attacking Katsinas. Every man went off alone or with trusted companions to uncover his mask and put it on, along with other moccasins. The former moccasins were wrapped in cloth and hung from the belt holding up a breechcloth. Masked, all the Katsina came together and rushed toward Acoma. Coming to a deep chasm, they jumped across one at a time. Sometimes, a Katsina would fall and die, to be left until secret burial later.

Near the town, Katsina pulled up shrubs and brandished them, yelling the war cry. At the base of the mesa, the Tiamunyi and other officers met them and replaced their heavy clubs with light, less dangerous weapons. While the officials held the others off with prayer feathers, two Katsina went up the trail to the barricade, leaned their forearms and heads against it, and prayed. After some time, the officials returned to the mesa top and the Katsinas rushed after them. Pausing once at the top of the trail, each Katsina then went to the barricade, prayed, and struck it four times with his weapon. When all the Katsinas had done this, the six men and the Opi dismantled the barricade, moved it to the next station of seven, and set it up again. Though the Katsinas were yelling and gesticulating, this movement of the barricade was solemn and stately.

At the third station, the Opi came around in front and cut the throats of some Katsinas. (Four days before each intended Katsina had gone to a particular Opi member with a feather offering and stated the time and place for this blood letting, along with some means of recognition. Around his neck each Katsina wore an intestine filled with sheep heart blood.) The Katsina fell face down so the blood drained into the ground as a sacrifice to the earth and a prayer for a saturating rain. After the blood drained, the war twins came to each one and placed flints and bows at the head, shoulders, back, and legs to revive him.

More throats were cut at the fourth station. At the seventh, the white Gomaiyawish were bound and castrated. Blood flowed from a filled intestine in their breech cloth. The twins relieved some of their pain, but these scouts sat for some time rocking back and forth. The battle ended.

Boys came from the Antelope clan house with baskets filled with prayersticks. Also inside each basket was a cotton ball filled with beads. Every Antelope found his or her own bundle of four prayersticks tied into corn husks holding corn meal, gave it to a Katsina, and they prayed together. A smudge fire was built on the west side of the mesa to call back the watchmen. All the Katsina left, the hostiles to the west and the friendly ones to the other three directions. They did not return to store the masks until nightfall. The barricade was taken down and each man took some of the parts home for storage until the next use. The Opi went to the town kiva. The Antelopes returned to their clan house to wash and dress.

Ritual chastity was an obligation for eight days before and after the fight. Acoma was quiet and sad for days while the bloody patches remained on the ground, but, in time, the stains faded away.

Signal Fires

Every five years at midsummer, at the end of July, the Corn clan hosted a ceremony called "Shuratsha Lights The Fires" (White 1932a: 94-96) which emphasized the modalities of fire and water symbolism among the Keresans.

The rite was announced eight days before by the head of the Corn clan at a meeting of the members in their house. Then the Outside Priest told the town the next morning. The first four days everyone purged and prepared prayersticks and regalia. Corn members recruited boys and girls they had sponsored at Katsina initiations and practiced songs and dances every night in the clan house. Meat, salt, and coitus were forbidden to the clanspeople. The day before the rite, masks and clothing were prepared. Some Corn men hunted rabbits to serve at the feast.

At midnight leading into the final day, sponsored boys went to nearby mountains and mesas, making wood piles. A pair waited in each direction, ready with a firedrill. Within Acoma, similar piles were also built, including one in front of the Corn clan house. During the eighth day, only small children could drink water, which was forbidden to everyone else.

Meanwhile the seven Katsina personifiers, carrying masks, walked toward a spring some miles west of Acoma, led by Shuratsha, a naked ten year old boy.[45] The others were two other pairs of men and a blind son and his mother (though a man wore the mask). The head of the clan and other Corn men and women also went along. Half way to the spring, they built a camp where women and masks remained as men continued to the spring.

At dawn, the two boys in the north ignited their fire. Then they moved west, building six fires along the way. When the west fire was lit, the other boys ignited their fires, as did the Katsinas at the spring. Then they converged on Acoma, building small fires along the way.

Before the Katsinas left the spring, Shuratsha filled a pottery canteen with fresh water, lit the end of a cedarbark firebrand, and carried it with a piece of charcoal. The canteen hung around his neck and down his back. When they reached the camp, the Katsina put on the masks and went to Acoma. Shuratsha also hung some dead rabbits on his back.

As they went into town, the adult Katsinas danced at the foot of the mesa, at the top, and at a series of stations. Shuratsha did not dance, but instead lit each wood pile until they reached the Corn house, where women

---

[45] Cf. *Shulawitsi*, the virgin boy fire god of the Zuni, who appears at the world renewing Shalako ceremony when he leads the Council of the Gods in a re-creation of the Zuni emergence from their sacred salt lake.

came out and took inside the canteen, rabbits, and charcoal. The dancers also went inside to bathe, unmask, and feast.

The Outside Priest met with the Corn leader to receive the canteen and take it to the cacique. From "her," at the center, a few drops of this water were taken to every household and town reservoir, and sprinkling prayers were made to each of the directions. Finally, Corn women took bits of the charcoal to every fireplace in Acoma. In this manner, fire and water, the balanced elements of life, were sanctified and renewed for the pueblo and its world.

Since there are strong Zuni parallels to this rite, it might be suspected that Acoma borrowed the idea for the rite and made it their own.

On the other hand, the Great North Road (Sofaer, Marshall, and Sinclair 1989) into Chaco Canyon included a mound and elaborate stairway at Kutz Canyon, and a signal fire station at El Faro and more than 20 other features "located on pinnacles, mesa tops, and steep ridge slopes" (1989: 370). Moreover, many of the roads lead not to ruins but to "pinnacles, springs, or lakes." The Ashlislepah Road from Peñasco Blanco to the northwest ends at a group of cisterns and now-evaporated Black Lake.

Chaco, Kashkachrutya, Katsinas, and Beyond

If Chaco Canyon were White House, the emphasis on roads to the north, rather than west or another direction, confirms the Keresan belief in emergence from ShipopU and subsequent migrations to the south and then, after several disasters, to other directions, particularly of late, to the east and the Rio Grande.

Indeed, as this examination began with my admiration of the Keresan Pueblos and my disappointment with academic, specifically archaeological, theories as depersonalized, abstracted, and reified, this speculation into Keres culture history serves, yet again, as a reminder that the Pueblos, both ancient and modern, have much to teach us about the meaning of culture, history, and meaningful existence.

Recently, as a result of oil and gas exploration on the Colorado Plateau, intensive archaeological efforts have been devoted to the surveying, mapping, and testing of sites throughout the region. In particular, archaeologists have walked the terrain to inspect the roads and the ruins associated with the rise and demise of the Chaco. As an east-west canyon in the center of Keresan distribution the reasons for its location is symbolic, rather than economic or political, although archaeologists remain baffled about why Chaco is located where it is (Doyel 1992: 3).

Nevertheless, some interesting reevaluations of this "Chaco phenomenon" have emerged.

First, the roads are not what they seemed. In fact, they may not even be roads because most could not have been used to transport logs and other bulky items.[46] Even before the rise of Chaco, linking roads were built in the 800s among the huge Basketmaker III sites in southeast Utah (Gabriel 1991: 71, Windes and Ford 1992: 75).

Second, the ruins are much more complexly planned and constructed than had been suspected. Each greathouse was part of an entire "built ritual landscape" of mounds, stairways, processional paths and rings, shrines, ramps, and earthen platforms. Chaco Canyon alone had 45 stairways (Gabriel 1991: 185) and, to the south, Llave de la Mano, which may have begun about AD 450, had a massive earth and rubble temple-like platform, over twelve feet high, set against a cliff edge.

The amount of time and labor involved was enormous, adding further support to my supposition that all of these construction projects were an important aspect of the religious training of young men (and women?) being initiated into the complex cult that supported Chaco Canyon and the outliers. Those clan which finished the training and received their "degree," before undertaking another period of training for a higher order one, were entitled to build a greathouse in their own home territory.

In this sense, the greathouses were every bit as significant as the "houses" (as in the House of Windsor, House of David, and House of Medici) that dominated European feudal estates and empires. The difference with the Chaco "houses," however, was that they were "religious houses" rather than political ones. The motivation that encouraged people to undertake the labor and fulfill the roles was that of a postulant working to become a bishop, where material wealth followed from spiritual preparation, rather than the reverse. In this regard, membership in the Chaco system required more of a personal, physical, emotional, and spiritual commitment than just working for compensation or building a home.

Among the important mechanisms for forging Keresan solidarity during the initiation of newer members into the Chaco phenomenon, the moving of logs to roof the buildings probably played a considerable role. While the ordeal of moving these trunks has not been detailed, a possible

---

[46] Among the Maya, the causeway (sakbe, "white road") "functioned principally as pathways for ceremonial processions and pilgrimages among related nobles. Such rituals were, in all the cases we have come across, political statements of obligation and responsibility" (Schele and Freidel 1990: 498, note 12).

parallel for this activity may be the "log races" held by the Sherente in Brazil (Maybury-Lewis 1965: 85-88, photos 5, 13). Teams of men race to carry 200 pound palm logs into the village, shifting the burden from one shoulder to the next to accomplish the task. The race was not competitive, but instead a gesture of fellowship and stamina very much in keeping with Pueblo ethos.

The sequencing of greathouses in one place has been superbly studied in Manuelito Canyon (Fowler and Stein 1992), where the unbroken succession – before, during, and after Chaco – consisted of Kin Hocho'i (AD 700-1150), Ats'ee Nitass (AD 1150-1250), and Big House/Naat'a'ani Bikin (AD 1250-1300). A "long row of slab houses and great kiva" occurred in the 800s, affirming the Keresan and slab link. Indeed, the hatchure designs so distinctive of Chacoan ceramics (Toll, Blinman, and Wilson 1992: 151) are another expression of this banding or layering so important in the Keresan cosmology of the underworlds. In Manuelito, some roads link with ancient ruins, suggesting that they were a "time bridge" between present and past, facilitating the ritual return to ancestral sites still performed by Keresan priests. Equally important, later sites seem to collapse the symbolism of the elaborately built ruin area into a single place and time (Fowler and Stein 1992: 111).

Because so much was involved, it was elderly clan and priestly leaders who lived in the greathouses and hosted the influxes of people who attended the public rituals. That the greathouses were occupied by married couples and families is indicated both by household artifacts and by the continued use of kiva chambers to separate men from women. While the smallhouses were an organic part of the Southwest landscape, located wherever farming and resources were practical; the established elders dwelt in the greathouses, where they were maintained by a regional community who cared for them physically in return for spiritual support. All of these people came together for scheduled rituals when the flow of power was directed from Chaco to their own communities. That is why most roads are not continuous, but are best defined near a greathouse or shrine. Indeed, these avenues are not roads, but landing strips for this transmission of power.

Yet power also had material manifestations, inhabiting either fetishes, effigies, images, shrines, emblems, or priests. Some of these probably followed along the route marked by roads at each end. Examples include tally sticks or knotted strings sent to each greathouse to count the days until the next major rite. During the spring, special sproutings of beans, as at the modern Hopi Puwamuya, could have been sent by runners from Chaco great kivas to local ones to sanctify the spring planting. Furthermore, snakes were probably carried over these roads and left in the rugged terrain where the roads noticeably fade out into the landscape. Since the Hopi attribute their own Snake priesthoods to the Keres, as the song words support, and several modern Keresan towns, such as Sia, have active Snake priesthoods, a snake cult in the Chaco seems a strong possibility. In fact, personally running a handful of consecrated rattlesnakes out of a plaza into the country would provide strong incentive for building a road section that was straight and smooth.

Like other communities throughout the Native Americas, Keres culture was and is based on intimate relationships with the landscape, particularly of men with animals and of women with plants. Clans took their names and identities from beings and places where ancestors had lived and interacted with the land. Similarly, priesthoods evolved from personal bonds between an ancestor and a spirit at a particular locale. Since the spirit was immortal but the human was not, the bond was passed on through later generations of males. The Pueblos, however, as a communal society, institutionalized this bond into a priesthood whose officials belonged to a patriline. With the shift from pithouse to kiva chamber during Late Basketmaker, many priesthoods were established in families. Presumably, men who married into a community also set up their own chambers to function as curers, rain makers, solar observers, star charters, crop enhancers, war magicians, spirit go-betweens, ritual managers, and many other specialties. Over time, the most successful of these family cults coalesced into leading priesthoods, who formed attachments with other elite families to create internal degrees, grades, or orders within the priesthood as a way of complicating the initiation process and expanding the membership. These intermeshed priesthoods then and now oversaw Keresan social arrangements, eventually centering themselves in Chaco Canyon at the heart of Keresan distribution.

As a total cosmological system the "Chaco phenomenon" would have had seven levels based on relations with more and more of the land. At present, these full seven compass points are the four horizontal directions, two vertical ones, and the center; that is, North, South, East, West, Up, Down, and Center. During the apogee of Chaco, however, these seven levels would have been increasingly more inclusive. As modern Keres still provide labor, supplies, and food for the Tiamunyi of their town, working and harvesting fields set aside for "her" family, so all Keresans probably once supplied food and other necessities to the priestly elite living in the Chaco greathouses. In return, the priests saw and see to the spiritual wellbeing of the town and its members.

As an approximation, from smallest to grandest, these territorial levels would have been a) the shrines and farmsteads at the fields, b) smallhouses of kin and in-laws c) chamber kivas of the local priesthood, d) great kivas of the local communities, e) Chacoan greathouse outliers where the ranking district clan and priests lived, f) Chaco Canyon greathouses community of clan and priestly elite, and g) Chaco Core (particularly Pueblo Bonito and Chetro Ketl) where everything came together, including international relations with elites and traders from as far away as the Valley of Mexico and the Maya.[47]

This Keres system, thus, ranged from the local to the global under the management of priests who kept the calendar and arranged the flow of power, both along its natural course and by periodic ritual renewals and redirections. For example, Chaco may have observed the 52 year renewals of the world dictated by the Mesoamerican ritual calendar when the different timing systems coincided. Two 52-year cycles (104 years) would match the episodes that seem to cover a century in the canyon. Some Chaco involvement in Mesoamerica (Weigand 1992) is suggested by the distribution of Cerrillos turquoise (found as manufacturing debris in many of the Chaco Canyon smallhouses) throughout Mexico, such as the sites (and states) of Guasave (Sinaloa), Las Cuevas and Zacoalco (Jalisco), Ixtlan del Rio (Nayarit), Casas Grandes (Chihuahua), and Maya sites (Yucatan).

By the time of Chaco, priests had formed an overall theology with a distribution of ranked spirits arranged over the landscape. Some remained local patrons, represented by the stone and other images kept by clan households and priesthoods, while others had pan-Keresan significance, such as the Koshari who had primary responsibility for all the winter ceremonials. Overarching and interlinking all of these was Consciousness Deity (Thought Woman), who must have been directly linked with Bonito if not the downtown Core.[48]

The other paramount deity was the Sun, also linked with the Core. In its heyday, the core consisted of Bonito, Chetro Ketl, and Pueblo del

---

[47] Keres-Mayan connections are suggested by the remarkable parallels between Kokopelli and Ek Chuah, the Maya god of merchants (Miller 1975).

[48] Bonito was so crucial to the overall global system that, after people stayed away from the canyon, Aztec West and Salmon have been described a "Bonito clones" at the center of the northern system (Stein and Lekson 1992: 91, Fowler and Stein 1992: 119). Moreover, since "The La Plata, Animas, and San Juan each have four great houses" (McKenna and Toll 1992: 134), a background for later San Felipe, Santo Domingo, and Cochiti similarities is suggested, along with a missing fourth manly town.

Arroyo. In terms of their shapes, Bonito was a northern and Chetro Ketl a southern semi-circle. Of particular note, based on the straight west wall, Arroyo was an eastern half but was located west of the other two ruins. Presumably, there was no pueblo ruin on the east side so as not to obstruct the direct rays of the rising sun. As holy allies, the Core towns would have relied on these fresh daily rays to empower their purposes.

As a cosmic center, Chaco would have influenced all of the Anasazi, and, most particularly, the Keresans. All avenues to power would have been welcomed so ancestors of other Pueblos probably acted within the Chacoan system and even maintained a smallhouse in the Canyon. Ethnographic evidence from modern Pueblos indicates the profound impact that Keresan priesthoods have had on the others, presumably during the Chacoan period.

What does seem to be limited to Keresans, however, was the great kiva, the Keres badge of community solidarity and membership, now as in the past. Since their modern day equivalent is the paired town kiva wings, ancestral great kivas must have had seasonal associations based on winter use linked with the Chacoan global system or local summer congregations.

In the aftermath of Chaco, the global system drew inward, if not collapsed, into an arrangement of regional towns, each with two kivas and a population moving seasonally into farming colonies and farmsteads. The overall linkages provided by Chaco apparently now only exist among the priestly elites of these modern towns. Indeed, such priesthoods have always been involved in aspects of international cooperation. For example, during a visit to Zuni, the medicine maker of the Ant Priesthood exchanged sacred breaths with Edward Tylor, British founder of modern anthropology (Stevenson 1904: 211, note a).

In lieu of the Chacoan integration for the Pueblos, another organization arose with wider popular appeal. This new integrator was the Katsina cult, which began to spread about AD 1300 from the Upper Little Colorado Valley, a border area between Anasazi and Mogollon that had been part of the "Chacoan phenomenon." Located between the Zuni, Keres, Hopi, and Pimans, the Little Colorado was a fertile region for such a new cultural synthesis.

Charles Adams (1991), who has examined the archaeological evidence for the Katsina cult, which he viewed as a replacement for the great kiva (1991: 153), noted that like Puebloan society generally, Katsina are divided into priestly and ordinary grades, but the priestly leaders appear only at the major rites and, presumably, their masks are worn by the priests themselves or with their sanction, thus enhancing the rank of both human and spirit elites.

The cult emerged along the Upper Little Colorado between 1275 and 1325, marked by the joint occurrence of Fourmile (glaze polychrome) pottery, open plazas separated by houseblocks, rectangular kivas, and depictions of masks (1991: 83). Each of these traits began in other traditions. Thus, the enclosed plazas can be traced to the Salado of southern Arizona and the square kiva to the Mogollon. Secondary associations are duck (slipper) pot, piki (wafer bread) griddle, square medicine bowls with terraced sides, and more trade of obsidian (1991: 79).

Masks themselves had a long prehistory in the Southwest and Mexico. Body disguises with paint and costume are even older, as shown by the painted flayed human head skin found by Kidder and Guernsey (1919: 190-192) in Northeastern Arizona in a Basketmaker context. Modern Koshare painted in bands of black and white harken back to this practice. Basketry half masks, such as those worn by modern Katsina line dancers, are about a thousand years old. Only the cask ~ helmet masks worn by modern Katsina and made of bison hide may originate in the cult.

The impetus for the rise of the cult was a 1275 population displacement of Anasazi from the Four Corners area of the Colorado Plateau moving south of the Mogollon Rim. To integrate these migrants into existing communities, the cult provided a common focus for cooperation between old and new villagers.

Over time, two other versions developed among the Hopi, about 1400, and among the Jornada Mogollon of the Lower Rio Grande, about 1450. The Hopi aspect emphasized rain making and spread to areas where moisture was precarious (1991: 142). The Jornada version had warfare ~ protective overtones.

Thus, at a time when populations were shifting and aggregating because of climate change or Ute and Athapaskan enemies moving into the region (1991: 160), the Katsina cult provided a mechanism for integration. Of note, it arose in a former Chacoan area and received another input from the Hopi region, where Keres were present. Moreover, the very word Katsina is Keresic, strongly suggesting that the Keres again were in the forefront of the revitalization of Anasazi religion in the post-Chaco period.

By means of the cult, huge towns were formed of disparate peoples, allowing the orderly transmission of land ownership and usage, safety in numbers, intermarriages, and on-going stability (1991: 149). In addition, while most Pueblos adopted the cult, except along the upper Rio Grande, town specializations were helped not hurt by this inter-town system (1991: 159). Mutually interdependent towns, each with its own specialty, were encouraged by the common bond of the cult. Then as now, distinctive types of pottery (bowls, jars, mugs) and decorations, weavings, baskets, jewelry, and ritual items were traded within this larger pattern of cooperation.

The modern cult is distinguished by masks, group performance, a plaza surrounded by occupied roomblocks, square kivas, line dances, rectangular designs, cloud terrace forms, depictions in rock art and kiva murals, and general membership by all men (and sometimes also women) (1991: 14). It fulfills a variety of community functions, like priesthoods, but on a more democratic basis. In particular, the cult is associated with clouds and rain, as well as curing, fertility, military strength, and the ancestors.

Most importantly, while the cult and the priesthoods overlapped in function to some extent, the existence of Katsina priests and leaders served to reinforce Puebloan theocracies into the present.

The other major work to suggest a link between Chaco and Animas (Aztec complex) is Stephen Lekson's The Chaco Meridian (1999: 71, 137, 160; 2015:), tracing transfer of regional authority from Chaco ~ AD 800-1125 (300y +) to Animas ~ AD 1110-1275 (165y), both in New Mexico, to Paquime ~ AD 1250-1450 (200y) in Chihuahua, northern Mexico. Among their similarities are "colonades, room-wide platforms, stone disk post foundations, platform mounds, and tri-walls" in each of these "ceremonial cities," consisting of dispersed, distinctive building blocks and geoforms made of dirt, adobe, and layered stone walls.

Thus, positioned along the same meridian are the complexes of Chaco ruins, of Animas just to the north, and of Paquime (Casas Grandes) far to the south. These relocations allowed for improved farming, from Chaco dry waffle field farming to Animas ditches to Paquime irrigation canals, as "The political prestige economy of Chaco and Aztec exploded into a mercantile economy at Paquime," especially in breeding and trading macaws. As Lekson (1999: 50, 158) remarks, it is a "case of macaws and effects," after "Aztec fell, like Chaco, because rainfall didn't."

Yet it is easier to observe the priesthood's proliferation of small kivas and kihus (chambers) at Chaco and Animas than at Paquime, where mounds, rooms, ballcourts, and plazas indicate important roles of priests and shamanic curers (Di Peso 1974 1: 223, 2: 574).

While the 1980s Chaco Project began with the hypothesis that apartment-like greathouses served as food banks for storing crops in a desert region of fluctuating rainfall and harsh weather conditions, excavations proved otherwise. Greathouses had only a few hearths indicating dwelling rooms and middens showed distinct thick layers of smashed pottery, marking huge periodic gatherings. Plazas had huge kitchens and cooking pits, presumably roasting maize, to feed periodic seasonal influxes of many pilgrims.

At Pueblo Bonito in downtown Chaco, beautiful but problematic tall cylindrical jars with lugs were found in a single room cache of 192 (of 210 known), and Lekson (1999: 97, 98) dubiously compares them to open ended hand drums at Paquime, assuming a dry hide drum when a water drum, like that used in the Woodlands, is a better percussion analogy. That these jars were special containers seems assured, but of what? _Chayainyi_ wear a left bear paw during cures, and use more easily handheld rattles but not drums. The most likely jar contents, therefore, are dry herbs and other remedies sanctified by Chaco clergy. Anyone who has taken sacred soil from the shrine at Chimayo, New Mexico, or holy water from a church font understands the need for a closed container that remains spotless after use, though their wide mouths seem to preclude liquids in this arid environment.

But these movers and shakers remain mute in Lekson's analysis, language locales and speech communities are ignored. Paquime is in a Uto-Aztecan region. Pilgrims were multilingual. Yet Chaco greathouses were Keresan, as Paris is French, despite a mix of worldwide peoples. In Great Kivas their priests conducted periodic, seasonal, astronomical public rituals which, then as now, "keep the world moving" (Nabokov 2015: 476 #2; Aztecs famously fed it with sacrificial blood). Some from other Pueblos attended public rites hosted by Keres, especially renewal of the world they all shared. At Chaco's heart, though, were the more private kiva chambers of the priesthoods, caring for the dis-ease of patients and the cosmos.

Over time, Chacoan priesthoods entered other Pueblos via successful cures because, then as now, to be healed by a priesthood was to be initiated into it. Patients in need might be inlaws ~ pilgrims ~ desperate, yet once healed they received further instruction in songs and prayers in Keresic, and formed the core of a new priesthood in another Pueblo. Such chains of initiation provided insurance to allow the revival of a town's lapsed priesthood via one of its prior offshoots, as needs arose.

Surrounded by branches of Uto-Aztecan, along with the remarkable migration of Tanoans from south to north along the Rio Grande, Keres held their own because of respect (and fear) of their priesthoods (and enforcers). Indeed, the shift of the theocracy tradition that "perpetuated their power through architectural and landscape symbolism" (Lekson 1999: 141), but not population shifts, from Animas to Paquime may have been motivated by this Tanoan influx into the north, leading to Tewa climax at Mesa Verde. The sightline for the meridian was probably less on the ground and more in the sky, using some astronomical feature overhead. To his credit, Lekson (1999: 145) disagrees with Florence Hawley Ellis, my own revered professor, that the mythic _Kashkachrutiya_ ~ Keresic White House was not Mesa Verde or the Four Corners, but indeed Chaco itself, and I concur.

Lekson and Cameron (1995) are particularly insightful on the reoccupations of the greathouses that changed them from monastic centers into all too familiar Pueblo-style apartments.

Most remarkable of all are the Pueblo I sites along the Dolores River, abandoned over a thousand years ago after sacrificing obviously engendered couples. This coherent Keresan population occupied secular villages on the east, while "four western villages – McPhee, Cline Crest, Windy Ruin, and 5 MT10-12 – are consistently arranged in a horseshoe shape and enclose associated plazas on threesides" enabling public ceremonies for priesthoods (Wilshusen and Ortman 1999: 383, 386-7).

> McPhee had several group burials with evidence of violent death, as well as a striking pattern in the abandonment of pit structures. Three distinct classes of pit [387] structures have been identified at McPhee on the basis of associated ritual features, and pit structures at each level of this hierarchy were abandoned in different ways. The most ritually important community pit structures were intentionally burned, secondary ritual pit structures were abandoned with their roofs intentionally collapsed on paired (male and female) adult burials on the pit structure floor, and pit structures that exhibit little evidence of use in community ritual were left to fall down on their own.

The abandoning of Dolores villages coincided with the growth of villages in the Chaco, strengthening its rise as the premier religious center of its time, with echoings that continue to this very day.

Since religion was and is the dominant institution of the Pueblos, the Keresans could have had no greater impact than they clearly did because their contribution to the Anasazi tradition was the ranked esoteric priesthoods, the most crucial of all Puebloan – and Keresan – institutions.

GLOSSARY

Anasazi = The array of archaeological sites and remains – distributed in Arizona, New Mexico, and adjacent portions of Utah, Colorado, and Mexico – ancestral to modern Pueblos. Conventionally spanning 2500 years, the sequence is divided into stages of Basketmaker (I, II, III) and Pueblo (I, II, III, IV, V). Other comparable Southwestern archaeological traditions were the Mogollon, Hohokam, and Hakatayan.

Archaic = Archaeological time when people lived in camps or rock shelters and used only stone tools to hunt and gather food.

Aztec-Tanoan = A segment of the Uto-Aztecan stock spread from New to Old Mexico.

Basketmaker = Archaeological periods before people used pottery.

Benavides, Fr. Alonso = Official Visitor to the New Mexico missions and missionary among the Rio Grande Pueblos and Navahos, who wrote an Memorial about the missions in 1630.

Chaiyaanyi = priests initiated in the Keresan religious guilds, whose apogee was the many kivas and chambers in the greathouses of Chaco Canyon.

Clan = A kinship grouping traced through the mother or the father and named for a plant, animal, or other entity from nature or culture. Most Pueblos have matrilineal clans, traced through mothers and daughters. Therefore, a man is more closely related to his sister's children than to his own and, as mother's brother, had primary responsibility to train and discipline his nieces and nephews.

Cochise = Archaic period complex of southern Arizona, ancestral to Mogollon.

Context = A three-part relationship basic to the organization of Keresan culture. The outside, inside, and center are each occupied by members as symbolic expressions of Man, Woman, or both.

Entrada = Spanish word for the arrival or entrance of expeditions into the New World.

Esoteric = Sacred and secret information protected by leading members of priesthoods and clans to enable them to sustain their members and conduct proper religious observances.

Gauwatsaishoma = The hole in our earth that leads through three underworlds to Shipop.

Gender = The cultural concepts related to males and females.

Gomaiyawish = Spirits who act as scouts. Red ones are friendly, but white

157

ones are not. They look like Zuni Mudheads.

Gowiye = The official successor of the cacique.

Hakatayan = Archaeological tradition of the upper Colorado River between Arizona and California leading to the Yumans.

Hohokam = Archaeological tradition of southern Arizona leading to the Pimans (O'otam).

Hokan = a stock or collection of remotely related native languages spoken by widely scattered populations in California and southern Mexico.

Hosta Butte = tabletop mesa south of Chaco Canyon whose name is applied to scattered, unit, Bc, or small house ruins found throughout the Southwest.

Hydraulic = Waterworks to enable irrigation either by diversion to channel runoff or by conservation to retain it in reservoirs or some combination of both.

I = Iatiku, spirit of the Earth, who is represented by the perfect cornear fetish of initiated priests.

Iyaanyi = Keresic term for the all-pervasive, powerful energy animating the universe.

Katsina = Spirits, both males and females, who live under a lake in the west and bring rain to Pueblos who perform masked dances in their honor.

Keres = Seven modern Pueblo towns in central New Mexico.

Keresan = Comparative term for all the towns.

Keresic = Language family of these towns, lacking any closely related languages, although a distant origin with the Hokan stock has been proposed.

Kiva = A religious building or church, which evolved from the pithouse, used by modern Pueblos. Either round or square, it is entered by a ladder through a hatchway in the roof to represent the emergence from the underworlds. On the floor are a hearth, standing slab altar, and a sipapu hole. Around the sides is a built-in bench, called the "fog seat" to represent billowing clouds, where sacred items are kept. Modern towns have large moiety kivas and smaller chambers used by the priesthoods. Archaeological kivas include the Great Kiva, which served a community, and regional styles known as Chaco, with a subfloor ventilator, or Mesa Verde, with a keyhole shape.

Kiva Wing = An alignment linking together certain priesthoods, clans, and buildings to articulate the organization of a Keres town.

Kopishtaiya = Celibate spirits who live in the east.

Koshari = Sacred clowns of winter, painted in black and white bands, who were the first of the managing priesthoods (See p 55).

Kwirena = Sacred clowns of summer, each side painted a different color, with sparrow hawk feathers in the hair (See p 55).

Linebreak = The gap in the painted line that rims the lip of a pot.

McElmo = Archaeological style associated with Mesa Verde, from the canyon of the same name.

Maiyanyi = Spirits of the earth.

Marked = Specific instance of a relationship in which the generic example is called unmarked. For Keresans, Man is marked, exclusively manly, and Woman is unmarked, with both male and female attributes.

Masawi = Elder war god twin and senior war captain.

Mesa Verde = Archaeological style of southwestern Colorado, noted for its cliff-dwelling ruins in caverns in the canyon walls.

Moiety = A kinship or social group that divides a society into two halves or sides. Tewa moieties are called Summer and Winter.

Mogollon = Archaeological tradition along the border of Arizona and New Mexico noted for its brownware pottery.

N = Younger sister at Shipop during the creation and later patron of Europeans and Navahos. Variant spellings include Naotsiti ~ Nutsityi ~ Nowutset ~ Nowshsiti (See p 45).

Numic = Native language family throughout the Great Basin of Nevada and Utah.

Opi = War ~ Warrior priesthood.

Oshara = Archaeological sequence within the Anasazi tradition distinctive of the Keresans.

Oyoyewi = Younger war god twin and second war captain.

Pecos = Important Towa ruin, easternmost of the Pueblos, excavated by Alfred Kidder, who hosted a 1927 conference there that established the Anasazi sequence from Basketmaker to Pueblo.

Picosa = Southwestern manifestation of the Desert Archaic, beginning 7,000 years ago, and composed of the Pinto Basin, Cochise, and San Jose.

Pinto Basin = Archaic complex of southern California.

Piro = Tanoan speakers of southern New Mexico, cf Tompiro.

Priesthood = A religious grouping of men dedicated to a specific task (managing, curing, protecting) dealing with power and spirits. Leaders, members, and novices are distinguished, based on their access to ritual knowledge. Presumably the complex degrees and orders of membership are ancient, growing out of ancestral shamanic abilities passed to the men of a family.

Pueblo = A native farming town or one of its inhabitants of the Southwest.

Puebloan = Comparative term for the towns and people noted for raising corn, beans, squash; conducting elaborate ritual dramas in open plazas and church-like kivas to pray for rain; and living communally in planned buildings.

Reconquest = Reimposition of Spanish government into the Southwest by Diego de Vargas in 1692.

San Jose = Archaeological complex of only stone tools, dated as 5200-3800 years ago.

San Juan Basin = The drainage area of the San Juan River, a tributary of the Colorado River, that serves as the northern state border of Arizona.

Shalako = Six, ten-foot high, bird-like beings who are welcomed into the Pueblo of Zuni each year for a world renewal ceremony named after them. Each Shalako represents a direction. Two other new houses are occupied by the Council of the Gods and by the Mudheads (Koyemshi).

ShipopU = The original underworld home of the Keres.

Shiwana = Cloud spirits who live in the sky, associated with lightning.

*Shuratsh*a = Spirit patron of a ceremonial fire lighting at Acoma sponsored by the Corn clan.

T = The Creatress of the Keresan universe, often called Thought Woman. Variant spellings are Tsityostinako, Tsichtinako, Sussistinnako, and Ts'its'ts'ciinaak'o (See p 45).

Thought Woman = The Keresan deity of mind and creation.

Tiamunyi = The leader ~ cacique of the internal and religious aspects of a Keres town.

Tompiro = Tanoan speakers living in the highlands above the Piro.

Tradition = Something sustained over a long time, such as lithics (stonework) of the Archaic or pottery of the Ceramic, which includes variations such as the brownware of the Mogollon, yellowware of the Hopi, or whiteware of the Chacoans.

Triwall = Ceremonial building made with two rings of rooms around a central kiva.

U = Elder sister of the creation who became patron of the Keres. Variant spelling include Uretsiti ~ Utctsityi ~ Utset ~ I'tc'ts'ity'i (See p 45).

War Captains = Annually appointed officials who represent the war god twins and assume their names.

Wenimatsa = The lake in the west, filled with weeds, where the Katsina live.

White House = The Keresan ancestral home where all of them lived together, assumed to be Chaco Canyon and its outposts.

Wing Walls = Dividers ~ radials across the floor of a pithouse, stretching from the central fire to the outer wall to separate the domain of women, near the fire and front, from that of men, in the back near the sipapu.

List of Abbreviations

AA = American Antiquity.
AA-M = Society for American Archaeology, Memoirs.
AAA = American Anthropologist.
AAA-M = American Anthropological Association, Memoirs.
AE = American Ethnologist.
AMNH-AP = American Museum of National History, Anthropological Papers.
BAE-AR = Bureau of American Ethnology, Annual Report.
BAE-B = Bureau of American Ethnology, Bulletin.
Eth = Ethnology.
ENMU-CA = Eastern New Mexico University, Contributions to Anthropology.
EP = El Palacio
IJAL = International Journal of American Linguistics.
FMNH-AS = Field Museum of Natural History, Anthropology Series.
JAR = Journal of Anthropological Research, formerly SWJA
PAES = Publications of the American Ethnological Society.
PMASAL = Papers of the Michigan Academy of Science, Arts, and Letters.
PP = Peabody Papers of Harvard University.
SMC = Smithsonian Miscellaneous Collections.
SWJA = Southwestern Journal of Anthropology.
UA-AP = University of Arizona, Anthropological Papers.
UC-PAE = University of California Publications in American Archaeology and Ethnology.
UNM-AP = University of New Mexico, Anthropological Papers.

BIBLIOGRAPHY

Aberle, Sophie 1948 The Pueblo Indians Of New Mexico; Their Land, Economy, and Civil Organization. AAA-M 70.

Adams, E. Charles 1991 The Origin and Development of the Pueblo Katsina Cult. Tucson: University of Arizona Press.

Akins, Nancy 1986 A Biocultural Approach to Human Burials from Chaco Canyon, New Mexico. National Park Service, Branch of Cultural Research, Reports of the Chaco Center 9.

Allen, Paula Gunn 1986 The Sacred Hoop. Recovering the Feminine in

American Indian Traditions. Boston: Beacon Press.

Altschul, Jeffrey 1978 The Development of the Chacoan Interaction Sphere. JAR 34 (1): 10-146.

An-Che, Li 1937 Zuni: Some Observations and Queries. AAA 39.

Anderson, Frank 1955 The Pueblo Katsina Cult: A Historical Reconstruction. SWJA 11 (4): 404-419.

Ascher, Robert 1961 Analogy in Archaeological Interpretation. SWJA 17.

Baer, Marjorie and Ann Baggerman Frej 1983 Pueblo of Laguna. A Project Report. US Department of the Interior, National Park Service, Historic American Buildings Survey.

Bandelier, Adolph 1890-2 Final Report Of Investigations among the Indians of the Southwestern United States, Carried on mainly in the Years from 1880-1885. Parts 1 and 2. Papers of the Archaeological Institute of America. American Series III. John Wilson and Son University Press.

    1946 The Delight Makers. Dodd, Mead, and Co.

Bannister, Bryant 1964 Tree-Ring Dating of the Archaeological Sites in Chaco Canyon, New Mexico. Southwestern Monuments Association, Technical Series 6, part 2.

Beidelman, TO 1961 Right and Left Hand among the Kaguru: A Note on Symbolic Classification. Africa 31.

Benavides, Alonzo 1954 Benavides Memorial of 1630. Washington, D.C.: Academy of American Franciscan History. Translated by Peter Forrestal, CSC.

Benedict, Ruth 1931 Tales of the Cochiti Indians. BAE-B 98.

Bice, Richard and William Sundt 1972 Prieta Vista. Albuquerque Archaeological Society Report.

Boas, Franz 1925, 1928 Keresan Texts. PAES VIII, 1 & 2.

Brew, John Otis 1946 Archaeology of Alkali Ridge, Southeastern Utah. PP 21.

Bryan, Kirk and Joseph H. Toulouse 1943 The San Jose Non Ceramic Culture and Its Relation to a Puebloan Culture in New Mexico. AA 8 (3): 269-280.

Bullard, William 1962 The Cerro Colorado Site and Pithouse Architecture in the Southwest United States Prior to A.D. 900. PP44 (2).

Chapman, Kenneth and Bruce Ellis 1951 The Line Break, Problem Child of Pueblo Pottery. EP 58 (9): 251-289.

Cohen, Yehudi 1964 The Transition from Childhood to Adolescence. Chicago: Aldine Publishing Co.

    1969. Social Boundary Systems. CA 10 (1): 103-126.

Cordell, Linda 1979 Middle Rio Grande Valley, New Mexico. Cultural Resources Overview. Government Printing Office, Bureau of Land Management (BLM).

Crane, Leo 1926 Indians of the Enchanted Desert. London: Leonard Parsons.

Crown, Patricia, and W. James Judge, eds 1991 Chaco and Hohokam. Prehistoric Regional Systems in the American Southwest. Santa Fe: School of American Research Press.

Curtis, Edward 1926 The North American Indian, Volume XVI. Plimpton Press.

Cushing, Frank 1892 Manual Concepts: A Study of the Influence of Hand-Usage on Culture Growth. AAA 05 (4): 289-317.

Daifuku, Hiroshi 1961 Jeddito 264. PP33 (1).

Davenport, William 1959 Nonunilinear Descent and Descent Groups. AAA 61 (4): 557-572.

Davis, Emma Lou 1963 The Desert Culture of the Western Great Basin: A Life-Way of Seasonal Transhumance. AA 29 (2): 203-212.
    1965 Small Pressures and Cultural Drift as Explanations for the Abandonment of the San Juan Area, New Mexico and Arizona. AA 30 (3): 353-355.

Davis, Irvine. 1959 Linguistic Clues to Northern Rio Grande Prehistory. EP 66 (3): 73-84.
    1963 Bibliography of Keresan Linguistic Sources. IJAL 29 (3): 289-293.
    1964 The Language of Santa Ana Pueblo. BAE-P 191 (69): 53-190.

Densmore, Frances 1938 Music of Santo Domingo Pueblo, New Mexico. Los Angeles: Southwest Museum Papers 12.
    1957 Music of Acoma, Isleta, Cochiti, and Zuni Pueblos. BAE-B 165.

Di Peso, Charles 1974 Casas Grandes. A Fallen Trading Center of the Gran Chichimeca 1, 2, 3. Flagstaff: Northland Press.

Dittert, Alfred 1959 Culture Change in the Cebolleta Mesa Region. University of Arizona: Ph.D. Dissertation.

Dittert, Alfred, Frank Eddy, and Beth Dickey 1963 Evidence of Early Ceramic Phases in the Navajo Reservoir District. EP 70 (1-2): 5-12.

Douglas, Mary 1970 Purity and Danger. London: Pelican Books.

Doyel, David, ed 1992 Anasazi Regional Organization and the Chaco System. Maxwell Museum of Anthropology, Anthropological Papers 5.

Dozier, Edward 1967 Hano, A Tewa Indian Community in Arizona. Case Studies in Cultural Anthropology. New York: Holt, Rinehart and

Winston.

   1970   The Pueblo Indians of North America.   Case Studies in Cultural Anthropology. New York: Holt, Rinehart and Winston.

Dumarest, Noel 1919 Notes on Cochiti, New Mexico. AAA-M 6 (3): 137-236. Translated by Elsie Clews Parsons.

Dumont, Louis 1970 Homo Hierarchicus. University of Chicago Press.

Durkheim, Emil and Marcel Mauss.   1963   Primitive Classification. Translated by Rodney Needham. University of Chicago Press.

Eddy, Frank   1966   Prehistory in the Navajo Reservoir District, Northwestern New Mexico. Santa Fe: Museum of New Mexico, Papers in Anthropology 15, parts 1 and 2.

Eggan, Fred 1950 Social Organization of the Western Pueblos. University of Chicago Press.

   1979. Pueblos: Introduction: 224-235 in Ortiz, ed.

Ellis, Bruce   1953   Vessel-Lip Decoration as a Possible Guide to Southwestern Group Movements and Contacts. SWJA 9 (4): 436-457.

Ellis, Florence Hawley 1951 Patterns of Aggression and the War Cult in Southwestern Pueblos. SWJA 7 (2): 177-202.

   1952 Jemez Kiva Magic and Its Relation to Features of Prehistoric Kivas. SWJA 8 (2): 147-163.

   1953 Authoritative Control and the Society System in Jemez Pueblo. SWJA 9 (4): 385-394.

   1959 Outline of Laguna History and Social Organization. SWJA 15 (4): 325-347.

   1964   A Reconstruction of the Basic Jemez Pattern of Social Organization, With Comparisons to Other Tanoan Social Structures. UNM-AP 11.

   1966   The Immediate History of Zia Pueblo as Derived from Excavations in Refuse Deposits. AA 31 (6): 806-811.

   1967a The Use and Significance of the Tcamahia. EP 74 (1): 35-43.

   1967b Where Did the Pueblos People Come From? EP 74 (3): 35-43.

   1974. Anthropology of Laguna Land Claims. American Indian Ethohistory, Indians of the Southwest, Pueblo Indians III. New York: Garland Publishing Co.

   1979 Laguna Pueblo: 438-449 in Ortiz, ed.

   1983 Foreword: xxiii-xxxviii. The Architecture and Dendro chronology of Chetro Ketl, Chaco Canyon, New Mexico. Stephen Lekson, ed. Albuquerque: Reports of the Chaco Center 6.

   nd Twelve Centuries in Northern New Mexico: A Quick Glimpse of

Twelve Centuries of Human Adaptation in New Mexico's Difficult Northern Area. Ghost Ranch.

Ferdon, Edwin 1954 A Surface Jacal Site in the Chaco Basin. EP 61 (2): 35-42.

   1955 A Trial Survey of Mexican-Southwestern Architectural Parallels. Santa Fe: Society For American Research, Monograph 21.

Fewkes, Jesse Walter 1893 A-wa-to-bi: An Archaeological Verification of a Tusayan Legend. AAA 06: 363-375.

   1899. The Alosaka Cult of the Hopi Indians. AAA 1, 522-544.

Ford, Richard, Albert Schroeder, and Stewart Peckman. 1972. Three Perspectives on Puebloan Prehistory. pp 19-39 in Ortiz, ed.

Forde, Daryll 1963 Habitat, Economy, and Society. New York: E.P. Dutton.

Fowler, Andrew, and John Stein 1992 The Anasazi Great House in Space, Time, and Paradigm. pp. 101-122 in Doyel, ed.

Fox, Robin (J.R.) 1967a The Keresan Bridge. London: Athlone Press, London School of Economics, Anthropological Monograph 35.

   1967b Kinship and Marriage. London: Pelican Books.

   1972 Some Unsolved Problems of Pueblo Social Organization: 71-86 in Ortiz, ed.

Frazier, Kendrick 1986 People of Chaco. A Canyon and Its Culture. New York: W.W. Norton and Company.

Freidel, David, Linda Schele, and Joy Parker 1993 Maya Cosmos. Three Thousand Years on the Shaman's Path. New York: William Morrow and Co.

Fritz, John 1978 Paleopsychology Today: Ideational Systems and Human Adaptation in Prehistory: 37-59, Chapter 3, in Charles Redman, ed.

Gabriel, Kathyrn 1991 Roads to Center Place. A Cultural Atalas of Chaco Canyon and the Anasazi. Boulder, CO: Johnson Books.

Gabriel, Kathyrn, ed 1992 Marietta Wetherill. Boulder, CO: Johnson Books.

Garcia-Mason, Velma 1979 Acoma Pueblo: 450-466 in Ortiz, ed.

Gardiner, Howard 1974 The Quest For Mind. New York: Vintage Books.

Gearing, Fred 1958 The Structural Poses of Eighteenth Century Cherokee Villages. AAA 60 (6): 1148-57.

   1960. Priests and Warriors: Social Structures for Cherokee Politics in the Eighteenth Century. AAA 64, part 2.

   1970. The Face of the Fox. Chicago: Aldine Publishing.

Geertz, Armin W. and Michael Lomatuway'ma 1987 Children of Cottonwood. Piety and Ceremonialism in Hopi Indian Puppetry.

American Tribal Religions, Vol. 12. Lincoln: University of Nebraska Press.

Gillespie, William 1979 An Overview of The Archaeology of Chaco Canyon. 7 page manuscript in the Chaco Center Library, University of New Mexico.

Gladwin, Harold 1945 <u>The Chaco Branch</u>, Excavations at White Mound and in the Red Mesa Valley. Gila Pueblo: Medallion Papers 33. 159pp.

 1957 <u>A History of the Ancient Southwest.</u> Portland, Maine: Bond and Wheelright.

Goldfrank, Esther Schiff 1927 <u>The Social and Ceremonial Organization of Cochiti.</u> AAA-M 33.

Greenberg, Joseph 1966 <u>Language Universals.</u> The Hague: Mouton

Grebinger, Paul 1973 Prehistoric Social Organization in Chaco Canyon, New Mexico: An Alternative Reconstruction. The Kiva 39 (1): 3-23.

 1975. Prehistoric Social Organization in Chaco Canyon, New Mexico; Postscript 1975. 15 pp. manuscript.

Gunn, John 1917 <u>Schat-Chin: History, Traditions, and Narratives of the Queres Indians of Acoma and Laguna.</u> Albuquerque: Albright and Anderson.

Haas, Mary 1969b <u>The Prehistory of Languages.</u> The Hague: Mouton.

Hackett, Charles 1937 <u>Historical Documents Relating to New Mexico, Nueva Vizcaya, and Approaches Thereto, to 1773.</u> Washington: Carnegie Publications 330, III.

 1942 <u>The Revolt of the Pueblo Indians of New Mexico and Otermin`s Attempted Reconquest, 1680-82.</u> Albuquerque: University of New Mexico Press.

Haile, Fr. Berard, OFM 1981 <u>Men Versus Women</u>. A Conflict of Navajo Emergence. American Tribal Religions 6. Lincoln: University of Nebraska Press.

Hall, Robert 1977 An Anthropocentric Perspective for Eastern United States Prehistory. AA 42 (4): 499-518.

Hallowell, A. Irving 1967 <u>Culture and Experience.</u> Schocken Books.

Harlow, Francis 1973 <u>Matte-Paint Pottery of the Tewa, Keres, and Zuni Pueblos.</u> Santa Fe: Museum of New Mexico.

Harris, Arthur, James Schoenwetter, and A.H. Warren 1967 <u>Archaeological Survey of the Chuska Valley and the Chaco Plateau, New Mexico.</u> Santa Fe: Museum of New Mexico Research Records 4, Part 1.

Harvey, Byron 1963 Masks at a Maskless Pueblo: The Laguna Colony

Katsina Organization at Isleta. Eth 2 (4): 478-489.

Hawley, Florence 1934 The Significance of the Dated Prehistory of Chetro Ketl. Santa Fe: School of American Research, Monograph 2.

1937 Pueblo Social Organization as a Lead to Pueblo History. AAA 39 (3): 504-522.

1946 The Role of Pueblo Social Organization in the Dissemination of Catholicism. AAA 48 (3): 407-415.

1950a Big Kivas, Little Kivas, and Moiety Houses in Historical Reconstruction. SWJA 6 (3): 2 86-302.

1950b Keresan Patterns of Kinship and Social Organization. AAA 52 (4): 499-512.

1951 Pueblo Social Organization and Southwestern Archaeology. AA 17 (2): 148-151.

Hawley, Florence and George Hawley 1938 Classification of Black Pottery Pigments and Paint Areas. UNM-AP 321, 2 (4): 1-27.

Hawley, Florence, Michael Pijoan, and C.A. Elkins 1943 An Inquiry into Food Economy and Body Economy in Zia Pueblo. AAA 45 (4): 547-556.

Hayes, Alden c.1973 Pithouses Y and Z at Shabikeschee (29 SJ 1659). 10 pp. manuscript in the Chaco Center Library, University of New Mexico.

1974 The Four Churches of Pecos. Albuquerque: University of New Mexico Press.

1981 Part One: A Survey of Chaco Canyon Archeology: 1-68 in Hayes, Brugge, and Judge.

Hayes, Alden, David Brugge, and W. James Judge 1981 Archaeological Surveys of Chaco Canyon, New Mexico. Washington: National Park Service, Publications in Archaeology 18A. Chaco Canyon Studies.

Helm, June 1965 "Bilaterality in the Socio-Territorial Organization of the Arctic Drainage Dene. Eth 4 (4): 361-385.

Helm, June, ed 1966 Pioneers in American Anthropology. Seattle: University of Washington Press.

Hertz, Robert 1960 Death and the Right Hand. Glencoe Free Press. Translated by Rodney and Claudia Needham.

Hewett, Edger 1909 The Excavations at Tyuonyi, New Mexico in 1908 AAA 11 (3): 434-455.

1936 Chaco Canyon and Its Monuments. Albuquerque: University of New Mexico Press.

1943 Ancient Life in the American Southwest. New York: Tudor Publishing Co.

Hibben, Frank and Herbert Dick 1944 A Basketmaker III Site in Canyon Largo, New Mexico. AA 9 (4): 381-385.

Hickerson, Nancy 1994 The Jumanos ~ Hunters and Traders of the South Plains. Austin: University of Texas Press.

Hill, James 1966 A Prehistoric Community in Eastern Arizona. SWJA 22 (1): 9-30.

Hodge, Frederick 1910 Handbook of American Indians North of Mexico. BAE-B 30, parts 1 and 2.

Hodge, Frederick, George Hammond, and Agapito Rey 1945 Fray Alonso de Benavides' Revised Memorial of 1634. Albuquerque: University of New Mexico Press.

Hoebel, E. Adamson 1952 Keresan Witchcraft. AAA 54 (4): 586-589.
    1953 Underground Kiva Passages. AA 19 (1): 76.
    1968 The Character of Keresan Pueblo Law. Proceedings of the American Philosophical Society, Volume 112 (3): 127-130.
    1969 Keresan Pueblo Law: 92-116 in Law in Culture and Society. Laura Nader, ed. Chicago: Aldine Publishing Co.
    1979 Zia Pueblo: 407-417 in Ortiz, ed.

Hough, Walter 1903 Archaeological Field Work in Northeastern Arizona; The Museum Gates Expedition of 1901. Smithsonian Annual Report for 1901. United States National Museum, pp. 297-385. 100 plates.

Hrdlicka, Ales 1903 A Laguna Ceremonial Language. AAA 5 (4): 730-732.

Hunt, Edward Proctor 2015 The Origin Myth of Acoma Pueblo. Peter Nabokov, ed. NY: Penguin Classics. [Stirling 1942]

Hurt, Wesley 1947 The Development of Architecture, Canyon de Chelly. AA 12 (4): 270-272.

Hymes, Dell, ed 1967 Studies in Southwestern Ethno-Linguistics. The Hague: Mouton.

Irwin-Williams, Cynthia and Vance Haynes 1970 Climatic Change and Early Population Dynamics in the Southwestern United States. Quaternary Research 1: 59-71.

Irwin-Williams, Cynthia and Henry Irwin 1966 Excavations at Magic Mountain. Proceedings of the Denver Museum of Natural History 12.

Irwin-Williams, Cynthia 1967 The Picosa: The Elementary Southwestern Culture. AA 32 (4): 441-457.
    1972 The Structure of Chacoan Society in the Northern Southwest: Investigations at the Salmon Site. ENMU-CA 4 (3): 1-144.
    1973 The Oshara Tradition: Origins of Anasazi Culture. ENMU-CA 5 (1): 1-28.
    1980 A View of the Chaco from Salmon Ruin, Update 1980. Paper

given at the Pecos Conference, Mesa Verde, Colorado.

Jackson, William 1887 Ruins of the Chaco Canyon, Examined in 1877. Tenth Annual Report of the United States Geological and Geographical Survey: 431-450.

Jelinek, Arthur 1967 A Prehistoric Sequence in the Middle Pecos Valley, New Mexico. University of Michigan, Museum of Anthropology, Anthropological Papers 31.

Jennings, Jesse and Edward Norbeck 1964 Prehistoric Man in the New World. University of Chicago Press.

Jessup, David. 1985. From Science to Understanding: A Reanalysis of Chacoan Social Structure. University of Chicago: MA Thesis.

Jett, Steven 1964 Pueblo Migrations: An Evaluation of the Possible Physical and Cultural Determinants. AA 29 (3): 281-300.

   1965 Comments on Davis' Hypothesis on Pueblo Indian Migrations. AA 31 (2): 276-77.

Judd, Neil 1954 The Material Culture of Pueblo Bonito. SMC 124.

   1959 Pueblo del Arroyo, Chaco Canyon, New Mexico. SMC 138 (1).

   1964 The Architecture of Pueblo Bonito. SMC 147 (1).

   1967 The Bureau of American Ethnology, A Partial History. Norman: University of Oklahoma Press.

   1968 Men Met Along The Trail, Adventures in Archaeology. Norman: University of Oklahoma Press.

Judge, W. James 1991 Chaco: Current Views of Prehistory and the Regional System: 11-30 in Crown and Judge, eds.

Kaut, Charles 1957 The Western Apache Clan System: Its Origin and Development. UNM-AP 9.

Kidder, Alfred 1927 Southwestern Archaeological Conference. EP 23 (2): 554-561.

   1962 Introduction to Southwestern Archaeology. Yale University Press. [1924]

Kidder, Alfred and Samuel Guernsey 1919 Archaeological Explorations in Northeastern Arizona. BAE-B 65.

Kroeber, Alfred 1917 Zuni Kin and Clan. AMNH-AP 18 (2).

   1928 Native Cultures of the Southwest. UC-PAE 23 (9): 375-398.

   1963 Cultural and Natural Areas of Native North America. Berkeley: University of California Press.

Kroeber, Theodora 1965 Ishi. Berkeley: University of California Press.

Kubler, George 1940 The Religious Architecture of New Mexico. Colorado Springs: Taylor Museum Publications.

Kupferer, Harriet 1962 Material Changes in a Conservative Pueblo. EP 69

(4): 248-251.

Kuhn, Thomas 1964 The Structure of Scientific Revolutions. Chicago: Phoenix Books.

Lambert, Marjorie 1967 A Kokopelli Effigy Pitcher from Northwestern New Mexico. AA 32 (3): 398-401.

Lane, Michael, ed 1970 Introduction to Structuralism, New York: Basic Books.

Lange, Charles 1953 A Reappraisal of Evidence of Plains Influence Among the Rio Grande Pueblos. SWJA 92 (2): 212-230.

   1958   The Keresan Component of Southwestern Pueblo Culture. SWJA 14 (1): 34-50.

   1968a   Cochiti, A New Mexico Pueblo, Past and Present. Carbondale: Southern Illinois University Press, Arcturus Books. [1959]

   1968b The Cochiti Dam Archaeological Salvage Project. Santa Fe: Museum of New Mexico Research Records 6, part 1.

   1979a Cochiti Pueblo: 366-378 in Ortiz, ed.

   1979b Santo Domingo Pueblo: 379-389 in Ortiz, ed.

Laski, Vera 1958 Seeking Life. American Folklore Society, Memoir 50.

Leach, Edmund 1967 Political Systems of Highland Burma. Boston: Beacon Press.

   1970   Claude Levi-Strauss. New York: Viking Press, Modern Masters Series.

Leblanc, Steven 1983 The Mimbres People. Ancient Pueblo Painters of the American Southwest. New York: Thames and Hudson.

Lee, Richard and Irvine Davis 1968 Man the Hunter. Chicago: Aldine Books.

Leinau, Alice 1934 Sanctuaries in the Ancient Pueblo of Chetro Ketl. Master's Thesis, University of New Mexico.

Lekson, Stephen, Thomas Windes, John Stein, and James Judge 1988 The Chaco Canyon Community. Scientific American (July).

Lekson, Stephen 1991 Settlement Patterns and the Chaco Region: 31-56 in Crown and Judge, eds.

Lekson, Stephen 1994 Thinking about Chaco: 11-42. Peck, Lekson, Stein, and Ortiz. Chaco Canyon ~ A Center and Its World. Santa Fe: Museum of New Mexico Press.

   1999   The Chaco Meridian ~ Centers of Political Power in the Ancient Southwest. Walnut Creek, CA: Altamira Press.

   2015   The Chaco Meridian ~ One Thousand Years of Political and Religious Power in the Ancient Southwest. Lanham: Rowman &

Littlefield Publishers.

Lekson, Stephen, ed 1983 <u>The Architecture and Dendrochronology of Chetro Ketl, Chaco Canyon, New Mexico</u>. Albuquerque: Reports of the Chaco Center 6.

Lekson, Stephen, and Catherine Cameron 1995 The Abandonment of Chaco Canyon, The Mesa Verde Migrations, and the Reorganization of the Pueblo World. Journal of Anthropological Archaeology 14: 184-202.

Leroi-Gourhan, Andre 1968 The Evolution of Paleolithic Art. Scientific American 218 (2): 59-70.

Levi-Strauss, Claude 1944 Reciprocity and Hierarchy. AAA 46, 266-8.

   1963 <u>Totemism.</u> Boston: Beacon Press.

   1967 <u>Structural Anthropology.</u> New York: Anchor Books.

   1968 <u>The Savage Mind.</u> University of Chicago Press.

Lister, Florence and Robert 1968 <u>Earl Morris and Southwestern Archaeology.</u> Albuquerque: University of New Mexico Press.

   1981 Chaco Canyon ~ Archaeology and Archaeologists. Albuquerque: University of New Mexico Press.

Longacre, William, Ed 1970a <u>Reconstructing Prehistoric Pueblo Societies</u>. Albuquerque: University of New Mexico Press for the School of American Research.

Longacre, William 1970b <u>Archaeology As Anthropology: A Case Study.</u> UA-AP 17.

Lyons, Thomas 1976 Remote Sensing Experiments in Cultural Resources Studies, Non-Destructive Methods of Archaeological Exploration, Survey, and Analysis. University of New Mexico: Chaco Center, Report 1.

McGregor, John 1941 <u>Southwestern Archaeology</u>. New York: John Wiley and Sons.

   1943 Burial of an Early American Magician. Proceedings of the American Philosophical Society 86: 270-298.

McKenna, Peter, and Wolcott Toll 1992. Regional Patterns of Great House Development among the Totah Anasazi, New Mexico: 133-146 in Doyel, ed.

Marshall, Michael, John Stein, Richard Loose, and Judith Novotny 1979 Anasazi Communities of the San Juan Basin. Albuquerque: Public Service Company of New Mexico.

Martin, Paul 1936-9 <u>The Archaeology of Southwestern Colorado.</u> FMNH-AS 23.

   1962. <u>Chapters in the Prehistory of Eastern Arizona.</u> Fieldiana,

Anthropology 53, part 1.

Martin, Paul, and Fred Plog 1973 The Archaeology of Arizona. A Study of the Southwest Region. New York: Natural History Press.

Mathien, Frances Joan 1991 Political, Economic, and Demographic Implications of the Chaco Road Network: 99-110 in Trombold, ed.

Mauss, Marcel 1967 The Gift. New York: Morton and Co.

Maybury-Lewis, David 1965 The Savage and the Innocent. Life with the Primitive Tribes of Brazil. New York: The World Publishing Company.

Meggars, Betty and Clifford Evans 1955 New Interpretations of Aboriginal American Culture History. The Anthropological Society of Washington.

Miller, Jay 1972 The Anthropology of Keres Identity. Ph.D. Dissertation, Rutgers University.

1972a Priority of the Left. Man 7 (4): 646-7.

1974 The Delaware as Woman: A Symbolic Solution. AE 1 (3): 507-514.

1975 Kokopelli: 371-380 in The Collected Papers in Honor of Florence Hawley Ellis. Theodore Frisbie, ed. Santa Fe: Papers of the Archaeological Society of New Mexico 2.

1979 A Struckon Model of Delaware Culture and the Positioning of Mediators. AE 6 (4): 791-802.

1980 The Matter of the (Thoughtful) Heart: Centrality, Focality, or Overlap. JAR, 338-342.

1983 Keres Culture and Prehistory. Models of Pueblo Prehistory Symposium C-015-00. XI International Congress of Anthropological and Ethnological Sciences. Phase II (Vancouver). Sunday 21 August.

1989 Deified Mind among the Keresan Pueblos: 151-156 in General and Amerindian Ethnolinguistics. In Remembrance of Stanley Newman. Mary Ritchie Key and Henry M. Hoeningswald, eds. Berlin: Mouton de Gruyter.

2001 Keres: Engendered Key to the Pueblo Puzzle. Ethnohistory 48 (3), 495-514, Summer.

Miller, Wick 1959 Some Notes on Acoma Kinship Terminology. SWJA 15 (2): 179-184.

1964. Acoma Grammar and Texts. Berkeley: University of California Publications in Linguistics 40.

Miller, Wick and Irvine Davis 1963 Proto-Keresan Phonology. IJAL 29 (4): 310-330.

Mindeleff, Cosmos 1897 The Cliff Ruins of Canyon de Chelly, Arizona.

BAE-AR 16: 73-198.

Mindeleff, Victor 1891 A Study of Pueblo Architecture: Tusayan and Cibola. BAE-AR 8, 3-228.

Money, John, Joan Hampson, and John Hampson 1957 Imprinting and the Establishment of Gender Role. American Medical Association, Archives of Neurology and Psychiatry 77 (3): 333-336. March.

Morris, Earl 1921-8 The Aztec Ruin. AP-AMNH 26, parts 1-5.

Morris, Earl and Robert Burgh 1941 Anasazi Basketry: A Study Based on Specimens from the San Juan River Country. Washington: Carnegie Publications 533.

Morris, Elizabeth Ann 1980 Basketmaker Caves in the Prayer Rock District, Northeastern Arizona. UA-AP 35.

Nabokov, Peter 1986 Architecture Of Acoma Pueblo. The 1934 Historic American Buildings Survey Project. Santa Fe: Ancient City Books.
      2015 How the World Moves ~ The Odyssey of an American Indian Family. NY: Viking.
      2015a Introduction: xi-xiv. Edward Proctor Hunt, The Origin Myth of Acoma Pueblo. NY: Penguin Classics.

Needham, Rodney 1960 The Left Hand of the Mugwe. Africa 30.
      1969 Structure and Sentiment. University of Chicago Press.

Needham, Rodney, ed 1973 Right and Left. University of Chicago Press.

Newman, Stanley 1954 American Indian Linguistics in the Southwest. AAA 56 (4): 626-634.

Obenauf, Margaret 1991 Photointerpretation of Chacoan Roads: 34-41 in Trombold, ed.

O'Bryan, Deric 1967 The Abandonment of the Northern Pueblos in the Thirteenth Century: 153-7 in Indian Tribes of Aboriginal America. Sol Tax, ed. New York: Cooper Square Publishers.

Ortiz, Alfonso 1965 Dual Organization as an Operational Concept in the Pueblo Southwest. Eth 4 (4): 389-96.
      1969 The Tewa World. University of Chicago Press.

Ortiz, Alfonso, ed 1972 New Perspectives on the Pueblos. Albuquerque: University of New Mexico Press for the School of American Research.
      1979 Southwest. Smithsonian: Handbook of North American Indians, Volume 9, Pueblos.

Ortiz, Simon 1994 What We See: A Perspective on Chaco Canyon and Its Ancestry: 65-72. Chaco Canyon ~ A Center and Its World. Peck, Lekson, Stein, Ortiz. Santa Fe: Museum of New Mexico Press.

Parsons, Elsie Clews 1917 The Antelope Clan in Keresan Custom and Myth. Man 17: 190-3, article 131.

1919 Mothers and Children at Laguna. Man 19, 34-8, article 18.

1920 Notes on Ceremonialism at Laguna. AMNH-AP 19 (4): 83-130.

1923 Laguna Genealogies. AMNH-AP 19 (5): 131-282.

1925 The Pueblo of Jemez. Yale University Press.

1928 The Laguna Migration to Isleta. AAA 30 (4): 602-613.

1932 Isleta, New Mexico. BAE-Ar 47, 193-466.

1933 Some Aztec and Pueblo Parallels. AAA 35 (4): 611-631.

1936 Early Relations Between the Hopi and Keres. AAA 38 (4): 554-60.

1939 Pueblo Indian Religion. 1 & 2. University of Chicago Press.

1940 Relations between Ethnology and Archaeology in the Southwest. AA 5 (3): 214-20.

1962 Isleta Paintings. Esther Goldfrank, ed. BAE-B 181.

1968 The House-Clan Complex of the Pueblos: 229-31 in Essays in Anthropology Presented to A. L. Kroeber. Freeport, NY: Books for Libraries. [1936]

Patterson, Carol 1990?? Uretsete and Naotsete Genesis Myth from Cochitit Pueblo. Artifact 26 (1): 1-23.

Paytiamo, James 1932 Flaming Arrow's People. By An Acoma Indian. New York: Duffield and Green. 158pp.

Peck, Mary, Stephen Lekson, John Stein, Simon Ortiz 1994 Chaco Canyon ~ A Center and Its World. Santa Fe: Museum of New Mexico Press.

Pepper, George 1906 Human Effigy Vases from Chaco Canyon, New Mexico: 320-334. Boas Anniversary Volume, New York: G.E. Stechert.

1909 The Exploration of a Burial Room in Pueblo Bonito, New Mexico: 196-252. Putnam Anniversary Volume. New York: G.E.Stechert.

1920. Pueblo Bonito. AMNH-AP 27.

Stein, John, and Stephen Lekson 1994 Anasazi Ritual Landscapes: 45-58. Peck, Lekson, Stein, Ortiz Chaco Canyon ~ A Center and Its World. Santa Fe: Museum of New Mexico Press.

Perry, Richard 1991 Western Apache Heritage. People of the Mountain Corridor. Austin: University of Texas Press.

Plog, Fred 1978 The Keresan Bridge: An Ecological and Archaeological Account: 349-71, Chapter 15, in Redman and others, eds.

Radin, Paul 1970 The Winnebago Tribe. Lincoln: University of Nebraska Press.

Redman, Charles and others, eds 1978 Social Archaeology, Beyond

Subsistence and Dating. New York: Academic Press.

Reed, Erik 1946 The Distinctive Features and Distribution of the San Juan Anasazi Culture. SWJA 2 (3): 295- 305.

1955 Painted Pottery and Zuni History. SWJA 11 (2): 178-93.

1962 Human Skeletal Material from Bc 59, Chaco. EP 69 (4): 240-7.

Reher, Charles, Ed 1977 <u>Settlement and Subsistence Along the Lower Chaco River</u>, The CGP (Coal Gasification Project) Survey. Albuquerque: University of New Mexico Press.

Reichel-Dolmatoff, Gerardo 1971 <u>Amazonian Cosmos.</u> University of Chicago Press.

Reyman, Jonathan 1976 Astronomy, Architecture, and Adaptation at Pueblo Bonito. <u>Science</u> 193 (4257): 957-962.

1978a Winter Solstice at Pueblo Bonito, Parts 1 and 2. Griffith Observer 42 (12): 16-9, 43 (1): 2-9.

1978b Pochteca Burials at Anasazi Sites? pp. 242-273 in <u>Across the Chichimec Sea</u>. Essays in Honor of J. Charles Kelley. Carroll Riley and Basil Hedrick, eds. Carbondale: Southern Illinois University.

1989 The History of Archaeology and the Archaeological History of Chaco Canyon, New Mexico. pp. 41-53 in <u>Tracing Archaeology's Past</u>: The Historiography of Archaeology. Andrew L. Christenson, ed. Center for Archaeological Investigations, Southern Illinois University at Carbondale.

Roberts, Frank H.H. and Jean Jeancon 1924 Archaeological Research in the Northeastern San Juan Basin of Colorado during the Summer of 1922. Colorado Magazine 1: 108-118.

Roberts, Frank HH 1929 <u>Shabik'eshchee Village.</u> BAE-B 92.

1930 <u>Early Pueblo Ruins of the Piedra District, Southwestern Colorado.</u> BAE-B 96.

1932 <u>The Village of the Great Kivas on the Zuni Reservation.</u> BAE-B 111.

1939 <u>Archaeological Remains in the Whitewater District of Eastern Arizona.</u> BAE-B 121. Part I: House Types.

Roediger, Virginia More 1961 <u>Ceremonial Costumes of the Pueblo Indians.</u> Berkeley: University of California Press.

Roney, John 1992 Prehistoric Roads and Regional Integration in the Chacoan System: 123-132 in Doyel, ed.

Rossi, Ino, ed 1974 <u>The Unconscious in Culture.</u> New York: E.P. Dutton.

Saile, David 1977 `Architecture´ in Prehispanic Pueblo Archaeology; Examples from Chaco Canyon, New Mexico. <u>World Archaeology</u> 9 (2): 157-173.

Santa Ana 1994 Santa Ana. The People, the Pueblo, and the History of Tamaya. Laura Bayer, Floyd Montoya, and the Damayame, eds. Albuquerque: U of New Mexico Press.

Schelberg, John Daniel 1982 Economic And Social Development As An Adaptation To A Marginal Environment in Chaco Canyon, New Mexico. Ph.D. Dissertation: Northwestern University.

Schele, Linda, and David Freidel 1990 A Forest of Kings. The Untold Story of the Ancient Maya. New York: William Morrow.

Schoenwetter, James and Alfred Dittert 1968 An Ecological Interpretation of Anasazi Settlement Patterns: 41-66 in Anthropological Archaeology in the Americas. Anthropological Society of Washington.

Schroeder, Albert 1979 Pueblos Abandoned In Historic Times: 236-254 in Ortiz, ed.

   1985 Hopi Traditions and Rio Grande Pueblo Migrations: 105-112 in Prehistory and History in the Southwest. Essays in Honor of Alden C. Hayes. Papers of the Archaeological Society of New Mexico 11.

Schroeder, Albert and Dan Matson 1965 A Colony on the Move: Gaspar Castano de Sosa`s Journal, 1590-1. Santa Fe: School of American Research.

Sebastian, Lynne 1991 Sociopolitical Complexity and the Chaco System: 109-134 in Crown and Judge, eds.

   1992 The Chaco Anasazi. Sociopolitical Evolution in the Prehistoric Southwest. Cambridge University Press.

Service, Elman 1968 Primitive Social Organization. New York: Random house

Sever, Thomas, and David Wagner 1991 Analysis of Prehistoric Roadways in Chaco Canyon Using Remotely Sensed Digital Data: 42-52. Trombold, ed.

Shiner, Joel 1964 Dating Bc 50. EP 71 (3): 15-17.

Silko, Leslie Marmon 1977 Ceremony. New York: Viking Press.

Simmons, Leo and Don Talayesva 1969 Sun Chief. Yale University Press.

Smiley, Terah, Stanley Stubbs, and Bryant Bannister 1953 A Foundation for the Dating of Some Late Archaeological Sites in the Rio Grande Area, New Mexico. University of Arizona: Laboratory of Tree-Ring Research, Bulletin 6.

Smith, Estellie 1969 Governing A Taos. ENMU-CA 2 (1): 1-41.

Smith, Watson 1952 Kiva Mural Decoration at Awatovi and Kawaika'a. PP 37.

Sofaer, Anna, Michael Marshall, and Rolf Sinclair 1989 The Great North Road: a cosmographic expression of the Chaco culture of New

Mexico: 365-376 in <u>World Archaeoastronomy</u>. Anthony Aveni, ed. Cambridge University Press.

Speck, Frank 1927 <u>Symbolism in Penobscot Art.</u> AMNH-AP 29 (2): 25-80.

Spencer, Robert 1940 A Preliminary Sketch of Keresan Grammar. University of New Mexico, Master`s Thesis.

1946. The Phonemes of Keresan. IJAL 12 (4): 229- 236.

Spier, Leslie 1917 <u>An Outline for a Chronology of Zuni Ruins</u>. AMNH-AP 18, 207-331.

Stanislawski, Michael 1963 Extended Burials in the Prehistoric Southwest. AA 38 (3): 308-319.

Starr, Frederick 1897 A Study of a Census of the Pueblo of Cochiti, New Mexico. Proceedings of the Davenport Academy of Natural Sciences VII: 33-44.

Stein, John, and Stephen Lekson 1992 Anasazi Ritual Landscapes: 87-100 in Doyel, ed.

Stevenson, James 1883 <u>Illustrated Catalogue of the Collections Obtained from the Indians of New Mexico and Arizona in 1879 and 1880</u>. BAE-AR 2 (3-4): 311-465.

Stevenson, Matilde Coxe 1894 <u>The Sia.</u> BAE-AR 11: 3-157.

1904 <u>The Zuni Indians.</u> BAE-AR 23, 3-608.

Steward, Julian 1937 Ecological Aspects of Southwestern Society. Anthropos 32 (1-2): 87-104.

1970 The Foundation of Basin-Plateau Shoshonean Society: 113-151 in <u>Languages and Cultures of Western North America.</u> Earl Swanson, ed. Pocatello: Idaho State University Press.

Stirling, Matthew 1942 <u>The Origin Myth of Acoma.</u> BAE-B 135.

Strong, Pauline Turner 1979 San Felipe Pueblo: 390-397 in Ortiz, ed.

1979a Santa Ana Pueblo: 398-406 in Ortiz, ed.

Strong, William Duncan 1927 An Analysis of Southwestern Society. AAA 29 (1): 1-61.

1972 <u>Aboriginal Society in Southern California.</u> Classics in California Anthropology II. Banning: Malki Museum Press. [1929]

Stubbs, Stanley 1950 <u>Bird's Eye View of the Pueblos.</u> Norman: University of Oklahoma Press.

Taylor, Walter 1954 Southwestern Archaeology, Its History and Theory. AAA 56 (4).

1967 <u>A Study of Archaeology.</u> Carbondale: University of Southern Illinois Press, Acturus Books.

Toll, H. Wolcott 1991 Material Distributions and Exchange in the Chaco System: 77-108 in Crown and Judge, eds.

Toll, Wolcott, Eric Blinman, and Wilson Dean 1992 Chaco in the Context of Ceramic Regional Systems: 147-158 in Doyel, ed.

Trombold, Charles 1991 Ancient Road Networks and Settlement Hierarchies in the New World. Cambridge University Press.

Turner, Christy and Nancy Morris 1970 A Massacre at Hopi. AA 35 (3): 320-31.

Turner, Victor 1967 The Forest of Symbols. Ithaca: Cornell University Press.

Turner, Victor, Ed 1969 Introduction: 3-25 in Forms of Symbolic Action. American Ethnological Society, Papers of the Spring Meeting.

Underhill, Ruth 1944 Pueblo Crafts. Lawrence, Kansas: Bureau of Indian Affairs.

 1948 Ceremonial Patterns in the Greater Southwest. American Ethnological Society, Monograph 13.

 1972 Red Man's Religion. Beliefs and Practices of the Indians North of Mexico. University of Chicago Press.

Upham, Steadman 1982 Politics and Power: An Economic and Political History of the Western Pueblo. New York: Academic Press.

Van Dyke, Ruth 2007 The Chaco Experience ~ Landscape and ideology at the Center Place. Santa Fe: School for Advanced Research Resident Scholar Book.

Vivian, R. Gordon. 1959 The Hubbard Site and Other Tri-Wall Structures in New Mexico and Colorado. National Park Service, Archaeological Research Series 5.

Vivian, Gordon and Tom Mathews 1964 Kin Kletso. Globe, Arizona: Southwestern Monuments Association, Technical Series 6, Part 1: 1-115.

Vivian, Gordon and Paul Reiter 1965 The Great Kivas of Chaco Canyon. Santa Fe: School of American Research, Monograph 22.

Vivian, Gwinn 1970 An Inquiry into Prehistoric Social Organization in Chaco Canyon, New Mexico: 5-83 in Longacre, ed.

 1972 Prehistoric Water Conservation in Chaco Canyon. Final Technical Letter Report to the National Science Foundation. Grant GS-3100.

 ms. Conservation and Diversion: Water Control Systems in the Anasazi Southwest.

 1990 The Chacoan Prehistory of the San Juan Basin. New York: Academic Press.

 1991 Chacoan Subsistence: 57-76 in Crown and Judge, eds.

Vivian, Gwinn, and Bruce Hilpert 2002 The Chaco Handbook. An

Encyclopedic Guide. Salt Lake City: University of Utah Press.

Vivian, R. Gwinn, Dulce Dodgen, and Gayle Hartmann 1978 <u>Wooden Ritual Artifacts from Chaco Canyon, New Mexico; The Chetro Kelt Collection.</u> UA-AP 32. 152pp.

Wallace, Anthony 1970 <u>Culture and Personality.</u> New York: Random House.

Watson, James 1968 <u>The Double Helix.</u> New York: Signet Books.

Wauchope, Robert. 1965. Alfred Vincent Kidder, 1885-1963. AA 31 (2): 149-171.

Weigand, Phil 1992 The Macroeconomic Role of Turquoise within the Chaco Canyon System: 169-176 in Doyel, ed.

Weltfish, Gene 1971 <u>The Lost Universe</u>; The Way of Life of the Pawnee. New York: Ballantine Books.

Wendorf, Fred and Erik Reed 1955 An Alternative Reconstruction of Northern Rio Grande Prehistory. EP 62 (5-6): 131-173.

Wheat, Joe Ben 1955 <u>Mogollon Culture Prior to A.D. 1000.</u> AA-M 10.

White, Leslie 1928 A Comparative Study of the Keresan Medicine Societies: 604-19 in <u>Proceedings of the International Congress of Americanists</u> 23.

    1932a <u>The Acoma Indians.</u> BAE-Ar 47, 17-192.

    1932b <u>The Pueblo of San Felipe.</u> AAA-M 38.

    1935 <u>The Pueblo of Santo Domingo.</u> AAA-M 60.

    1942 <u>The Pueblo of Santa Ana.</u> AAA-M 60.

    1943 <u>New Material from Acoma.</u> BAE-B 136 (32): 301-59.

    1944a A Ceremonial Vocabulary among the Pueblos. IJAL 10 (4): 161-167.

    1944b Notes on the Ethnobotany of the Keres. PMASAL 30: 557-68.

    1947 Notes on the Ethnozoology of the Keresan Pueblo Indians. PMASAL 31: 223-43.

    1948 Miscellaneous Notes on the Keresan Pueblos. PMASAL 32, 365-73.

    1962 <u>The Pueblo of Sia.</u> BAE-B 184.

    1964 The World of the Keresan Pueblo Indians: 53-64 in <u>Culture in History</u>, Essays in Memory of Paul Radin. Stanley Diamond, ed. Columbia University Press.

    1973 Correspondence. Newsletter of the American Anthropological Association. June 14 (6): 2.

Whitely, Peter 1988 <u>Deliberate Acts</u>. Changing Hopi Culture Through the Oraibi Split. Tucson: University of Arizona Press.

Whorf, Benjamin Lee 1967 Language, Thought and Reality. Cambridge, Massachusetts: MIT Press.

Willey, Gordon 1956 Prehistoric Settlement Patterns in the New World. Viking Fund Publications in Anthropology 23.

1966. An Introduction to American Archaeology: North and Middle America. Englewood Cliffs: Prentice Hall.

Wilshusen, Richard, and Scott Ortman 1999 Rethinking the Pueblo I Period in the San Juan Drainage: Aggregation, Migration, and Cutlural Diversity. Kiva 64 (3): 369-399, Spring.

Windes, Thomas 1977a Typology and Technology of Anasazi Ceramics: 279-370 in Reher 1977.

1977b Preliminary Investigations at the Pueblo Alto Complex, Chaco Canyon, 1976. Manuscript (84pp) in the Chaco Center Library, University of New Mexico.

1978 Stone Circles of Chaco Canyon, Northwestern New Mexico. Reports of the Chaco Center 5.

1991 The Prehistoric Road Network at Pueblo Alto, Chaco Canyon, New Mexico: 111-131 in Trombold, ed.

Windes, Tom, and Dabney Ford 1992 The Nature of the Early Bonito Phase: 75-87 in Doyel, ed.

Winship, George 1896 The Coronado Expedition, 1540-42. BAE-AR 14 (1): 329-613.

Wittfogel, Karl and Esther Goldfrank 1943 Some Aspects of Pueblo Mythology and Society. JAF 56 (219): 17-30.

Wormington, Hannah Marie 1957 Ancient Man in North America. Denver Museum of Natural History, Popular Series 4.

1964. Prehistoric Indians of the Southwest. Denver Museum of Natural History, Popular Series 7.

The Zuni People 1972 The Zunis: Self-Portrayals. Albuquerque: University of New Mexico Press.

Acknowledgements

A life-long project incurs many debts, beginning with the Keres themselves, who allowed a child to witness the public aspects of their culture and encouraged him to be intrigued. James and Charlotte Toulouse and family made a place for me, and Carmie Lynn Toulouse, with a critical eye, suffered through early revisions of this effort. Laura Lee, Charlotte Mary, Jeremy Alan, Tamaya Lynn, Trent, Marie, Ella Mae, Randy Bock, and many others also helped.

As an undergraduate at the University of New Mexico, Stanley Newman, WW "Nibs" Hill, Philip Bock, Bruce Rigsby, and, especially, Florence Hawley Ellis and Mary Elizabeth Smith set my academic course. Outside the classroom, Cynthia Irwin-Williams and the Anasazi Origins Project gave me first-hand experience as an archaeologist on Sia Pueblo Land tracing over ten millennia of local developments. Later as an advisor at Salmon Ruin, I was introduced to Chaco outliers and reoccupations.

As a graduate student at Rutgers and Princeton, my dissertation, the basis for this updated work after forty years of hindsight, benefitted from the efforts of Robin Fox, my chair, Yehudi Cohen, Warren Shapiro, and Mark Leone. Margaret Bacon, Jane Lancaster, and Martin Silverman encouraged. Alfonso Ortiz advised me throughout, often by providing contrasting Tewa examples. Along the way, Esther Goldfrank and Karl Wittfogel fed and hosted me. Merle Williams and Richard O'Connell gave timely support.

My parents and siblings aided as needed, as did fellow students Janet Pollak, Michele Teitelbaum, Cheryl Wase, Edward Deal, Nina Versaggi, Nancy Trembly, Ken & Mark Wilkie, Fiona Anders, Corinne Black, Karen & Tom Reynolds, John & Luceen Dunn family, Glenn & Dorothy Williams family, Andrew & Nancy Core family, Roland Wildman, Darlene & Jay, and Kathy Caprario.

Over the years, Elizabeth Brandt, Wick Miller, Tom Windes, Anna Sofaer, Peter Nabokov, Ray Fogelson, and John Stein offered insightful comments. Along the way, elders of the Delaware, Lushootseed, Tsimshian, Colville, and Creek tribes have provided comparative perspectives on Keresan culture in time and space.

Many thanks to all.

Sold @ Amazon.com

Index

#f = scattered entries on pages on either side of this page
#0f = scattered entries over this ten page span, 10f, 20f, etc

Please Help Zap Out Typo Gnomes

Sold @ Amazon.com

Jay Miller's books & E-books @ Amazon.com

JONA Memoirs

University of Nebraska Press